Y0-AGE-880

C¹-100

A Library of Modern Religious Thought

THE MIND OF
THE OXFORD MOVEMENT

A LIBRARY OF
MODERN RELIGIOUS THOUGHT
General Editor: Henry Chadwick, D.D.

S. T. COLERIDGE
CONFESSIONS OF AN INQUIRING SPIRIT
Edited by H. StJ. Hart

LESSING'S THEOLOGICAL WRITINGS
Selected and translated by Henry Chadwick

DAVID HUME
THE NATURAL HISTORY OF RELIGION
Edited by H. E. Root

S. KIERKEGAARD
JOHANNES CLIMACUS and A SERMON
Translated and edited by T. H. Croxall

JOHN LOCKE
THE REASONABLENESS OF CHRISTIANITY
Edited and abridged by I. T. Ramsey

THE MIND OF
THE OXFORD MOVEMENT
Edited by Owen Chadwick

THE MIND OF
THE OXFORD MOVEMENT

EDITED AND INTRODUCED

BY

OWEN CHADWICK

STANFORD UNIVERSITY PRESS
STANFORD, CALIFORNIA

STANFORD UNIVERSITY PRESS
STANFORD, CALIFORNIA
©1960 A. AND C. BLACK LTD.
ORIGINAL AMERICAN EDITION 1961
REPRINTED 1967

PRINTED IN THE UNITED STATES OF AMERICA

CONTENTS

Part II. THE AUTHORITY OF THE CHURCH

CONTENTS

CONTENTS

ABBREVIATIONS

KEBLE   *U.S.*   Sermons Academical and Occasional

NEWMAN   *Arians*   Arians of the Fourth Century
                  Prophetical Office. Lectures on the Prophetical Office of the Church viewed relatively to Romanism and Popular Protestantism
                  P.S.   Parochial Sermons
                  U.S.   Sermons, chiefly on the Theory of Religious Belief, preached before the University of Oxford
                  Tracts   Tracts for the Times (ed.)

PUSEY   *A.W.*   Sermons during the season from Advent to Whitsuntide
                  P.S.   Parochial Sermons
                  U.S.   Nine Sermons preached before the University of Oxford

INTRODUCTION

1. *The Oxford Movement*

In a library of modern religious thought, no apology will be needed for the inclusion of illustrations from the thought of the Oxford Movement. That movement was of decisive importance to the religion of the English, and not only to the Church of England, not only within the Church of England to the "high church group" which gave birth to the movement, nurtured it, and was transformed by it.

Of decisive importance to the *religion* of the English—no doubt, not to their philosophy, perhaps not so markedly to their apprehension of Christian doctrine. The mind of the Oxford Movement is not a mind which can be best studied or examined by asking for its philosophical conclusions (if any); even though at least two of its principal thinkers had the training and the makings of a philosopher. Nor can it best be studied or examined by asking for a list of its doctrinal propositions—for example, by observing that its leaders at first suspected the doctrine that saints should be invoked in prayer. As well might we seek to comprehend John Wesley by asking what he thought of the theories of Locke and Berkeley, or by setting forth his hostility to Calvinistic doctrines as the key to understanding his whole work. Like its predecessor the Evangelical Movement, it was more a movement of the heart than of the head. If the generalization be allowed, it was primarily concerned with the law of prayer, and only secondarily with the law of belief. It was aware that creed and prayer are inseparable. It was not concerned for religious "experience" while being unconcerned about religious language—on the contrary, it was earnestly dogmatic. But the movement, though dogmatic, was not dogmatic simply because it possessed or shared a particular theory of dogma. It always saw dogma in relation to worship, to the numinous, to the movement of the heart, to the conscience and the moral need, to the immediate experience of the hidden hand of God—so that without this attention to worship or the moral need, dogma could not be apprehended rightly. The Creed was creed—the truth; not a noise of words to evoke prayer. But it roused the mind to prayer, and only through prayer and life was it known to be truth. The Oxford men did not affirm, that which helps men to be saints must be true. But they had much sympathy with the proposition, and would probably have agreed that it contained more than a seed of truth. And in this modified sense, it is right to see the Oxford Movement as an impulse of the heart and the conscience, not an inquiry of the head. Certainly the principal changes which it brought in English life were changes in the mode of worship, or in the understanding of sanctity, or in the consequent methods of religious practice; and the changes of theological or philosophical thinking were by comparison less far-reaching.

Though the leaders were not so extreme in their antagonism to Reason as their opponents sometimes believed, the Oxford Movement was one part of that great swing of opinion against Reason as the Age of Reason had understood it and used it. Through Europe ran the reaction against the aridity of common sense, against the pride of rationalism. There is little in common, of religion, between Keble and Goethe, between Pusey and Victor Hugo. The scepticisms of Hume and Kant, the romantic poets or novelists, the new historians, the shock of Robespierre and the temple of reason, the evangelical or pietistic theologians, the desire to justify the past and to value tradition and history in the face of the critical cuts of rationalism—the revolt against Reason and "enlightenment" cannot rightly be seen in terms of a few simple forces. But the Oxford Movement was part of this reaction. They wanted to find a place for the poetic or the aesthetic judgment; their hymnody shared in the feelings and evocations of the romantic poets; they wished to find a place and value for historical tradition, against the irreverent or sacrilegious hands of critical revolutionaries for whom no antiquity was sacred; they suspected the reason of common sense as shallow; they wanted to justify order and authority in Church as well as State.

It is safe to say that the Movement would not have taken the form which it took without the impetus of ecclesiastical and secular politics. For example, one characteristic doctrine of the Oxford men was that high doctrine of the episcopal and priestly ministry which is usually described in the phrase *apostolic succession*. This high doctrine of the ministry was lent power in Church and State because in *1833* dissent from the Church of England and Ireland seemed more potent than at any time since the surrender of King Charles I to the armies of the Scots. Irish Roman Catholics (or English Roman Catholics, but less commonly and less vociferously) had begun (since the Roman Catholic Emancipation of *1829*) to sit in the Parliament at Westminster and to use their freedom against the Church of Ireland, still linked indissolubly to the Church of England. The Reform Act of *1832*, in revising the constituencies and abolishing the rotten boroughs and extending the franchise, weakened the Tory traditions upon which ecclesiastical authority seemed to rest politically; and who knew what would happen when the Whigs began to "reform" the Church according to their own notions? It was necessary, politically necessary, that the clergy of the Church of England should look to leaders who would declare that the authority of the Church does not rest upon the authority of the State; that the Church possesses a divine authority whatever the State may do, even if the State should be represented by an indifferent or a persecuting government; that the authority of the bishop or the vicar rests not upon his national nor his social position, but upon his apostolic commission. All this was politically necessary; it happened, *mutatis mutandis*, among the Presbyterians of the Church of Scotland for the same reasons, and among the Ultramontanes of the Church of France for similar reasons. If the government, which has for so long given privileges and fetters, seems to be at last neutral amidst the religious divisions of Ireland; if the government seems to lay rough hands upon ancient church endowments without consulting the authorities of the Church; if the government must henceforth take serious account of the demands or even the prejudices of non-Anglicans in the House of Commons—then it is time to assert that even if the Church were disestablished and disendowed, even if there were a complete separation between Church and State, even if the State followed the example of the United States of America and became outwardly and constitutionally indifferent to religion, the Church of England has still a claim upon the allegiance of Englishmen; a claim upon their allegiance not simply because they are Englishmen and this is the Church of England; not simply because this religion is part of national tradition or is suitable to the national character; not simply because this is the religion of their forefathers. It still has a claim upon the allegiance of Englishmen because this Church is teaching Catholic truth, and as such is the authorized and commissioned agent of Christ and his apostles to the people of this country.

There was, then, a political impetus; a revolution in the relations between Church and State, even if the extent and consequences of this revolution were still half known or half perceived.

But a political impetus does not create religious thought. It affords it opportunity, gives it point and purpose, establishes it as effective. The high Anglicanism of the Oxford Movement was not quite identical with the high Anglicanism which had existed for two hundred years and more. But the difference was not the result of the political crisis. The power of the Movement's religious ideas sprang from somewhere deeper in men's souls and minds than their contemporary ideas of ecclesiastical expediency.

2. The High Church Tradition

The word *high* began to be used in this connexion shortly before the Revolution of *1688*. It meant, in its original intention, strict; a man who was "stiff for the Church of England"; rigid; careful and precise in observing the rules of the Church about prayer and fasting, even perhaps when those rules had begun to seem archaic; a man who stood for the privileges of the Church against the dissenters; a strong defender of the Establishment. The phrase *high churchman* had once a political tang to it, and was easily prefaced by the word *Tory*. This kind of high churchmanship was potent or impotent with the fortunes of the Tory party. In crude outline, it was weak under William and Mary, powerful under Queen Anne, impotent under the first two Georges, and rising to power again at the end of the century with the growing fear of radicalism and the dissent which radicalism was held, not without reason, to accompany.

But the high church tradition in religious thought contained more than this.

A "high churchman" in (for example) *1800* would probably reverence King Charles I and keep the day of his death as a day of martyrdom. He would think that Charles died for the maintenance of the Church of England and its episcopal or apostolic ministry; that the responsibility for his death lay with the Roundheads who were the ancestors of the Whigs, and with the presbyterians and independents who were the ancestors of the modern dissenter.

He would probably think that the Revolution of 1688 was far less "glorious" than the Whig historians portrayed it; and he might well sympathize with those who, having taken their allegiance to King James II, refused to take an oath of allegiance to King William III—he might even have sympathies with the Jacobites, however archaic and dead their cause seemed by now to be. He might resent the safeguards for the presbyterian religion of Scotland, established in consequence of the Revolution of 1688, and befriend or honour the little groups of Scottish episcopalians.

He would probably think ill of any arrangement which might be held to suggest that the Protestants of the continental churches and the members of the Church of England were national allies, or equally, and without distinction, common members of a "Protestant Church". In the later years of the eighteenth century, the S.P.C.K. had begun using German missionaries in India; some English high churchmen openly disapproved of the arrangement.

Here, at least, is a conviction which cannot be explained merely in terms of political churchmanship. Though there was some connexion between its growth and the suspicion of Dutch William and his natural affection for the Presbyterians, or of German George and his natural affection for his own Lutherans, the conviction would be inexplicable only on these terms. It is explicable only as a doctrine, as a conviction based upon principles of religious authority, and grounded not in political need but in theological thought.

How was it that an important wing of English churchmen, whose Reformation had accepted the impetus and influence of the Reformation in Germany and Switzerland, could so sharply distinguish between themselves and the contemporary heirs of the German and Swiss Reformations?

The first Elizabethan archbishop of Canterbury, Matthew Parker, talked of a golden mediocrity (that is, a golden mean or via media) which his more continentally minded friends thought to be a leaden mediocrity, a mingle-mangle, an unfortunate compound of Popery and the Gospel. In the intention of Parker, a golden mediocrity was aimed to preserve within the fold of the one Church both the extreme parties which divided English religion, the continentally trained Protestants who were faithful to their masters in Geneva or Zürich, and the leaders of Queen Mary's Church, who had been convinced by events in the reigns of Edward VI and Mary herself that Catholicism included allegiance to the See of Rome. To some extent moderation succeeded. A Protestant of "Swiss Reformed" sympathies like John Jewel at first accepted it with reluctance and later, if not with enthusiasm, at least with loyalty. The number of persons who felt that their allegiance to the Pope prevented them from participating in the communion of the Church of England was at first comparatively small. But the decisive adherent of Geneva on the one side, and the decisive adherent of Rome upon the other, could do nothing else but work for change in the constitution and doctrine of the Church of England. Golden mediocrity never commanded the affections of the whole country. What is significant for our purpose, however, is that within the Protestantism of England, circumstances, political and religious needs, had created more room for the traditionally minded than was possible anywhere outside Lutheranism. The church historian of the seventeenth century, Thomas Fuller, said that the Thirty-Nine Articles were like children's clothes, made of a larger size so that the children might grow up into them. Whether the original authors of the articles were looking for that breadth and liberty, assigned to them by a more Latitudinarian age, is doubtful. The statement effectively represents the way in which Anglican moderation was seen to have room for persons attached, in mind or affection or devotion, to tradition. The more conservative and medieval elements in Cranmer's prayer books, or the continuation of the ancient mode of consecrating bishops, were perhaps important only to a few of the leaders of religion during the first twenty years of Elizabeth's reign. They became increasingly important thenceforth, to an always growing and influential section of English opinion.

One of the encouragements to the conservatives was the advance of scholarship during the later sixteenth century and after; especially the advances made by students of the early Church and the Fathers. It is hardly too strongly put, if we say that scholarship discovered the Fathers to support the Calvinists less, and the conservatives more, than the scholars of the middle sixteenth century had thought or expected. The great Reformers had all appealed to the Fathers. Their appeal had been subsidiary and secondary to the appeal to the Bible; but they had not supposed that the Christian Church had, from the very beginning, misunderstood the Biblical message, and therefore the evidence of the early Church possessed a theological and controversial importance. Calvin, indeed, had won a measure of his influence through the depth and readiness of his patristic scholarship.

But, as the sixteenth century drew towards its end, patristic scholarship became more effective. The Lutherans led the way; the Catholics followed. Great editions of patristic sources were printed, better texts were slowly made available, newly discovered manuscripts were published. The critical methods were still in embryo; it was still, in *1600*, difficult, if not impossible, to determine with security whether many of the works purporting to be ancient were, in fact, ancient or were spurious productions of a later age. Not until the second half of the seventeenth century was the scholarly method becoming sound in its treatment, assisted by printed collections, by comparison of texts, by study of linguistic style and environment, and all those means with which modern scholarship is familiar. But already, in *1600*, the knowledge of the texts was making a momentous difference to the study of the early Church. St Augustine, to whom everyone looked back for guidance in the doctrines of justification, grace, and predestination, had once risen head and shoulders above the other teachers of the ancient Church. In *1630* he was still a giant; but he had been placed in a wider context of learning, and especially against a background of Greek thought. It was found that the Fathers, taken as a whole, were not so clearly unanimous upon the doctrine of predestination as some authors had at one time contended. It was found that St Jerome, who had contended for the essential parity between bishop and presbyter, was not in agreement with all other teachers of the ancient Church, and that in St Ignatius, and even in St Cyprian, the primitive Church had allowed high honour and order to the bishop as distinct from the presbyter. The ancient Church, when seen by the historians, was found to have valued the single life, thought private confession and spiritual direction to be useful, bestowed reverence upon the Blessed Virgin Mary and the saints, used formal and sometimes elaborate liturgies.

In short, it may be repeated, the advance of patristic scholarship befriended the conservative and traditionalistic elements everywhere in Protestantism; and nowhere more significantly than within the Church of England.

If we look at the group of Anglicans between (say) *1610* and *1640*, we find that they are Protestants, and, in many respects, within the normal inheritance of Reformed thought; just as Hooker, for all his knowledge of Aristotle and St Thomas Aquinas, and for all his desire to controvert Calvinism, had been unmistakably a disciple (though not an uncritical disciple) of Swiss Reformed thought. And yet the atmosphere was curiously different from the atmosphere anywhere else in Protestantism, even if parallels may be found among the Lutherans. In George Herbert, John Donne, Nicholas Ferrar, Launcelot Andrewes, John Cosin, Thomas Jackson, William Laud, there is an air which is somehow redolent of Catholicism while it is still Reformed. In Herbert, or in Donne, we may find some of the best of Reformed theology, whether pastoral or dogmatic. There is no question of repudiating the Reformation. And yet the air is fresh, and not blowing simply from the usual quarters in Protestant thought. Part of this freshness springs from patristic study; part from a measure of Platonic philosophy, which was infused into contemporary minds with revolutionary impact after the long reign of nominalism throughout the unmetaphysical epoch of the Reformation, and which (in this group of men) may be found at its most theological in Thomas Jackson. In their attitude to the visible world is a sacramentalism which is not easy to find among the Protestant authors of the sixteenth century.

> The man that looks on glass
> On it may stay his eye
> Or, if he chooseth, through it pass
> And then the heaven espy.

Both these elements—an appeal to the Fathers as interpreters of Scripture, and a sacramentalism of nature and the world, into which the sacraments of the Church fitted easily—were to be fundamental to the mind of the Oxford Movement. From this background came Laud's quest for the "beauty of holiness", for altars in their old places, and protected by rails in a sanctuary; Andrewes' book of private prayers, wonderfully drawn from the ancient liturgies as well as from Scripture; Cosin's desire to utilize traditional ornaments in the chapel of Peterhouse or the cathedral at Durham.

The higher value placed upon the episcopal ministry in the Church of England came from the patristic background. But its contemporary importance arose from a more ecclesiastical and less theoretical question, the struggle with the Puritans.

The earliest Elizabethan bishops had not invariably exacted ordination by a bishop as a condition for holding posts in the Church of England. The known exceptions are very few, but they show, what would on other grounds be expected, that the bishops at first recognized the sufficiency for this purpose of (for example) presbyterian ordination overseas. The Puritans, however, believed that the presbyterian ministry was of divine right; and therefore that it was their duty to persuade the magistrate to overthrow the episcopal ministry among the other reforms to which he was called. In its extremist form, this programme created enemies to the bishops on grounds of conscience —or, at the practical level, trouble-makers in several dioceses. It was soon natural that the bishops, as administrators, should seek to control or restrain extremists. One chief measure of such control was to insist upon episcopal ordination; for otherwise an extremist, denied ordination in England, might seek it in Amsterdam or Geneva, and return. This control was, at first, an administrative act, based more upon pastoral expediency than upon theological doctrine. Only as the controversy sharpened, did it seem necessary to assert the rightness of an episcopal ministry; and when (from *1589* or *1590* onwards) this was asserted against the Puritans, Anglican theologians found the resources of the new patristic scholarship ready to hand. By *1610* there was an influential body of thought which believed, on grounds of historical study and historical continuity, that the episcopal ministry in its traditional form was "God-given". They did not deny that the ministries of the continental Protestants were good; but they believed that this ministry was the best, the complete ministry as God had intended his Church to be ordered.

The Civil War and the Commonwealth and the Protectorate achieved for this body of opinion a new and persuasive status. In the minds of non-Calvinists. Calvinism was now associated with disloyalty to the Church of England. Whatever might be said of extremists, this had not been true of Calvinists before *1640*. Three out of the six archbishops of Canterbury from Parker to Laud would not have disdained the theology of Switzerland: one of the most eminent English theologians of the early seventeenth century, Davenant, was a moderate Calvinist, and also Bishop of Salisbury. After *1640* there was not to be another archbishop of Canterbury as "Reformed" as Grindal, or Whitgift, or Abbott, until Sumner during the middle of the nineteenth century. This theology was associated, however unjustly and however faintly, with the killing of the king, with the overthrow of the constitution of the Church of England, with religious strife, and wrong-headed zeal and business, with disloyalty in Church and State. This was to have long consequences in English religious history. The descendants of the Puritans found it difficult to feel as fully at home in the Church of England as their ancestors had felt before *1640*. There was a barrier of psychological association, too rarely recognized, for the Evangelical Anglicans of the eighteenth century to overcome. Many Evangelicals of *1800* were altogether loyal to the Church of England as they understood it, and for themselves felt completely at home in it. The high churchman had some half-conscious association in his mind which prevented him from recognizing them to be truly at home. To him they seemed to bring with them a touch of the alien intruder. The "Anglican tradition" had come to be conceived as a tradition which did not include Calvinism. That tradition ran through Hooker, and Laud, and Thorndike, and Bull, and Jeremy Taylor; not through Whitaker, and Davenant, and Hall, and Baxter. When the men of the Oxford Movement claimed to be representing the "authentic" Anglican position in theology, they meant this. To them, Calvinism seemed by its history to have sacrificed any right which it might once have possessed, to be counted an authentic portion of the tradition. And it has to be confessed that the rigidities of the Restoration settlement in *1660–2*, by excluding men like Baxter from the ministry, and then by imposing severe restrictions upon dissent, had taken the most effectual step towards removing them.

The theology of the Church of England, though weakened by these rigidities, was preserved from impoverishment by a succession of remarkable thinkers. On the one side were the Platonists of Cambridge, continuing and extending brilliantly if sometimes perilously, that Christian philosophizing which we have observed early in the century in minds like Jackson. On the other were the great students of the Fathers—Henry Hammond, Herbert Thorndike, Bramhall, Jeremy Taylor, Pearson, Gunning. These latter no longer looked for their inspiration to the school of Zürich, or of Geneva, or even of Wittenberg. They looked to antiquity, and systematically attempted to draw out the implications of antiquity for religious doctrine and religious practice. It was, therefore, natural that their thought should diverge increasingly from the thought of the continental Protestants; and thence begins that strange air of isolation which Clement Webb used to notice as a particular feature of much Anglican thought between 1650 and 1850.

The divergence was most marked, at the time, in Luther's *articulus stantis aut cadentis ecclesiae*, the doctrine of justification. It was hardly conceivable that a church, Lutheran or Reformed, should not hold to the doctrine of justification by faith alone; and this is the interpretation of which the Thirty-Nine Articles of the Church of England are most readily patient. But Reformed theology was no longer the chief guide; and on the left of the Calvinists the anarchies of Civil War had thrown up a chaos of sects, few of them important (as the Quakers were to be) but some of them seeming to tend towards an antinomian interpretation of the doctrine of justification by faith—"provided that I cling to Christ's Cross, it matters not what works I do". To Luther and his contemporaries, the peril seemed to be a works-religion, to the neglect or destruction of the Gospel of faith. To the theologians of the Restoration the peril seemed to be an antinomian religion, to the neglect or destruction of good works. They, therefore, attempted to frame their doctrine of justification in language which allowed more to the necessity of good works and human endeavour than had been common among Protestant divines. Few went as far as Jeremy Taylor, who seems sometimes to minimize the doctrine of original sin until it can hardly be observed. Few (contemporaries) went as far as George Bull, who argued that St Paul must be understood in the light of St James, and not vice versa. But this veering away from the old, sharp, language of *sola fide* became, in some measure, characteristic of high Anglican thought in the later seventeenth century. Those divines sought to preserve what they believed the Reformation to have rightly defended; in particular, they eschewed the doctrine of merit. But they were eager to call attention to the needs of the soul's growth in sanctification, needs which they felt the extreme forms of the doctrine of "faith alone" to have underestimated, by implication if not by intention.

There were now three main differences of emphasis, therefore, between the non-Calvinist tradition of Anglican thought and the main stream of Protestant thought and practice upon the continent, whether Lutheran or Reformed. The English divines looked for their divinity in Scripture and the Fathers, and though they found Luther or Calvin to be sometimes useful, not inevitably more useful than (for example) St Thomas Aquinas; the continental divines (if it may be permitted thus to generalize, while we remember that any such generalization must be liable to exceptions) still saw the ancient Church through the eyes of the Reformation, and though they found the Fathers sometimes useful, not inevitably more useful than St Thomas Aquinas. The English divines believed in justification by faith in such language as to insist upon the necessity of good works; the continental divines might assent to the language as a matter of theory, but (when fully representative of their own tradition) preferred the more vigorous expressions of *sola fide*. The English divines affirmed episcopacy to be, though not the only "good" ministry (for the Reformation upon the continent, they said, had been less fortunate in its circumstances than ours), at least the best, the God-ordained ministry, and the historic mode of its transmission to be part of that divine ordinance. The continental divines (when they were rather Lutheran than Reformed) might recognize the episcopate to be a reasonable arrangement of the church administration, might sometimes allow that, for purposes of reunion and peace, it could be good for a Lutheran Church to accept episcopal orders. Together with these three main points of difference, there was a further difference between the high Anglican and the Reformed (though not between the high Anglican and the Lutheran). Since Hooker's demonstration *Of the Laws of Ecclesiastical Polity* (1593-7), the high Anglican claimed with confidence that the Church could order "things indifferent" to edification; that unless Scripture explicitly excluded a practice or ordered a practice, the Church might (under God) make arrangements for the due ordering of decent worship; that it was no sound argument against the surplice, or incense, or the sign of the Cross in baptism, to affirm that the papists had misused them. If that had once been a plausible argument when men and women had been trained in erroneous ideas, it was a plausible argument no longer. And while no one wished the churches of the land to be clothed in a "meretricious gaudiness" it was almost more important now to beware of an opposite extreme. And therefore high churchmen in England of the later seventeenth century continued to desire that altars should be in their ancient places, and that confession might be available to those who desired it. These desires were not, however, exclusive to English high churchmen, among Protestants. They were still to be found among some of the Lutherans.

The gap between high English churchmen and the Protestants of the continent was widened by the age of reason. As the seventeenth century turned into the eighteenth, came the age of Locke and of the reasonableness of Christianity. Reason by its nature, is not kindly to history, or at least thinks little of arguments from history. The question that matters is not whether anyone has believed x in the past, but whether x is true. All that complex of new science, and mathematics, and invention, and empirical philosophy, worked the revolution throughout European divinity. Neither the Reformers nor the Fathers were any longer obligatory as spectacles with which to examine the Scripture, not even (according to some eminent thinkers) useful. Improved philosophy and improved knowledge of nature had rendered these guides old-fashioned if not obsolete or misleading. We should find more help, in understanding St Paul, from Locke than from Luther or from St Augustine—so argued Latitudinarians in England.

The high churchmen, or their remnant, were sundered from the dominant Latitudinarians by a wide gulf. Their thought was now liable to the charge of archaism. But so far as they stood by the principles of their predecessors, they were further sundered, not only from the leading English divines of the Latitudinarian school, but from the equally rationalizing theology of the continent. During the eighteenth century even the Lutherans seemed to be departing from their own tradition. Now, at last, the practice of confession was falling into disuse in the Lutheran churches, their sacramental theology seemed to be less sacramental as it sought to become more rational, their more daring men were making tentative efforts at the higher criticism of the Bible. By 1800 the remnant of English high churchmen, though they avowed themselves still to be Protestant, saw little in common between their Protestantism and the Protestantism of Geneva or Wittenberg, which they were now inclined, more than at any previous epoch since the Reformation, to repudiate.

The Latitudinarian dominance in English thought widened the area of belief possible for English churchmen. It so reinterpreted the Thirty-Nine Articles as to make them no longer the doctrinal hedge or guide which once, perhaps, they had successfully formed.

The first widening had been due, not to the Latitudinarians, but to the Laudian divines who wished for stronger language about the necessity of good works in the doctrine of justification, and were called by their opponents "Arminians". The Thirty-Nine Articles had been intended, above all, to enshrine the doctrine of justification by faith alone. They had not been intended to be rigid or exclusive upon the point; but such an article as number XIII, with its teaching that the works of the heathen cannot be good in God's sight, was only compatible (in its obvious sense) with that Augustinian idea of justification which Luther had proclaimed. George Bull and others, in their attempt to interpret St Paul by St James, had wished to find room for the good works of the heathen as truly good; and Bull had, therefore, manipulated the article, by dividing the title from the text in order to discover in it what might later have been called a "non-natural" sense. There was nothing dishonourable or even casuistical about this interpretation, for it was beginning to be agreed, by the end of the seventeenth century, that any dogmatic formula, at least of "human" construction, may need re-interpretation in the light of future thought. The Latitudinarians continued to widen the opinion permissible to one adhering to the Thirty-Nine Articles—first, and moderately, in Gilbert Burnet's exposition of the articles, and later in the century by theologians like Blackburne or Paley or Hey or Watson, who held their places in the Church of England, subscribing to the Thirty-Nine Articles, but certainly not subscribing to all of them in their natural sense; and it was argued by some that the articles could not have been intended to bind all English minds for all time, whatever the results of Scriptural study, and that they were, therefore, intended to be articles of peace in the Church, not to be articles exacting an *ex animo* assent to the doctrines individually contained therein.

The men of the Oxford Movement naturally disapproved of these endeavours, by a left wing, to widen the basis of communion. It seemed to them to be an attempt to weaken that authority of the Church which they were eager to proclaim. But it must be observed that this widening made it easier for them to affirm or even to speculate. It would have been anachronistic, or at least ineffectual, to accuse their doctrine of justification of incompatibility with the Thirty-Nine Articles, as once George Bull had been accused by his opponents. When Newman published Tract XC and showed, incidentally, that the articles need not be so contradictory to all the doctrines of the

Church of Rome as had formerly been believed, he shocked a wide public, and led to charges of insincerity, and casuistry, and dishonesty. Whether or not Newman's method was sound is a question. But the novelty was not in his handling the articles to extract the maximum breadth from their language. The novelty lay in his handling the articles in a Catholic direction. It was natural that liberals like A. P. Stanley should support Newman's right so to interpret the articles, and warmly resist any attempt by authority to condemn Tract XC. The widening of the area of belief, and the turning of an assent or subscription to the Thirty-Nine Articles into a general assent rather than a particular adherence to every clause (even before such general assent received a measure of recognition by Parliament in the Clerical subscription Act of 1865), were appropriate and perhaps necessary for the Oxford men. Their tradition had long sought to draw its divinity from the wells of antiquity, and assumed that the articles of the sixteenth century would be found to be in agreement with the divinity thence drawn. The mode of the church's worship, and the forms of the Prayer Book, and the corporate mind of Church and bishops, were more important to them than the external propositions of faith declared by the divines of 1571, confronted as they were by particular circumstances and problems of the Reformation, not all of which were applicable to the nineteenth century. The articles were not as expressive of the living mind of the Church, as was its tradition of prayer; they must be conformable, but need not be directive.

The high churchmen of the Restoration had associated their churchmanship with another doctrine, declared to be derived from Scripture —the doctrine of the divine right of kings. King James I had said, "No bishop, no king", and the Civil War had seemed to prove the case. The doctrines of Calvinists had often included the right or duty of resistance to an ungodly sovereign; the restoration of King Charles II, in being the restoration of a truer religion, included as part of its orthodoxy the belief that resistance to a lawful sovereign was an offence against God as well as man.

In some circumstances, such a doctrine was near to being self-destructive. It needed only the accession of a Roman Catholic sovereign to put high churchmen into something of the predicament of a Cranmer, who believed in the supreme headship of the Crown and was ordered by the Crown (in the person of Queen Mary) not to believe in the supreme headship of the Crown. After the revolution of *1688*, several of the best high churchmen went into the non-juring schism; some were suspect of Jacobitism; and after the accession of George I in *1714*, the whole tradition was weakened, its adherents scattered, its doctrine neglected.

The high church party was slow to perceive the consequence. Its continued reverence for King Charles the Martyr was but an external and devotional sign of a memory and a stance which remained firm. But it was inevitable that some high churchmen should feel after a doctrine of a Church, as independent of the State. While the non-jurors were contending for the independent rights of the Church against the State, where the law of Caesar conflicted with the law of God, a few who would not carry their protest to the length of refusing communion were concerned to state a doctrine like apostolic succession, not so much as a doctrine in relation to dissent, or validity of sacraments, or faithfulness in Church order, but as a sign that the spiritual powers of the Church were not derived from the State and might have a claim upon the soul's allegiance superior to the claim of the State.[1] But with the exception of the leading non-jurors, these writers cannot be affirmed to have influenced the leaders of the Oxford Movement. Faced by a parallel revolution in Church and State, high churchmen of different epochs were inclined to assert the same contentions. But they were parallels, there was no descent from one to the other.

For, in the meantime, during the period from *1715* to *1830*, the assertion of a spiritual independence was no characteristic of the high tradition. That tradition was content to be conservative; still stiff with dissent, still politically Tory, still deeply attached to the Prayer Book, still concerned about sound doctrine—but it was coming, in the unemotional age, to be "high and dry" as the Oxford leaders called it. Its ethics were guided by *The Whole Duty of Man*; and its piety tended to be sober, earnest, dutiful, austere, or even prosaic in expression. Take such a parson, and place him in the atmosphere of a new age, where feeling is permissible, where poetry is a high road to truth, and you would no longer find a "high and dry" churchman. You would find a John Keble.

The Evangelicals contributed to the formation of the high church

---

[1] E.g. Hill in *Municipium Ecclesiasticum* (*1697*), and cf. George Every, *The High Church Party 1688–1718* (*1956*), pp. *85* ff.

party both by influence and by reaction. As they preached their way into the hearts of rich and poor, neglectful of parish boundaries, friendly with dissent, calling for conversion, putting the Bible before the simplest people, teaching the necessity of faith, favouring the conviction of assurance in salvation, and distrusting language about good works, they encouraged by reaction the "stiff quality", the *high* element in high churchmanship. The high churchman believed that evangelical language about conversion might mislead Christian men into forgetting the regenerating grace which had been bestowed upon them in baptism; that their language about justification might minimize the growth of the soul in sanctification; that their language of assurance might lead to complacency, whereas the soul should work out its own salvation in fear and trembling; that thus to set forth the Bible, without reference to the historic community of Christians, to whom the Scriptures had been given, was to breed error and individualism; that the rights of the parish and of the incumbent should be preserved. On the other hand, the Evangelicals contributed perhaps more than any other group to transforming the high and dry men into the new high churchmen of the nineteenth century. There is a certain continuity of piety between the Evangelical movement and the Oxford Movement. There were other reasons why the high churchmen should learn not to be afraid of the feelings—romantic literature and art, the sense of affection and the sensibility of beauty pervading European thought, the flowering of poetry, the medievalism of the novel or of architecture. But in religion the Evangelicals taught the Oxford men not to be afraid of their feelings—indeed, both Newman and Pusey brought into the movement a strong element of Evangelical sensibility and language, whether or not they may rightly have been called Evangelicals, at any stage of their lives (Newman, perhaps, more rightly than Pusey). The poetry of Keble's *Christian Year* is the outward sign of the new sensibility in the piety of high churchmen:

> "Sun of my soul, thou Saviour dear,
> It is not night if thou be near"—

such language would have seemed "enthusiastic" and strained to the old-fashioned high churchman, and to the piety of *The Whole Duty of Man*. It was not difficult for an Evangelical like Samuel Wilberforce, the son of the great slave-emancipator, to pass from an Evangelical world to the world of high churchmanship, in the crisis of the eighteen-thirties when the revival of the Church as a divine society seemed imperative in the face of a Parliament that was no longer wholly Anglican.

Probably it is this element of feeling, the desire to use poetry as a vehicle of religious language, the sense of awe and mystery in religion, the profundity of reverence, the concern with the conscience not only by way of duty, but by growth towards holiness, which marks the vague distinction between the old-fashioned high churchmen and the Oxford men. It was not so much a difference of doctrine, a difference in the adherence to certain propositions. It was primarily a difference of atmosphere, a concern for the evocative and the reverent, a sense of the whispering beauty and truth of divinity as its presence surrounded the soul. The difference may be seen in a man who is sometimes regarded (and with reason) as a member of the Oxford Movement, William Palmer, Fellow of Worcester College. Palmer was one of the most learned high churchmen in Oxford, and by his liturgical studies enriched and inspired many of the Tractarians. He possessed a clear, cool head, a coherent and well-arranged mind, a knowledge of logic and of the scholastic method. In *1838* he published his treatise *Of the Church*, an exposition of the high doctrine of the Church which is formally the ablest exposition provoked by those times, and won the respect of Perrone, the leading theologian of the contemporary Roman schools. The book is marked by all the qualities of Palmer's mind, cool reasoning, system, relentless logic, such intelligibility as to be impossible to misunderstand. And yet it should be classed, perhaps, rather with the thought of the high and dry school than with the thought of the Tractarians themselves. Its scholastic qualities rely upon the clear proposition and the syllogism. There is no mystery, no sense of depth, no feeling—all is tidy, the mystery is cleared away, the system propounded in its rigidities, the ends are rounded so that truth may not seem rugged. It is a conscientious book; but it is not quite what Newman, or Keble, or Pusey, or Froude, or Williams would have written. Apostolic succession is soberly stated; but it is stated somewhat as though it was a cold piece of machinery for averting heresy and schism, and in it there is nothing of the personal, nothing evocative of historical continuity in the power of the Gospel.

In his *Apologia*, Newman wrote an unfriendly picture of Palmer, one of the few unfriendly pictures among the generous portraits of his former colleagues in the Church of England:

> Mr Palmer had many conditions of authority and influence. He was the only really learned man among us. He understood theology as a science; he was practised in the scholastic mode of controversial writing; and, I believe, was as well acquainted, as he was dissatisfied, with the Catholic schools. He was as decided in his religious views as he was cautious and even subtle in their expression, and gentle in their enforcement. But he was deficient in depth; and besides, coming from a distance, he never had really grown into an Oxford man,[1] nor was he generally received as such; nor had he any insight into the force of personal influence and congeniality of thought in carrying out a religious theory—a condition which Froude and I considered essential to any true success in the stand which had to be made against Liberalism. Mr Palmer had a certain connection, as it may be called, in the Establishment, consisting of high church dignitaries, archdeacons, London rectors and the like, who belonged to what was commonly called the high-and-dry school. They were far more opposed than he was to the irresponsible action of individuals. Of course, their *beau ideal* in ecclesiastical action was a board of safe, sound, sensible men. Mr Palmer was their organ and their representative; and he wished for a committee, an association, with rules and meetings, to protect the interests of the Church in its existing peril.

Palmer had turned the artillery of his logic upon the thought of Newman during his last two or three years as an Anglican, perceiving the precipice ahead and wishing to fence it; and perhaps this application of cold scholasticism helped to create in Newman's mind the touch of bias which marks this brilliant portrait and renders it something of a caricature. But if allowance is made for the element of caricature, it is an excellent and illuminating example of a criticism of the high-and-dry by the high. They were shallow; their theory attempted to rest upon the reasoning of its propositions and took no account of the force of personality; they were far too concerned with defending the Church, maintaining the privileges of the establishment; they

[1] Palmer came from Trinity College, Dublin.

were sober, sensible men, suspicious of extremism or (in its eighteenth century sense) enthusiasm. And by contrast, Newman thought of the Oxford men as men of personal influence and enthusiasm, suspicious of sobriety and common sense, anxious to strive after depth and to penetrate mystery even at the expense of clarity, content to be less coherent so long as they were not shallow, using propositions rather as means than as ends, more concerned with truth than with the defence of the Establishment, more content even to let the Establishment go so long as truth prevails. The contrast was exaggerated by Newman. But it represents a real and momentous difference in habit or cast of mind.

3. Keble

In trying to represent the mind of a movement, we are faced with the difficulty that movements have no mind. If we sought to present the mind of the Reformation, Bossuet would soon have something to say with his book on the variations of Protestantism. Froude, or Pusey, or Rose, or Newman, or Keble, each contributed something distinctive to a store which was not always common. Froude believed the doctrine of the Real Presence and brought Newman to value it; a poem in Keble's *Christian Year* seemed to deny it. Even the closest of associates may sometimes contradict each other, and on matters which are not unimportant. If we try to illustrate the mind of the Oxford Movement, we are not portraying the individual minds of its authors. But if we are not describing individual minds, it is doubtful whether anything else is describable or, at least, worth describing.

Yet we may approach the task from the other end, and say that at least individual idiosyncrasies may be excluded. William Palmer of Magdalen College (not to be confused with Palmer, above, of Worcester College) held strange, perhaps bizarre, ideas about the Eastern Orthodox Church; and it is clear that his particular ideas, so far as they were exceptional, are inappropriate as illustrations of any movement, even though something may often be learned about historical groups from the eccentricities which appear in their vicinity. William George Ward is another, more directly to the purpose. For he was equipped with a philosopher's training and a fine mind, and in his doctrine of conscience as the sole vehicle of religious knowledge he claimed only to be rendering coherent and systematic the doctrine of conscience which Newman was already setting forth; and certainly he was able to give a point, and an intelligible frame, to what Newman had suggested in stumbling language. And yet, when Newman found himself made intelligible, he refused to recognize himself; and there is little doubt that he was correct in so refusing. Can a statement which Newman repudiated be regarded as a true illustration of the movement?

Let us therefore take, as a provisional guide, the principle that the mind of the Oxford Movement from 1833 to 1841 is not rightly illustrated by any speculation, doctrine, position, or argument which Newman, or Keble, or Pusey, would (at that date) have rejected. Such a principle is open to the accusation of leaving nothing but a lowest common denominator between the religion and theology of three men. It forces removal of Keble's then cleaving to a near-receptionist doctrine of the Eucharist. It forces the removal of those later arguments of Newman as he deserted the standing-ground of Pusey on his road towards Rome. More seriously, it forces the removal of a few speculations or theories of real interest for religion but which were characteristic only of Newman's bold mind. But it is a sign that this was a movement of minds, and not an alliance of individual minds, that the doctrine and theology thus left between the three men has certain recognizable features, of details as well as of type; and this doctrine and theology forms the centre of a far wider group of writers and preachers, rooted in the old tradition of high churchmen, receiving fresh impetus both from the crisis of the times and from their leaders in Oxford, but so substantially coherent that it is not misleading to speak of "the theology of the Tract-Writers". The writers of the Tracts themselves did not think this misleading, for with the Tracts they issued lists of books declared by them to contain the principles which they were seeking to assert.

Each of these three—Keble, Newman, Pusey—contributed something characteristically his own, as to the success, so to the thought, of the movement.

Newman believed that Keble was "the true and primary author" of the movement, although "as is usual with great motive-powers", he was "out of sight". After achieving the highest rewards of scholarship which the University of Oxford had to offer, he retired to be his father's curate in Gloucestershire, and remained in country curacies until he became vicar of Hursley near Winchester in 1836; from 1823

Oxford knew him only as a visitor. But the visitor, though a country clergyman, did not share in the traditional obscurity of that profession after 1827. If he was "out of sight", as Newman wrote, it was not in the sense that he was out of the public eye. In 1827 he published, with the utmost reluctance, the volume of poetry entitled *The Christian Year*. Its immense popularity as a handbook of devotion was a surprise to him and made no difference to his life or character. He was a deeply modest, quiet, meek man, with no trace of self-confidence, nor assertiveness, going about his country parish conscientiously, unobtrusively, unexcitingly, engaging otherwise only in the scholarship for which he was well fitted, but in which his modesty made him shrink from publication, and which issued, as its most appropriate fruit, in an excellent edition of Hooker's works. He was not, in spite of Newman, "out of sight" of the world. From 1831 to 1841 he held the (non-resident) Professorship of Poetry at Oxford. But it was a true judgment in a moral sense. He gave the impression of seeking obscurity, of being fearful of publicity. He eschewed all the arts that gain popular applause; he would allow nothing that might merely captivate, even in the sermons which he preached to his simple parishioners. And there was something about him, perhaps, connected with this, which unfitted him to be the author or leader of a movement. It was once said of him by one who had known and admired him, that he had "no go". What is the force of the criticism, if it is a criticism? Was there just a hint of dullness being round the corner, to the lively minds which were his equals? Or was it that he seemed to dislike speculative fire and energy? For Keble, in spite of his poetry and his prayer of feeling, was a Tory high churchman of the old school, and thought it the supreme duty to stand in the ancient ways and avoid novelty. Was it the rigidity of the high churchman, who was hostile to dissent or to evangelicals ·or to Whigs within the Church of England? If he was gentle and meek, he could nevertheless be roused to indignation by any person or policy that seemed to be trampling upon his Church, which he truly loved (the word is not too strong) as the authentic representative of his Master. And he identified the cause of the Church of England with the cause of Tory high churchmanship. If there is a distinction between decisive adherence to principles and rigidity, then, alone of the four original leaders of the Oxford Movement, Keble seemed at times to pass from the one into the other. It is evident in his University sermons, in the sermon on Tradition which is quoted in this volume. His own person was the chief link between the Oxford men and the high churchmen of *1688*. He represented in the movement that symbolical reverence for King Charles the Martyr which had been one of the principal elements composing the traditional churchmanship of the school.

"There was nothing in him to foreshadow the leader in a bold and wide-reaching movement. He was absolutely without ambition. He hated show, and mistrusted excitement. The thought of preferment was steadily put aside both from temper and definite principle. He had no popular aptitudes, and was very suspicious of them. He had no care for the possession of influence; he had deliberately chosen the *fallentis semita vitae*, and to be what his father had been, a faithful and contented country parson, was all that he desired. . . . He had not many friends and was no party chief. He was a brilliant University scholar overlaying the plain, unworldly country parson; an old-fashioned English Churchman, with great veneration for the Church and its bishops, and a great dislike of Rome, Dissent and Methodism, but with a quick heart; with a frank, gay humility of soul, with great contempt of appearances, great enjoyment of nature, great unselfishness, strict and severe principles of morals and duty."[1]

His contribution to the mind of the Movement is more difficult of analysis than his personal place and influence within it. Newman kept the day of Keble's assize sermon upon *National Apostasy* (14 July *1833*) as the day when the Oxford Movement began. Yet that sermon is untypical of the movement as it later developed. It denounced the government for its neutrality between the religions of Ireland, represented by its plan for the suppression of Irish bishoprics. The sermon is more akin to the sermons of high churchmen in Queen Anne's reign, than to the high churchmanship of Hurrell Froude or Newman. It is high churchmanship with regard to the State and dissent, a claim to retain the rightful privileges of the Establishment, and less markedly the type of high churchmanship which asserted the independent and divine status of the Church, whether the Church was established or disestablished. The sermon collected no disciples, raised no

[1] R. W. Church, *The Oxford Movement* (*1891*), pp. *21–3*. I cannot think Church's use of the epithet "brilliant" to be justified. It suggests qualities which Keble distrusted, and which should not be attributed to him by a sober judgment.

party-standard, asserted nothing but what other high churchmen were saying through the country. The importance of the sermon to the Movement was only in its signal within Newman's mind. The trumpet was sounded, and the warriors began to gather, when Newman started to publish the *Tracts for the Times*. Nor did the trumpet at first sound a sufficiently loud, or at least sufficiently distinctive, note to collect many warriors. The transformation of a few like-minded persons into a "movement" was not the work of an instant.

Keble collected round him pupils—Isaac Williams, Robert Wilberforce, Hurrell Froude—and won their allegiance by personal stature. It was Froude who persuaded Keble that he ought not to be suspicious of Newman, despite Newman's dialectic, his friendship with the liberal philosopher Whately, the evangelical forces in his early life. Keble distrusted dialectic. He had learned to think of Whately the logician as shallow, and irreverent. He was altogether out of sympathy with that school of rational theology which treated Christian truth as though it were a philosophy of life, God as though he were a theory to be demonstrated, and faith as though it were the assent of the mind to proven, or to highly probable, propositions. Faith was a gift, its source the Holy Spirit acting through the authoritative teaching of the Church, its medium the sacraments of the Church. Reason was to expound a given truth; to criticize, or to prove (supposing the latter possible) savoured to Keble of irreverence. In Keble this distrust of the dialectician was more a feeling than a clearly articulated conclusion. But in Hurrell Froude he captured a mind, it is true from an old-fashioned high church family, resembling his own in its outlook, but a mind that was dialectical and critical and original. "Froude was a bold rider", wrote Newman, "as on horseback, so also in his speculations." Rose said of him, "with quiet humour" after a long conversation, "he did not seem to be afraid of inferences". He brought to bear upon the old tradition, represented by Keble, an inquiring and even revolutionary spirit, "a free elastic force and graceful versatility of the mind, brimful and overflowing with ideas and views, which were too many and strong even for his bodily strength, and which crowded and jostled against each other in their effort after distinct critical expression", the opposite of all that could be described as "wooden". Keble alone could never have understood Newman, the dialectician who had helped Whately to compose his treatise upon Logic. It was Froude who brought Newman to reverence Keble, and Keble not to be afraid of Newman.

In this way Keble helped to form the moral ideal of the movement, more by his person than his thought; and the moral ideal was essential and integral to its theological development. The fact that he was not a don but a country pastor—this alone was momentous for the movement. It was never to be a movement of mere speculation (which Keble abhorred), a mere movement of the upper mind. It was to be a movement of pastoral and moral care (without which the movement of the mind would stray). The mental picture of pastoral care was still, in the England of *1830*, the parson in the country parish. Since *1714*, or since *1688*, the lower clergy of the Church of England had been "higher" than their bishops and their flocks. *They* were confronted with the dissenter in their parish, or the itinerant preacher, as the bishop was not. *They* had sought vainly (and sometimes foolishly) to maintain the rights of Convocation. And the Church of England in *1830*, despite the Industrial Revolution and the spreading populations of London and the North, was still pre-eminently (and too much) a church of country parishes. The movement reached out so forcibly from Oxford because it understood the needs of the country parish, because its teaching passed into the shelves of the vicarage library and the ideas of its sermons (or the sermons themselves) into the village pulpit. Keble represented for the movement this anchor in the parochial clergy of the country. In some ways the most "typical" figure of the whole movement is none of the leaders but Isaac Williams—pupil of Keble; poet; quiet and obscure country parson; avoiding noise and publicity and controversy (though he found it without intending to find it). The truth, Keble had taught the clergy, will not be popular. We must not expect more than a remnant of faithful men. We must expect criticism and even abuse, that is always the way of truth. And we must go about our parishes quietly, diligently, unassertively, but faithful to our commission, leading our people into the community of Christ which is the Church, and therefore keeping from them nothing of that body of truth which the Church declares to us authoritatively, in such a manner as they are each able, in their moral and spiritual condition, to receive it.

The mode of receiving or apprehending doctrine is believed, by all these men, as they react against the "merely" intellectual, the school of religious philosophy, to be related to moral and spiritual capacity. Though the full Gospel is to be declared, it can only be declared rightly to those who can apprehend it fully, and Christian teachers ought therefore to follow the apostolic example and begin with milk in order that the hearers may grow up and later receive meat. This was a doctrine which the Oxford Movement derived, or thought it derived, from the methods and practice of the primitive church in instructing its catechumens, the keeping back of the creed until the convert had reached a stage of his Christian education, the exclusion of the unconverted from the holiest rites of the sacraments. Their patristic scholarship dwelt much upon the *disciplina arcani* of the ancients, the "reserve in communicating religious knowledge", as two celebrated *Tracts for the Times* described it. But their interest in this patristic restraint arose from more contemporary considerations. They shrank from the newer methods of evangelism, used especially among dissenting bodies, where (so they thought) the preacher forcibly declared the holiest and deepest mysteries of the Christian religion before crowds in the effort to secure conversion. There seemed to them to be something irreverent in holding up (for example) the Cross of Calvary before persons whose impenitent or irreverent spirit caused them only to mock. How the impenitent were to be brought to penitence was another question, but they were sure that this was not the divinely given mode of doing so, and perhaps some of the old prejudices of the high church party of the last century also entered their dislike of these methods. Again, they possessed a strong theological interest in "reserve". Conscience, not logical reason—the ethical judgment rather than the argumentative judgment—is for all these Tractarians the chief road to religious knowledge. The soul is to grow into apprehending Calvary by doing right, by allowing grace to sanctify.

Despite these practical and theoretical reasons for an interest in the doctrine of reserve (apart from the interest aroused by the desire to follow an example in the early Church), Keble's person and outlook were powerful in this direction. "Publicity", or anything of the kind, was abhorrent to him. Religious truth was an aweful judgment, to be approached like the burning bush with the shoes from off the feet, to be approached with wonder and fear, not with the axe of the critical intellect, or the desire for novelty.

"Don't be original" was the advice which Keble gave to a friend (was it Newman?) in whose sermon he found new ideas. Against the rough hands of reformers, he wished to preserve the traditions which he had received in the Church; and therefore to Keble and to many conservatives of this time the word *tradition* is a word of good omen. The Protestant fathers of the Church of England, mindful of medieval corruption, had thought tradition to be an ill-sounding word, to be admitted if at all only under strict safeguards, had associated it with the traditions of the scribes and Pharisees. But now, in a time when the utility of all ancient institutions is in question, the value of tradition and custom is brought home to every Tory churchman. And among ancient institutions the Church was pre-eminent. It was natural that conservatives should again be ready to hear the word *tradition* upon the lips of theologians. The contemporary need of theology seemed to be a revival or reconsideration of the corporate authority of the Church. Men said, the Bible and the Bible only is the religion of Protestants; and they seemed to mean that every individual should extract from the Bible what his individual reason found there, without regard for the corporate judgment of the Christian community. It seemed to Keble, and to Newman and Froude, imperative to teach the authority of the corporate judgment of the Church, and therefore to understand aright what is meant by Christian tradition.

It was denied by none of the Tractarians (until they were ceasing to be Tractarian) that all things necessary for salvation are found in Scripture. But this was not to confess the Bible and the individual reason to be the sole guides to religious truth. The individual reason strayed and misjudged; the Scriptures had been addressed to primitive congregations which already received a faith from apostolic men, and were therefore never intended to be systematic expositions of doctrine, were never intended to be understood apart from the common faith of the Christians who received them. If this is to be summarized in an epigram (as it was summarized by Dr. Hawkins of Oriel College in a long and famous sermon of *1818*, preached to a congregation which included the undergraduate Newman) we may say that the Church is to teach, the Bible to prove. The Christian does not first fetch his faith by applying his reason to the critical study of the Bible, but by apprehending the truth from other Christians and thereafter being led by them to find the evidence and proof of these truths in the Scriptures. The Church can neither teach what is contrary to the Scriptures nor add doctrines to the truth taught in the Scriptures. But the individual will not understand the profundities of Scriptural truth, will have but a shallow and misleading notion, until he has advanced in the Christian way of life—that is, by sharing in the life of the Christian community and allowing the grace of God to sanctify him through its teaching and its sacraments.

Therefore we may say (and Keble is not afraid of it, though he was much criticized for saying it) that in understanding the Bible it is indispensable to consider the tradition of the primitive Church. The Church not only puts the Bible before our minds. It puts the Bible in a certain light before our minds, and prepares our minds to penetrate into its truth. It arranges the doctrines of the Bible into a system as it delivers them, distinguishes the essentials from the inessentials, gives us help by its treasures of interpretation, and a mode of government and worship which forms the context in which the Scriptures are declared.

Therefore we need, according to Keble, to keep tradition before us in three spheres;(1) the system and arrangement of fundamental articles —i.e. approach the Scriptures with the Creed in mind; (2) the interpretation of Scripture—establishing by the consensus of the early Church, for example, that Melchizedek's feast is rightly seen to be a type of the Eucharist, or the Song of songs rightly understood as an allegory of the mystical union betwixt Christ and His Church; (3) the discipline, formularies and rites of the Church—of which the New Testament, taken alone gives but fragmentary notices—the observance of Sunday, the mode of consecrating the Eucharist.

Therefore, what all the orthodox Fathers have agreed is authoritative. Keble was perhaps not fully aware that the phrase "all the *orthodox* Fathers" begs a further question with regard to tradition. Is a *universal* assent to be found by excluding the minority from consideration? Or is the judgment upon the orthodoxy of the Fathers, like the judgment upon the canon of Scripture, only to be found by reference to a judgment outside itself, and subsequent to it, the judgment of "posterity"? And in what manner should we seek to define "posterity", and must we again look for a *universal* assent only by excluding a minority from consideration? Like the Vincentian Canon *quod ubique quod semper quod ab omnibus*, to which all the Tractarians appealed and on which Keble's doctrine of tradition was at bottom founded, the doctrine is a working theory for practical and pastoral purposes of teaching, and could not aspire to being watertight as theory without running into a potential charge of being self-contradictory or at least self-modifying. But it was a pastoral purpose which he envisaged. He was not concerning himself with speculation.

There was a difference between Keble and Hawkins, not a difference of theory but of attitude, and it was a difference which divided the Tractarians from their predecessors, even from the highest of the high churchmen among their predecessors. Hawkins had a theory of tradition, partly because he believed it to be necessary if the existing teaching of the Church is to be defended against its adversaries, unitarian or philosophical. His theory was conservative, preservative. Keble's theory is also, in a manner, preservative—keep the deposit. But it is not only preservative. He has begun to compare the teaching and practice, common or popular in the present Church of England, with the teaching or practice of antiquity, and to find the present Church wanting. Therefore the idea of primitive tradition is not only a preservative idea, but a quest for reform (Newman's "second reformation"), for the restoration of, or re-emphasis upon, those beliefs or practices approved or authorized by antiquity but wanting or fragmentary in the present age. "Is there not a hope", asked Keble, "that by resolute self-denial and strict and calm fidelity to our ordination vows, we may not only aid in preserving that which remains but also may help to revive in some measure, in this or some other portion of the Christian world, more of the system and spirit of the apostolical age? New truths, in the proper sense of the word, we neither can nor wish to arrive at. But the monuments of antiquity may disclose to our devout perusal much that will be to this age new, because it has been mislaid or forgotten, and we may attain to a light and clearness, which we now dream not of, in our comprehension of the faith and the discipline of Christ." It is the more powerful in that it comes from the pen, not of Newman whose mental processes certainly did not run in tram-lines, but of the old-fashioned, retrospective, Tory pastor of a humble country parish.

This concern for the "tradition" of the ancient and undivided Church is the foundation of Tractarian thought. It is not that they were non-Scriptural, though Newman has been accused (unjustly) of being uninterested in Scripture. No one can read the sermons of Pusey or Newman without discerning how lovingly and reverently they turned the pages of their Bibles. But they believed the Bible could only be approached with the proper spirit of reverence when it was approached not with the fallen, objective, detached, intellectualist mind of the individual, but with the eyes of the ancient and undivided Church for which the Biblical texts were in fact written, and which selected some to be Biblical and others not. For this reason they set out to make the Fathers available to the English reader, with something of the same religious spirit in which the Reformers had sought to make the Bible available in the language of the people.

Newman (in Tracts *38* and *41*, published in *1834*, and in the *Lectures on the Prophetical Office of the Church*, published in *1837*) taught this theory in a lucid and extended form, amplifying it as vehemently against Rome as against the Latitudinarian Protestants towards whom its first formulations had looked. In Newman's exposition of the theory the new note of Tractarian thought, compared with the older high churchmen is still more evident.

There were three charges (in particular) to which this theory of tradition was open; first that the difficulty of finding out what was tradition was worse than the difficulty of finding out what was in Scripture, the writings of the Fathers being a vaster, less coherent, less concordant body of material, and therefore that the argument from tradition removed the real authority in the Church from the faithful and from their pastors into the hands of the church historians, who could declare with expert information the teaching of the early Church; secondly that it could easily be made to sound like a piece of ecclesiastical machinery for disposing of dissent, as sometimes it sounds when expounded by a schoolman like William Palmer of Worcester College; and thirdly, the practical difficulty of *applying* antiquity, as a reforming measure, to the beliefs and practices of the Church of England in *1835*.

The second of these charges—that it is a device—misses the mark in the case of Newman and Pusey and Keble. It is not a negative, nor is it a mere form. It is (if the expression be allowed, for they would not have used it) a sacrament. The Church is seen to be like a living being, with its breath, and its limbs, and its head. And tradition is not like certain sentences spoken from the mouth, though the words of the mouth are part of tradition. It is more like the beating of the heart or the breathing of the lungs, or the character of the man, which is part hidden, part reflected in his appearance, part issuing in his conduct, part appearing in his words. "Prophets or Doctors", wrote Newman,[1] "are the interpreters of the revelation. . . . Their teaching is a vast system, . . . pervading the Church like an atmosphere, irregular in its shape, from its very profusion and exuberance. . . . This I call Prophetical Tradition, existing primarily in the bosom of the Church itself, and recorded in such measure as Providence has determined, in the writings of eminent men." This atmosphere is best expounded by Newman, because he possessed the most acute and sensitive mind among the leaders, and above all because he possessed by nature and by musical ear, and had developed by practice, a gift of writing haunting prose. He was incapable of representing tradition as an ecclesiastical device. It was sacramental of the life of heaven, the Church visible as a sign of the invisible. It was an earthly story of the communion of the saints in heaven. His feeling for historical continuity, his affection for the past, his reverence for an otherworldly sanctity, his love of "orthodoxy" not as orthodoxy or rigidity but as faithfulness to every truth revealed, his sense of the richness and exuberance of the Christian tradition—all these enabled him to set forth the implications of tradition in magical prose.

If Palmer was the clearest head, because the doctrine is mechanical, Newman, because the doctrine is not mechanical, gives most trouble to his commentators. Perrone, the leading schoolman of Rome, believed his expositions to be muddled—but unjustly. Everything is blurred, nothing has sharp edges; everything is irradiated with the light from heaven, nothing is lit by the bare, drab, light of a dull afternoon. He saw mystery lurking at every turn; he had learnt, intellectually from Bishop Butler, and emotionally from his quasi-evangelical upbringing and from the romantic environment of the day, that the mere intellect skims the surface of reality. He attributed to a mixture of influences from Butler and Keble his belief that "material phenomena are both the types and the instruments of real things unseen". Tradition is the life of the Church, which, though visible, is more invisible than visible. Tradition, apostolic succession, ministry, episcopate—despite the strength of his language against dissent, he seldom sees these as engines against dissent. He sees them as rungs in Jacob's ladder, where the angels ascend and descend.

[1] Lectures on the Prophetical Office (ed. *1838*), pp. *305–6*.

4. Newman and Faith

It is easy to exaggerate Newman's part in the movement and indeed to think of him as the whole. We so often see the Tractarians through the spectacles of Newman's *Apologia*, and read it as the development of a single mind. Clement Webb wrote to the contrary that though Newman was the greatest figure in the Movement, he was not "even typical" of it. I should not like to subscribe to this opinion, in spite of the authority of its progenitor. It appears to me that the Newman of the years until *1839* or *1840*, even if (like any individual) he had idiosyncrasies which cannot properly be described as belonging to the Movement, represents all its qualities—its sacramentalism and sense of mystery, its controversial confidence, its doctrine of authority, its theory of religious knowledge, its pastoral impetus—are not the Parochial Sermons of Newman the "typical" doctrine of the Movement at its highest, contributing to, rather than creating, a body of theological and devotional thought? It is of the essence of the Movement that its best writing should be enshrined in parochial sermons.

But (I have heard it said) he was a sceptic, not an honest doubter, not even a man with a *fides quaerens intellectum*, but a sceptic who held his scepticism about the rational intellect in a dual harness with religious credulity. And scepticism is not typical of the Movement, and can otherwise be attributed only to W. G. Ward.

It is one of the most intractable problems about his thought. He gives ground for the charge. There is a sceptical streak—the *Essay on Ecclesiastical Miracles* at the lowest, a jumble of twisted dialectic about historical evidence, which it is not too strong to describe as repellent, in a man who possessed (as Acton later confessed) the potentialities of a historian.[1] His teaching encouraged Ward to make the absolute division between the conscience and the metaphysical intellect, even though he rejected Ward's conclusions. James Froude, at one time his disciple, thought of him later as irrational and revolted against the irrationalism. Some of Newman's work upon the lives of the saints, and his Tract *85*, show something of the same streak. He had learned (too much?) from Bishop Butler's *Analogy*—had he almost learned that we need not shrink from paradox because the world is in any case full of paradox

---

[1] See the recent study by T. S. Bokenkotter, *Cardinal Newman as a Historian*, in *Recueil de Travaux d'Histoire et de Philologie;* IV, Fasc. *18* (Louvain *1959*), especially pp. *98* ff.

and so we must expect it? He enjoyed argument, was clever with the use of the *argumentum ad hominem,* and occasionally there is too much argument, too much cleverness.

Yet Newman's was the most profound exposition of the Tractarian doctrine of faith. Doubtless there must be confessed to be a streak of scepticism, about the metaphysical realm, in Pusey and Keble and the others. The whole Movement was fighting the aridity (as it believed) of Paley and Whately and the school of religious philosophers, was engaged in showing the lack of value, *for religious purposes,* of the logical intellect. Newman was untypical in that he possessed a dialectical mind for this purpose. He was not untypical as he formulated the doctrine of conscience and faith in his University sermons upon religious belief.

Faith is not, as Paley and the religious philosophers had taught or implied, an assent to argument, an assent after weighing the probable evidences. According to the New Testament faith is the gift of God, it comes by hearing the testimony of God and accepting it. Though nothing can be claimed to be true in faith which is rejected by the reason, it does not therefore follow that faith is the result of reasoning in the mind. Reason tests, and verifies faith, does not create it.

A child may act savingly on faith, though he cannot give reasons, knows nothing of logic or proof. Reason is always, for Newman, the analytical reason. And though faith is seen to be an act of the reason, he is anxious to demonstrate that it is no act of proof, or demonstration, or analysis, or syllogism; that it is an act, based partly upon the moral judgment of the conscience, which insists that we venture now because act we must, and which is content (like every other practical decision of our lives) with evidence short of the demonstration, perhaps far short. Faith is more a principle of action than of intellectual assent. Something must be done, and done now. Faith is acting upon what we hope for or desire—though this hope and desire are not simply conjured from our own heart, but are formed in response to the circumstances which we find. Therefore the same evidence (of the external kind, like the argument from design) will be weighed differently by different minds, in the measure that they allow moral considerations to enter. Faith is created in the mind, not by proofs but by probabilities, and probabilities will appear different according to the moral judgment and values of the person perceiving them.

In declaring that faith is not assent to the Evidences of Christianity, and that such a notion creates an attitude of mind irreverent and irreligious and detached, Newman did not therefore declare evidences to be valueless. They are an encouragement to believers, a stay and confirmation of their faith or hope. Newman, in a momentous admission, named the idea, that no reliable evidence is needed for the profession of Christianity, "a wild notion". He allowed that there could (theoretically) be evidence sufficient to disprove. But he will not say that evidence is the source of faith; for faith, though confirmed by evidences, has another source—in the moral judgment and the religious feelings, acted upon by the grace of God. "A mutilated and defective evidence suffices for persuasion where the heart is alive; but dead evidences, however, perfect, can but create a dead faith."

Then how is faith to be distinguished from credulity? How is faith to be seen as different from prejudice, bigotry, superstition, or fanaticism? The philosophers of religion replied, again, that as reason was the foundation of faith, so the safeguard was in reason. If the reason is cultivated, men will know why they believe, and how their belief differs from superstition or credulity. Educate men, and they will cease to be superstitious.

Newman denied it. Reason is not the safeguard of faith. Why not? Because he was afraid that, the moment reason is allowed to be the safeguard of faith, it will become detached from it, will hold the facts of religion at arm's length, instead of embracing them, will examine and dissect them, will pass into irreverence. God cannot be God if the proper human attitude is to dissect His qualities and prove His existence. Newman protested too much, for he had already allowed that reason had the duty of subsequently verifying faith, that nothing which reason rejected could be regarded as part of faith; and to verify faith by the reason is at the same time to safeguard it from fanaticism. He ought to have allowed that reason must enter into the appropriation or transmission of the Scripture and the Church's teaching. He ought, even upon his own principles, to have allowed some place for reason in his safeguard of faith, and his extreme statement is one of those which opened him to the charges of scepticism or fideism. But he was denying that reason is the safeguard of faith because he believed (with all the Tractarians) that there was a deeper and a better safeguard—a right state of heart. Holiness, or dutifulness, or love—that is the eye of faith, which keeps it from fastening upon unworthy objects; *fides formata*, faith working by love—there is the stability which prevents the faith from wandering after unworthy objects. Faith is "a movement from something known to something unknown, kept in the narrow path of truth by the Law of dutifulness which inhabits it, the Light of heaven which animates and guides it. . . . It is perfected not by mental cultivation, but by obedience."

Newman is only the most subtle expounder of this doctrine of faith and conscience, which is the second foundation (after the doctrine of authority) of all the Tractarian teaching. Keble and Pusey both taught it, in their different ways; W. G. Ward tried to codify it; Isaac Williams gave what is in some ways the most interesting account of it, even if the account is oversimplified, in his Tract on reserve in communicating religious knowledge. The doctrine of reserve, though much misunderstood and abused at the time, lies near the heart of Tractarian thought; partly because its connexion with Keble's own stamp of character is so intimate, and partly because it is inseparable from the doctrine that a right state of heart is the safeguard of faith.

Newman never expounded this doctrine of faith systematically, and it must be taken as a line of thought suggestive of the meaning of faith and its relation to evidence. There are those who see the systematic working out of this view in the *Grammar of Assent*, and it is plain that the relation between the university sermons upon faith and reason and that book is close, so close that the later book cannot easily be understood without reference to the sermons. But by the time he came to write the *Grammar*, his change of allegiance and the development of his mind have introduced new considerations, a concern for certitude, and for the nature of divine faith as distinguished from human faith. These later concerns are hardly present in the struggling paragraphs of the university sermons; and perhaps for this reason the sermons are more congenial to the mind of the twentieth century than the more systematic *Grammar*. We know more now of the relation of beliefs to attitudes, and are fully ready to go thus far at least with Newman, that evidences, however suggestive of faith, are not its source, and that in this kind of knowing the will is concerned as well as the intellect. Does a child believe in God simply because his parents tell him so? If that is all, then his belief in God is not faith: he may have learnt of God on evidence (their authority) but the trust in God must be his own, formed through the parents upon Him whom the parents trust, formed upon their own faith and their attitude, reaching out with the heart towards someone but dimly comprehended; the evidence is subsequent, and even when subsequent is not weighed with the disembodied detachment of the pure contemplative intellect, studying its probabilities. And therefore said Newman (too forcibly): "It is as absurd to argue men, as to torture them into believing"; and "first shoot around corners, and you may not despair of converting by a syllogism". For the deepest motive of faith is not the arguments presented to the head, but the harmony of Christian truth with the inner teachings, and inner growth, of the conscience. Faith is more a test of a man's heart than of his head.

Newman gave the movement leadership, and coherence, and influence, the form of a party. He was the decisive kind, he made opponents and disciples. He gave them a beauty of language in sacramental apprehension, a concern for forms of worship and for the ascetic modes of holiness, a love of the Fathers and their thought. He was not essential to the Movement; none of the main ideas would have been hidden if Newman had not been its leader. But it can hardly be denied that from 1840 his veering away from its main fortress, his loss of confidence in his own leadership, his emotional (on top of his earlier intellectual) awareness that the Tractarian Via Media was a paper religion, his resentment at episcopal and other attacks, his retirement from Oxford, and the rumour of his passage towards Rome, were (temporarily at least, probably more than temporarily) calamitous for the Oxford Movement.

5. Pusey and the Language of Mysticism

Dr Pusey was not a speculative theologian, nor the leader of a party by inclination, nor the representative of the parochial clergy. He was as retiring and popularity-hating as Keble, and like Keble he had none of the arts which captivate the many. His contributions to the *Tracts for the Times* were long, solid, documented, not easily readable, and were partly responsible for turning the *Tracts* from short and popular pamphlets into treatises for theologians. His name was attached to the Oxford Movement because he had a recognizable and senior position in the university; a man of the aristocracy, a man of wealth and place;

of rare and conscientious learning and accuracy, but withal a simple, unworldly, otherworldly soul, with a simple unquestioning faith. In the *Apologia* Newman ascribed to Pusey the power to be the centre of the party—"He was able to give a name, a form and a personality to what was without him a sort of mob." But this, as is evident from Pusey's career, is what Pusey could not, and what Newman himself could, do. Pusey could make disciples, but few, very few, and they profound and individual. Despite the name Puseyite which was so gratuitously bestowed upon the Tractarians, he could not lead a party. If he had thought a party to be following him, he would have shut himself in his house, said his prayers, and continued with his studies. Men looked upon him as somehow remote—beautifully strange, but still strange.

Newman did not recognize that Pusey had made any *intellectual* contribution to the Movement; or, if he recognized it, he was silent upon the subject. Most of what he attributed, in retrospect, to Pusey was but external—"he furnished the Movement with a front to the world". He allowed that Pusey had imported into it a weight of scholarship, a sobriety and a gravity which might otherwise have been lacking. Pusey looked, not for broadsheets, but convincing tomes, not for dialectic, but for massed information, not for controversial skill, but for a sense of responsibility. And it is true that at first sight Pusey's intellectual contribution was insignificant in comparison with that of Newman. He wished only to accept the teaching of the Bible as handed to him by the Church. He was content with an appropriation of it and fully shared, more than shared, Newman's view that to be critical and detached (and even argumentative) was to be guilty of irreverence. He was not subtle, had no intention of being subtle. His famous Tract upon Baptism, with its massed information, whatever its temporary success by way of confirming high churchmen in their belief that the ancient Church taught baptismal regeneration, succeeded only in clouding the issue for his successors; for amid all the texts and quotations about regeneration, he nowhere considered the meaning of the word *regeneration* itself, or defined carefully enough the sense in which he was using it, and thereby removed almost all permanent value from the volume, apart from its use as a work of reference. Like Keble, he distrusted originality and novelty. He desired only to stand in the ancient ways, and his sole intellectual weapon was information about the ancient ways. He was shocked to find that the professors in Germany seemed to read no book not published during the last twenty-five years. It was tragic that his biography should have been entrusted to the obvious author, the most intimate of his immediate disciples, H. P. Liddon. For Liddon treated Pusey's letters and papers with reverence, the reverence due to a great man (but not due to a great mind, for the mind is not that kind of mind), and the reiteration at inordinate length of detailed information, succeeded in concealing Pusey's stature behind a pile of paper, and rendered the biography readable only by the student.

It would be too sharp a dissection, but not therefore without its truth, to say that Newman represented the moral and intellectual force in the Movement, Keble the moral and pastoral, Pusey the moral and devotional. Newman left the Church of England, Keble and Pusey remained; and though this single fact is in no way a cause but only a symbol, the pastoral and devotional power in the Movement proved to be far more effective, in the long run, than its intellectual power. If it altered *lex credendi*, it altered it by first transforming *lex orandi*. If we think of the Catholic Movement in the Church of England as consisting in a doctrine of authority, a pastoral concern for worship, sacraments, and new modes of sanctification, derived from wider sources than those common within Protestantism (priestly ideals, retreats, confession, devotional books, ways of private prayer and the like), then Pusey should be principally associated with this last. He it was who in the years after *1841* and *1842* translated and adapted continental books of devotion for English usage. He did more than anyone to encourage the revival of the monastic life, and was in the closest touch with the new foundations of nuns.

Upon the doctrinal plane, Pusey's language imparted a new note to the common language of the Tractarians. The Church is the Body of Christ—that is common to them all. But Pusey almost *feels* the individual's incorporation into the Body. His language is more mystical (in the modern rather than the contemporary sense) than the language of any other Tractarian, and in its dwelling upon the participation of the Christian in the divinity of Christ, the union of the soul with its Redeemer, can rise to heights of beauty. Brilioth, indeed, named him the *doctor mysticus* of the Movement. Pusey fetched this language not from the French writers of devotion, but from the Greek Fathers, and the Christian Platonism which they represented, though its roots went down into the pietism of the Evangelicals. He made many disciples of the Movement familiar with the classics of mystical writing, from St Bernard onwards. The language of his sermons breaks forth in contemplative rapture as he meditates upon the unity of God and man. Never would you naturally use the word *ecstatic* of the published writings of Keble or Newman, not even when reading their poetry. The word springs naturally to the mind of one reading the sermons of Pusey. He loved to contemplate the presence of Christ in the soul; he conceived obedience, less as action, than as a quiet resting in the will of God; he thought of the Eucharist as the gate through which the Lord came to take up His habitation in the soul. In this aspect of Tractarian thought is to be found the chief source of that greater emphasis upon the Incarnation in its relation to the Atonement, which has often been noticed as characteristic.

In one other respect the atmosphere of Pusey's teaching was unique. More than the others, he felt able to use strong language, indeed the strongest language, about the responsibility of the human will for its choice between good and evil.

Since the days of the seventeenth century when antinomian doctrines of good works had shocked more sober churchmen, the high church tradition had usually favoured a moderate theology of justification by faith; a theology which preferred to avoid the phrase "faith alone", stressed the necessity of good works as an issue of faith, sometimes allowed that works could be "good" before justification or, (in other words) that justification could be a process rather than a single act of God, asserted that righteousness could not be imparted without beginning to be inherent, eschewed merit and works of supererogation, attempting to avoid the charge of teaching "salvation through good works" by recognizing the grace of God as the beginning and the accompaniment of the road to heaven, and by denying the doctrine (common in the Roman Catholic Church) that with the aid of grace, apart from the imputation of Christ's holiness, good works could qualify the soul for heaven. Newman, who, in his lectures on Justification (1837) reconsidered these traditional questions from the standpoint of the theologian, substantially taught this moderate or mediating doctrine. As a theologian, Pusey agreed—the main lines of his agreement are printed in this volume.

But as a devotional writer, rather than as a divine, Pusey seemed prepared to attribute still more to the powers of the human will to choose the good. Like Keble and Newman, he believed that the contemporary teaching of the Evangelicals, by attributing so much to faith alone and assurance, was underestimating the need to exhort men to obey, the need to show them that they were responsible for their lightest sin, that they could turn to God and could choose the right if they but would, that they were perpetually being confronted by the broad way which beckoned and the narrow way which appeared so steep. This moral earnestness is almost to be described as passionate. All the Tractarians, believing that sanctity had been undervalued by the latitude-men, were inclined to the other extreme, to press men to be saints quickly. Observers of the Roman Catholic Church, experienced in the guidance of monks and nuns, have commented that Newman's rule of life for his little group at Littlemore was too severe. If Newman at times pressed the immediate claims of holiness too earnestly, this was still truer of Pusey. It was not that he failed to recognize the workings of grace, or man's incapacity, or justification by faith. But he was zealous to remind the soul of its aweful responsibility as it stands under judgment before God, and he could perhaps create a sense of strain. The nursery of his own family was not a natural nursery; his wife, as she declined in health, became subject to a painful over-scrupulousness; his immediate disciples sometimes laboured under a similar strain.

This concern for responsibility, this devotional (not theological) undervaluing of grace, this reluctance to recognize naturalness and "the seed growing secretly", that sanctification was not only a supernatural life but a supernatural consecration of natural life, affected the young Liddon, Pusey's more intimate friend and follower. I have elsewhere written of the young Liddon's moral exhortations[1]—"Even when the presuppositions of another age in theology are put aside, something perhaps is still missing. Sin, judgment, grace, redemption—he proclaims them from the rooftops. But he cannot quite bring himself to say, O felix culpa quae talem ac tantum meruit habere Redemptorem! The reason seems to lie in a weakening of the childlike quality in him. In the young Liddon you feel, sometimes, that the burden of responsibility has weighed down youth's simplicity".

Dr Pusey, then, was not always wise. But he practised what he preached. If it was not always wise as advice, it was heroic as conduct.

[1] The Founding of Cuddesdon, p. 43.

6. The Teaching of the Tracts

Pusey once gave a simple summary of Tractarian teaching, in *1840*, when the word *Puseyism* was beginning to be commonly used to describe the Oxford Movement. Part of his reply went thus[1] (the italics are original):

"*What is Puseyism?*"

"It is difficult to say what people mean when they designate a class of views by my name; for since they are no peculiar doctrines, but it is rather a temper of mind which is so designated, it will vary according to the individual who uses it. Generally speaking, what is so designated may be reduced under the following heads; and what people mean to blame is *what to them appears* an excess of them.

(*1*) High thoughts of the two Sacraments.

(*2*) High estimate of Episcopacy as God's ordinance.

(*3*) High estimate of the visible Church as the Body wherein we are made and continue to be members of Christ.

(*4*) Regard for ordinances, as directing our devotions and disciplining us, such as daily public prayers, fasts and feasts, etc.

(*5*) Regard for the visible part of devotion, such as the decoration of the house of God, which acts insensibly on the mind.

(*6*) Reverence for and deference to the ancient Church, of which our own Church is looked upon as the representative to us, and by whose views and doctrines we interpret our own Church when her meaning is questioned or doubtful; in a word, reference to the ancient Church, instead of the Reformers, as the ultimate expounder of the meaning of our Church."

And after mentioning differences of attitude, and in the doctrine of justification, he continued:

"I am, however, more and more convinced that there is less difference between right-minded persons on both sides than these often suppose—that differences which seemed considerable are really so only in *the way of stating them;* that people who would express

[1] Liddon, *Life of Pusey*, ii, *140*.

themselves differently, and think each other's mode of expressing themselves very faulty, mean the same *truths* under different modes of expression."

This summary of Tractarian thought does not seem extreme, or extreme only in being unusually conciliatory. It is almost the old platform of the old high church tradition, and Pusey half-contends that it is nothing more, when he said that they were "no peculiar doctrines". The traditional and conservative mode of expression may be seen in such phrases as "the two Sacraments". The only part of this platform which might have been expressed otherwise by Hammond, or Thorndike, and the divines of the seventeenth century, is the sixth section, with its implied antithesis between Fathers and Reformers. This, though only an implied antithesis, made a momentous difference to the nature of the "temper" of mind. It might, for example, have a widely different effect upon section 5, upon what is intended by the phrase "regard for the visible part of devotion".

In the *Tracts* themselves, the conservative element is strongly marked, particularly because several of them are Catenas (Newman's idea, though probably under Pusey's general influence), that is, extracts from the Anglican divines of the High church tradition, illustrating for example how the doctrine of the eucharistic sacrifice had frequently been professed by loyal members of the Church of England; and others are designed to prove that the doctrines professed are the doctrines of the Book of Common Prayer, that the doctrine of Apostolic Succession, for example, is contained in, or at least implied by, the service of ordination; to emphasize the duty of fasting or of frequent Communion; to exhort the clergy to refuse an alteration in one jot or tittle of the liturgy. There is practically no "theology' properly speaking, to be found among the Tracts, except in Isaac Williams' Tracts on Reserve, Pusey's on Baptismal Regeneration, or Newman's last few Tracts. There is nothing original in the polemic against Rome —transubstantiation, purgatory; it is no more effective, and no less effective, than the traditional criticisms by Protestants, even though one or two of the Tracts (Newman's number 75 on the Breviary, for example) might be held by the nervous to have a devotional influence towards a Roman world of thought. Among the productions of the Tractarians, *The Tracts for the Times* cannot be regarded as those most significant for their religious thought. They were too slight, or too sensibly designed for other purposes, devotional, controversial, ecclesiastical, historical.

The controversy with Rome led to Tract 90; and the publication of Tract 90 (1841) led to the end of the Tracts, shattered Newman's self-confidence, and hacked away at those roots in Protestant tradition out of which the Movement had grown.

The unusual nature of the last Tract has tempted some to regard it as one of Newman's later idiosyncrasies on his Romeward path, to be rejected when estimating the mind of the Oxford Movement, a thesis no more authentic to the Tractarians than his Essay of 1845 on the development of Christian doctrine. But this view would not be in accordance with the facts. The idea behind Tract 90 was integral to the theology of the Movement. It was defended and applauded by Pusey and by Keble, and still more, by William Palmer of Worcester College, who had veered away in distrust from Newman since the publication of Froude's *Remains*, and who was the most solid, and among the most conservative, of the Oxford divines. These men did not agree with all the phrases of the Tract, and would have preferred alterations in detail. The principle behind the Tract they supported whole-heartedly. Indeed its seed was present in such a bare summary as Pusey's definition of *Puseyism* given above, with the phrase "reference to the Ancient Church instead of the Reformers"; the *instead of* which divided the high churchmen of the Oxford Movement from the high churchmen of the seventeenth century.

The aspect of the Movement which rankled in the public, or the academic, mind was the apparent hostility to the Reformation believed to be attributable to the Tractarians. This belief had been founded when Keble and Newman published Froude's *Remains* in 1838. There they had allowed to go forth to the world, together with sentences vehemently denouncing Rome, sentences which were shocking to the popular mind of the English. Froude had begun to study the Reformation at the beginning of 1832, during the constitutional crisis in the country. His visit to Italy in 1833 predisposed him to look upon reformers with a little more favour. By August 1833 he could write that "odious Protestantism sticks in people's gizzard", by December 1835 (now a dying man) "really I hate the Reformation and the Reformers more and more".

Newman, though he edited Froude's volumes, had not asserted publicly that he shared these extreme opinions (unless his editing of the *Remains* be taken as silent consent), and Pusey, who did not share them in this extreme form, was surprised when in *1841* he discovered Newman's deep dislike of the Reformers. It cannot be said that either Froude or Newman did more than dabble in the history of the Reformation, and neither was well qualified to make sound judgments upon the subject. But they had both formed an impression of an antithesis, perhaps an incompatibility, between the ancient Church and the Protestant leaders of the Reformation; and in Newman's more extreme, less sober disciples after *1838*, like W. G. Ward and Oakeley, this "hatred" of the Reformers created a genuine stumbling-block to subscription of the Articles *ex animo*. For subscription was not, to the Tractarians, a vague or general assent to articles of peace. They desired to re-assert the authority of the Church, to adhere to the liturgy and the rubrics; and no one could deny that the Thirty-Nine Articles were a significant part of the authority of their Church.

It was therefore necessary to prove that the articles might be interpreted, and subscribed, in a sense compatible with the faith of the ancient Church, and not in the sense intended by their reforming framers (if it were assumed that those senses were not identical). Newman was forced into Tract *90* by extremists like Ward, but it must not therefore be believed to be an idiosyncrasy of Newman. Some such explanation would have been necessary, sooner or later, upon the most sober principles of the Oxford Movement. That was why William Palmer welcomed and defended the Tract when it was published. And since, as Newman was well aware, Arminians or latitude-men had for two centuries or more been extending the meaning of the articles in various directions, and widening the number of opinions which might be professed under their shelter, it seemed to Newman that he was doing nothing disloyal to his Church in applying precisely the same principle to the particular needs of himself and his followers. Articles are the product of one age; and the theological needs of later ages make some readjustment or interpretation inevitable. The wisdom of the early Church must be allowed to speak to the contemporary mind, must not be narrowed and restricted by promulgations drafted when the knowledge of the early Church was less broad and less well grounded.

In the prevailing state of popular opinion, which resented the alleged

Tractarian hostility to the Reformation, and was peculiarly sensitive at the time because of its concern with Ireland and a government grant to the Roman Catholic College at Maynooth, this plan was delicate in execution. Newman was never imaginative in the realm of tact. In the introduction he described the Church as teaching "with the stammering lips of ambiguous formularies", a phrase by no means palatable even to Pusey. But it is perfectly clear, both from the Tract itself and from the subsequent explanations which he gave, that Newman in no way intended Tract 90 to be a reconciliation with Rome; and the fact that some still believe he intended this cannot be based on a reasoned study of the relevant documents, but can only be an inference from what happened subsequently, in 1845, or from the joyous deductions based on the Tract by extremists like Ward. "The only peculiarity of the view I advocate," Newman explained in a public letter to Jelf, "if I must so call it, is this—that whereas it is usual at this day to make the particular *belief of their writers* their true interpretation, I would make the *belief of the Catholic Church* such" (and by the Catholic Church he still meant the ancient and undivided Church). "That is, as it is often said that infants are regenerated in Baptism, not on the faith of their *parents* but of the *Church*, so in like manner I would say the Articles are received, not in the sense of their framers, but (as far as the wording will admit, or any ambiguity requires it) in the one Catholic sense."

It has not seemed necessary to include passages which relate in detail to that introduction of novelties in ritual and ceremonial which is so often regarded as the particular and influential outcome of the Movement.

The new ceremonial began modestly about 1837 and 1838, with little signs like the wearing of a scarf embroidered at the ends with crosses. In truth the movement for more elaborate ritual was a far wider movement than that of the Tractarians. Cambridge, as the original centre of that group of church-restorers and decorators and designers known as the Cambridge Camden Society, was till 1845 more important than Oxford in the matter. It was another part of that almost universal turning from the head towards the heart. Its roots lay in the desire to turn the churches into houses of prayer and devotion, where men would let their hearts go outward and upward in worship, instead of preaching-houses where their minds would be argued into an assent to creeds or to moral duties. "The desire that all things done in church should be done decently could not stay confined to the architecture. It must affect also the appurtenances and ornaments, the methods of conducting service. The restorers, influenced by the Romantic revival, looked to the medieval centuries to guide them. They were rebuilding chancels, favouring pointed arches, advocating frescoes instead of whitewashed walls. Inevitably, and without any leap of transition, they looked to antiquarian precedent to teach them how to restore the dignity of worship." As sanctity undervalued was now swinging towards sanctity in haste, so dilapidated altars, dirty cloths and hangings and surplices, were now swinging towards decorated altars, clean cloths and surplices, and ornamented hangings. This was a movement far wider than the Tractarian; the leaders thought these novelties to be then undesirable and improper, advised their disciples against them. Yet there was something in the thought of the Oxford Movement which cohered easily with this revival, came in part to dominate and guide it, and finally was itself part dominated and transformed by it, as the elaboration of *lex orandi*, running ahead of any justification in *lex credendi*, refused to be halted but forced *lex credendi* to accompany it.

One side of Tractarian theology "called the Church of England to revive the ancient ways. The ancient and undivided Church must be the model, not only in doctrine, but in liturgy and devotion. In appealing to antiquity they examined the Book of Common Prayer with microscopes and found that the rubrics of the Prayer Book, understood in their historical context, commanded daily worship, frequent celebrations, and more ornaments and vestures than were commonly to be found in English parish churches."[1] Had not the old high church tradition itself favoured a particular reverence for visible and external devotion? And now, with the Reformers on one side, and with the alleged aridities of Latitudinarianism believed to be repellent, antiquity and romantic aesthetics were both moving to give content to the nature of that reverence for visible and external devotion. "We", wrote Oakeley, "are for carrying out the symbolical principle in our own Church to the utmost extent which is consistent with the duty of obedience to the rubric";[2] and he amplified this dictum by suggesting that every church should be furnished with a prominent cross (not a crucifix); stained glass in the windows; penitential ornaments for the

[1] *The Founding of Cuddesdon*, p. 55. [2] *British Critic*, January–April *1840*, p. *270*

altar in Lent and rich hangings for a festival; flowers and two candle-sticks upon the altar (but lighting them "might give offence in these days and we do not advise it, though inclined to regard it as strictly Anglican"); bowing to the altar; facing east when consecrating the Holy Communion. "If to anyone some of these suggestions should seem trivial, let us remind that care about minutiae is the peculiar mark of an intense and reverent affection. Nobler task there can be none for a rational being than that of providing, with the most punctilious exactness, for the due celebrating of the Creator's honour; nor any worthier dedication of the offerings of nature and the devices of art, all alike His gift, than in the seemly adorning of His earthly dwelling place. At the same time we desire nothing less than that matters like these should be taken up without constant reference to "weightier" things; that were indeed to begin at the wrong end; nay, we would go farther, and say that there is something quite revolting in the idea of dealing with the subject of External Religion as a matter of mere taste."

Such was Oakeley's view. Dr Pusey would have expressed the warning more strongly. He disapproved of Oakeley's article. He believed that there was no time for anything else at present, than re-asserting Catholic truth, and that to devote energy or thought or con-troversy to the externals of worship (so that the externals of worship were reverent) was to divert the attention from what mattered. And he believed that the unadorned simplicity of the Church was fitting in its penitential plainness, representing humble sorrow at the divided and unsaintly condition of Christendom. Keble and Newman were no more concerned with ritual than Pusey. But it will be evident how easily and naturally the doctrine of faith and the doctrine of authority, the desire to avoid shallowness in worship and to seek the awe and the mystery of religious experience, cohered with the less guarded desires of younger men to experiment in liturgy and ecclesiastical art. The revival of ceremonial began with a few antiquarians. It was taken thence into parishes where the incumbent might have neither the knowledge nor the restraint of the academic liturgiologists, and was simply concerned with the pastoral effect upon his congregation.

On this doctrine of faith, the borderland between *lex orandi* and *lex credendi* is not always easy to determine. Therefore the mode of wor-shipping might begin to affect the credal propositions believed to be true. The Tractarians condemned the "Romish" doctrine that saints might be invoked in prayer. Was the *ora pro nobis* of some liturgies judged in that condemnation? In Tract *90* Newman argued this to be an open question, and it remained an open question for a long time among the descendants of the Oxford Movement. But if personal devotion in pursuit of enrichment adapts liturgical formulas where the *ora pro nobis* is used and assumed, then the question whether the Church of England condemns it begins no longer to be open.

7. The Influence of the Movement

The Oxford Movement changed the external face, and the internal spirit, of English religious life. But these changes were primarily religious, and only afterwards theological. They succeeded, far beyond the expectation of many, in transforming the atmosphere of English worship, in deepening the content of English prayer, in lifting English eyes, not only to their own insular tradition, but to the treasures of the Catholic centuries, whether ancient or modern.

They failed, beyond their own expectation and trust, in affecting the religious belief of Englishmen except so far as the new modes of worship helped to create an acceptance, or toleration, of more patristic or medieval modes of theological expression. In so far as the Oxford Movement was affirming a particular doctrine of authority, or a particular interpretation of the nature of dogma, or particular doctrines like baptismal regeneration to the exclusion from English religion of other interpretations of regeneration, the Movement failed. Dr Pusey's devotions for prayers during the day are still widely used and valued within the Church of England. His belief in an ancient and undivided Church that was infallible, or his particular mode of expressing a "branch"theory of the Church, now seem to many theologians to be obsolescent if not obsolete.

It might be reasonably argued that within the Church of England itself its doctrinal, as opposed to its religious consequences, were too significant to be described as failure. The proposed *1928* Prayer Book of the Church of England represented, as is the way of liturgies, the prevailing theology of many instructed Anglicans. There are other influences entering into that Prayer Book; but the influence of the descendants of the Oxford Movement is stronger than any other in dictating or suggesting theological changes from the legal Prayer Book of *1662*. The authors of the *1928* book were no longer frightened of the associations of certain words feared by the Reformers and restored by the Tractarians. They were ready to suggest the idea of a eucharistic sacrifice; to use a stronger language from the Fathers about the gift of the Holy Spirit in confirmation, to introduce a commemoration of the main Greek Fathers into their calendar, to strengthen the language which commemorates the faithful departed. And yet, despite such signal exceptions, the doctrinal consequences of the Movement were less momentous than its devotional. Indeed, one of the reasons for a certain untidiness or anarchy which seemed, in the years before and after *1900*, to be creeping into the Catholic Movement within the Church of England, was this distinction—the devotional "power" was still increasing at the moment that the doctrine of authority was weakening.

For it was not the withdrawal of Newman, or Ward, or Manning, or Robert Wilberforce, that was responsible for this comparative failure in doctrine. Those withdrawals, and especially that of Newman, who, despite his dialectic, his touch of irrationality, his wish to believe in ecclesiastical miracles of high improbability, and his later Ultramontanism, was a natural leader as well as a subtle thinker, weakened the force of the Movement and confirmed the suspicions which it had so inevitably aroused. But the Movement was meeting needs of the heart; it was only delayed by withdrawals which would have completed the destruction of any teaching which was superficial and nowhere touching the deeper chords of the soul. The failure in doctrinal influence was not caused because the teachers lost faith in their own teaching. It was caused by the appearance of altogether new stars in the firmament of Christian theology—the new science, Darwin, the new history, the Biblical critics. Intellectually, the teaching of the Oxford Movement upon authority was beginning to be an anachronism within a quarter of a century from its birth. Pusey believed that the monster which he termed "rationalism" was always due to a failure in morals. Such a view, if ever tenable, had become obviously untenable by *1870*.

To settle the thorny questions arising for the theologians from the new study of the Bible, to make terms with the new notion of revelation being forced upon sensible Christian thinkers, was an impossible task for the first disciples of the Tractarians. They had been plunged into the last ditch, and it needed a generation before any of them could lift their feet out and begin again. Liddon, ever faithful to Dr Pusey, devoted his later life to the maintenance of the Tractarian dogmatic against the rising tide; and since Liddon possessed an abler theological mind than anyone in the Movement except Newman and J. B. Mozley, this comparative waste is a measure of the temporary, intellectual, weakness of the successors of the Tractarians.

When the second and third generation came to be reconciled with the new notions of revelation, in Gore and Scott Holland and R. C. Moberly (especially in the volume of essays entitled *Lux Mundi*, published in *1889*) their intellectual endeavours again became fertile. They had abandoned most of the positions characteristic of Dr Pusey upon the authority of the Church. They had accepted a far looser idea of Biblical inspiration. They had rejected the belief that the ancient and undivided Church was inerrant. But in this sweeping revolution they sought to preserve what they believed to be of essential value in the position which Newman, Keble and Pusey had taken up. Though they no longer believed the Bible to be in the old sense inspired, they still looked to find the Word of God in the Bible. Though they no longer believed the ancient and undivided Church to be inerrant, they still believed the ancient and undivided Church to be authoritative. Though they could not accept Keble's statement of the doctrine of tradition, they nevertheless believed it necessary to Christian faith to see the New Testament as a document or documents addressed from faith to faith, the faith of the early Christians. And because they held a more traditional idea of church authority, they were less easily frightened by the revolution of thought about the Bible. They provided for the liberal movement in England a ballast which helped it not to be swept along by the excesses of evolutionary theology and philosophy. Though they no longer believed dogma to be infallible, they still cared mightily for dogma.

In a library of modern religious thought, the theology of the Tractarians ought still to be represented; primarily because of its influence, but not only because of its historical interest. Though their thought upon faith and its relation to conscience is still considerable despite the theological revolutions since their time, this is not because minds of the present day could wholeheartedly assent to it as it stands. The reaction against the rational thought of the eighteenth century swept them

along while it rendered some of Newman's arguments a strange mixture of philosophical weighing of probabilities and hostility to probabilities. Paley may have been superficial, Butler may have been
obsolescent (for the full efficacy of his analogy-argument rested upon
certain assumptions about natural theology, and the contemporary relations between science and religion, assumptions which were ceasing
to be valid by *1840*). But the philosophers of religion were at least not
liable to the charge of shutting religious thought within a high walled
garden, where Christians might believe as they liked while the world
went on its heedless way; a garden wherein Christian faith was preserved and deepened, but which was invisible to the supposed wilderness outside the wall. The Tractarians would have denied that their
doctrine of faith had these consequences. It cannot be said that the
denial would always have been justified; and yet it is not likely that
any sound Christian thinking will again lose that integral connexion
between faith and the conscience, that essential link between religious
propositions and moral judgments, which is one contribution of the
Oxford Movement to English thought. Nor is it likely that any sound
Christian thinking, however Biblical or however philosophical, can
afford to dispense in the long run with some attitude towards the early
Church and its understanding of the Bible. The Bible is the book of a
worshipping community, and that worshipping community can only
understand itself in the light of its own history and continuity.

8. Principles of Selection

A word is needed on the principles adopted in selecting passages to
illustrate the mind of the Movement. In every anthology personal
preference weighs heavily; and, while not leaving any of the main
doctrinal positions unrepresented or unmentioned, I have tried to select
passages which are forward-looking rather than backward-looking. I
have selected for the most part from the writings of the period *1833*
to *1841*, when the thought of the Movement was at its most coherent
and undistracted; but certain passages from a later date forced themselves into the book.

I have sought to eschew controversial writing. It might be argued
that I have thereby cut off a limb from the body. Newman was clever
when it came to polemic, far too clever for the liking of some of his

friends; and a man who is a good controversialist cannot help half-enjoying the battle. Somewhere deep down in Newman at this time of his life, was a feeling of pleasure, more perhaps at the justice and conviction of his own arguments than at conquest over an opponent. Pusey did not enjoy controversy. But he could not bear public untruth unchallenged, and therefore he blundered into controversy after controversy with a laborious and painful sense of duty. William Palmer was equipped by learning and by temperament to have held his own amidst the dialectics of medieval schools. Ward believed controversy to be the very life blood of intellectual advance, and danced upon the twinkling toes of his logic with an occasional snook of contempt round his lumbering antagonists. And if Ward had a rapier, Liddon kept a bludgeon, kept it for the most part mercifully behind his back.

Moreover, the dialectical theologian achieves finesse through his controversy. Just as the arguments over orthodoxy and heresy cleared the mind of the early Church upon the nature and implications of orthodoxy, so the theologian often acquires a point and decision in his language by means of his dialectic. A metaphysician, reaching upwards into the empyrean, ends at last in negatives; and these negatives sometimes negate another's positive assertions. It might be argued that to eschew controversy is to blunt the striking edge of Tractarian thought, even to blur its sharpest distinctions. Yet, for the most part, the controversial matter is either ephemeral, because addressed to a phase of thought which has passed away, or else so traditional as to be hardly worth repeating. The Anglican Newman was a vehement assailant of Rome. So were the Reformers of the sixteenth century; and despite his different point of view upon many matters, Newman did not significantly add to the sum total of effective polemic.

No excuse will be needed for the inclusion of extracts from the Movement's poetry. The inheritance of Keble's *Christian Year* was nearer to the heart of the Movement even than the inheritance of Bull, or Hammond, or Hooker. Nor is there a clear line of division between the theological poetry and the theological prose. With the sermons of Newman, or Pusey, or Isaac Williams, we are often in a realm of prose according to the print, in a realm of poetry in spirit and expression. The best theologian, in the narrowly technical sense of that word, was probably William Palmer of Worcester College. He is nothing if not prosaic, critical, unromantic, logical. And yet Palmer is less a man in the authentic spirit of the Movement than any, perhaps, of its leaders. If he leaves the impression that Church order, or the apostolic succession, or ordination, are pieces of machinery, that is because there is nothing evocative, symbolic, sacramental about his earthy writing. This method and this atmosphere was emphatically not the authentic method and atmosphere of the Movement; partly because its leaders had inherited a measure of Bishop Butler's scepticism about the metaphysical reason and its propositions, and partly because they perceived a connexion between theological language and poetry. Like poetry, the theological proposition was a door into a garden of Eden which could be glimpsed but not mapped. And this, surely, is one of the reasons why W. G. Ward's writing never gives the reader the impression that he is sitting comfortably with the doctrines of his friends, never gives the reader that evocative feeling conveyed so numinously by Newman, Froude, Pusey, Keble, Williams, and even Robert Wilberforce. Ward was a clever metaphysician, though his metaphysics were poles apart from those of Palmer. But he was essentially a man of prose.

In order to share in this poetry, it is necessary not to shrink from the Romantics as though they were harlots, but to engage them with head and heart as true lovers. It is necessary, perhaps, to be capable of pleasure in Wordsworth, or parts of Wordsworth. I will confess that I can only understand, with a bare assent of the intellect, the influence exerted by *The Christian Year*. Keble has moments of grandeur, moments of deep sincerity and simplicity; but the moments of bathos, or of superficiality, bring you down again to the dust too soon after you have soared above it. To read *The Christian Year* feels like seeing an honest and moral play where the illusion is often being broken. I give this only as a reflexion of personal taste. Perhaps there are men who can still, like their forefathers, elevate *The Christian Year* to the level of *Pilgrim's Progress* or *The Imitation of Christ*.

If Keble sometimes seems, paradoxically, unpoetic among the leaders, there is the Newman whose poetic gift, despite *Lead, kindly light* or *The Dream of Gerontius*, flowered most fully in his sermon. Pusey's sermons, though, like his letters, they can sometimes be too weighty and solid and therefore earthbound, at other times reach upwards into the clouds with a beauty of mystic apprehension. There is Isaac Williams, whose verse is to my mind more consistent than Keble's, and possesses in its moods a haunting note of inwardness, of a quality rare even among the Romantics; it was a minor literary, as well as theological, injustice that doctrinal odium prevented his election to the Professorship of Poetry at Oxford. Perhaps Williams, more than any of the others, was a disciple and lover of George Herbert.

This poetic strand is not an appendix to the Movement at its best, a tiara of jewels worn to sparkle but not needed for the hair. It is as natural and integral to the Movement as that study of antiquity which issued so fruitfully in the editions of the Fathers and the encouragement of patristic learning. It is as natural and integral to the Movement as the desire to make the churches numinous, to transform them from bare houses of preaching into temples evocative of prayer. It was as natural and integral because, like the desire to make the churches numinous, it was part of that symbolic and sacramental consciousness which formed the deepest link, perhaps the only true and valid link, between Romanticism and Catholicism. It is not an accident, I believe, that one of the most profound and sensitive and intelligent offspring of the Movement, R. W. Church, was also a delicate and perceptive interpreter at once of Dante and of Robert Browning.

PART I

FAITH

THE PURSUIT OF WISDOM

This hidden wisdom is entirely of a moral nature, and independent of any mere cultivation of the intellect. Indeed, the latter of itself would appear to be a hindrance to it—for such knowledge puffeth up. Even Aristotle cautions us that knowledge in morals can only be gained by practice. And that heavenly knowledge, of which St Paul speaks, he is cautious of disclosing to those who are carnally minded. . . . The character of this knowledge in all its fullness, its secret and hidden—its vast and infinite—nature, and its being entirely a matter of moral attainment, is sufficiently expressed in our blessed Lord's own words— "Judas saith unto him (not Iscariot) Lord, how is it that thou wilt manifest thyself to us and not unto the world?" Jesus answered and said unto him, "If a man love me, he will keep my words; and my Father will love him, and we will come unto him, and make our abode with him." It might also be considered that holiness in man is, in fact, nothing else but a sense of the divine presence; to improve in holiness, therefore, is to grow in the consciousness of God's presence. And this would again bring us to the same point, i.e. our blessed Saviour revealing Himself according to the state of each man's heart.

St John often mentions this knowledge in connexion with love, and such love as the result of obedience. And experience thus confirms it; actions of self-denial dispose the heart to prayer, prayer to the love of God, and the love of God to the knowledge of Him.

We find that we are in a striking way hedged in by ignorance respecting great truths, which we endeavour to gain the knowledge of by any way but that of practical obedience. Such have been attempts to explain the doctrine of the Trinity, which have ended in Arianism; to explain Christ's presence in the Holy Communion . . .; the mode of the new birth at Baptism, which seem, in great measure, to have been the cause of denying it: the incompatibility of free will with the divine foreknowledge is the conclusion which speculations on such a subject have come to. All these topics contain great sacred truths of the very highest possible importance that we should know; but if we attempt to arrive at any knowledge of them by speculation, or any other mode but that of practical obedience, that knowledge is withheld, and we are punished for the attempt: in the same manner that it was of the highest importance that they should know our Lord; but unless they were sincerely and humbly seeking Him, He was hid from them.

It appears as if pains were taken that, in the language of Pascal, "the understanding should not forestall the will"; as if knowledge was still the fruit of death, till the heart was prepared for it; that there is a knowledge boundless in extent, and infinitely good, and indeed, no other than that of acknowledging the divinity of our Lord, to the attainment of which we are urged as the great end of faithful obedience; but that unless that obedience lead us, as it were, by the hand, we shall never arrive at this inner temple. . . . After our Lord had publicly taught the people in parables, and such modes of speaking as, it is said, they did not understand, He said to His disciples *privately* (which privacy has been especially noticed) that their eyes were blessed, because they saw those glorious things which prophets and kings had in vain desired to see, i.e. the kingdom of heaven upon earth. Those glories of the kingdom, described in such glowing language in the Old Testament, were already thrown upon the world; but still they were only known, seen, and received privately by persons who are there described as having eyes to see and ears to hear, i.e. persons of a certain disposition and character; they were things which it is said in the same passage (Luke *10*) were "hid from the wise and prudent and revealed unto babes". And the expressions which describe that kingdom as established upon earth, still speak of it as a secret—a treasure hid in a field, which a man found, and for joy thereof sold all that he had to purchase it; as the pearl of great price, found by a certain person seeking goodly pearls, i.e. giving earnest heed to religious instructions.

The one great practical consideration is . . .
That Jesus Christ is now, and has been at all times, hiding Himself

from us, but at the same time exceedingly desirous to communicate Himself, and that exactly in proportion as we show ourselves worthy He will disclose Himself to us; that if we constrain Him He will come in and abide with us; that unsatisfactory as human knowledge is, and the increase of which is the increase of care, a knowledge which puffeth up; yet that there is a knowledge which humbleth, which is infinite in its nature, and is nothing else than deeper, and higher, and broader views of the mystery which is hid in Christ.

That although Scripture does not set before us any sensible joy or satisfaction to be sought for, as the end of holiness, yet it does this knowledge, which is attainable by nothing else but by making the study of divinity to consist in a divine life.

That with regard to any ways of doing good to the world, it is far too great a work for anything of human device, or any plans that partake of this world to perform; but if in the prescribed path of duty we shall be enabled to obtain this light, it will from us be communicated to others, but perhaps only in some secret way which is known to God, and which the world esteems foolishness, but a power which is of God, and therefore must overcome the world.

That all the means of grace faithfully cherished will lead us, as it were, step by step, into all these treasures, inexhaustible in their nature, limitless in their duration, and exceeding all conception of man, the blessing of the pure in heart, that they shall see God.

ISAAC WILLIAMS. *Tract 80.* pp. *40–1, 45, 47, 82–3*

OBEDIENCE THE CONDITION OF KNOWING THE TRUTH

Scripture gives us but one rule, one test, one way of attaining the truth, i.e. whether we are keeping God's commandments or no, whether we are conformed to this world, or whether we are, by the renewing of our mind, being transformed into His image, Who died for us that we might live to Him. It is not what we believe; the devils also believe: it is not what we feel; this may be the morning dew which passeth away: it is not what we know; knowledge alone puffeth up: it is not even what we speak in His Name; some who prophesy in His Name He will bid depart, as workers of iniquity. That whereon all depends is, what, believing and knowing, we do; whether by patient continuance in well-doing, we are seeking to have His image retraced in us, and ourselves, through His renewing Spirit, day by day, are made less earthly and more heavenly. "Be not conformed," says the Apostle, "to this world; but be ye transformed by the renewing of your mind, that ye may prove what is that good and acceptable and perfect will of God." The knowledge is not in our own power to attain. It is the gift of God, vouchsafed or withheld by Him, and each more or less according as man becomes conformed to the world and things earthly, or to God and things divine. It is in vain that men seek to obtain or to retain their belief in things divine, while they cleave to things of earth. "Whoredom (both spiritual and bodily, the idolatry of the flesh and that of spirit in loving aught besides God) and wine, and new wine," saith the Prophet,[1] "take away the heart." It is in vain (though it is a sad sight) that people will even strive to retain a belief in high and holy things, while their life is wrong. They will strive to convince themselves, but it is in vain; they study, but it is of no use. They will even strive to work themselves up to believe them, strive to believe them, but they cannot. As their thoughts are more and more occupied with the world, holy truth becomes fainter and fainter, even while they regret it and wish to retain or recover it. They look back mournfully to the belief of their childhood, but cannot recall or retrace it.

PUSEY. *P.S.* III. pp. *202–3*

RELIGIOUS LANGUAGE AND POETRY

There is . . . the studied preference of *poetical* forms of thought and language, as the channel of supernatural knowledge to mankind. Poetry, traced as high up as we can go, may almost seem to be God's gift from the beginning, vouchsafed to us for this very purpose: at any rate, the fact is unquestionable, that it was the ordained vehicle of revelation, until God Himself was made manifest in the flesh. And since the characteristic tendency of poetical minds is to make the world of sense, from beginning to end, symbolical of the absent and unseen, any instance of divine favour shown to poetry, any divine use of it in the training of God's people, would seem, as far as it goes, to warrant that tendency; to set God's seal upon it, and witness it as reasonable and true.

KEBLE. *Tract 89.* p. *189*

[1] Hosea iv, *11*.

POETRY AND TRUTH

[*The poet is among the moon-lit ruins of St David's*]

> I slowly wander'd through the site
> Of crumbling walls, half-falling tower,
> Mullions and arch, which darkly lower
> And o'er the intruder seem to frown,
> Putting on size beyond their own,
> Like giants in enchanted tale,
> As dimly seen through misty veil. . . .
>   And there was one who said that he
> (Speaking in his simplicity)
> Had oft been here at dead of night,
> But yet no form had met his sight—
> By that negation bringing nigh
> His secret deep expectancy;—
> But that the midnight tombs around
> Strange floatings by were said to sound,
> And through the aisled stillness deep,
> Strains indistinct were heard to sweep.
> Blest wisdom, dress'd in fancy's hue!
> Such legends, if they be not true,
> Speak what our nature here divines
> 'Mid holy sepulchres and shrines!
> Such thoughts in me a place have found
> 'Mid contemplations more profound,
> And seem to mingle with my themes
> More true than life such holy dreams;—
> I deem in them more truth to lie
> Than all man's cold philosophy.
>   ISAAC WILLIAMS. *The Baptistery*. pp. *194–5*

POETRY AND THEOLOGY

We cannot think that Poetry and Theology would be such close allies unless there were a hidden bond between them.

I have laid it down that Poetry is an art, given by God, for the especial purpose of refreshing and restoring burdened and troubled spirits. It follows that the more deeply anything penetrates the affections of man, the more evident and congruous is its link with Poetry. Everyone is agreed, and the experience of even a little true religion confirms, that nothing can take such utter possession of the heart as the thought of God and immortality; nowhere else does our nature feel so feeble under its burden; nothing so drives it to search about for healing and escape. Poetry offers help—by metre, or rhythm, or a use of words now serene and now passionate, by those means which cannot be precisely defined but which we all feel; and Religion is glad to avail itself of this help. These means will be of especial use to true devotion at times when it feels abased before the infinite universe—whether this is the devotion of ignorant men perceiving but a glimmer of the truth, or the devotion of educated men, who without such language could give no worthy expression, no expression whatever, to the greatness of the grace bestowed upon them.

Both Religion and Poetry struggle to express thoughts and feelings beyond the power of prose to describe; and this common weakness leads them to use alike the world of nature and sensation. It is marvellous how each can help the other here. Religion, searching for words and for every other means to express the movement of the soul, finds no help more welcome than that of Poetry. Poetry takes us by the hand and leads us into the hidden world of Nature, affording a wealth of natural analogies whereby the mind can grow beyond its incapacity for speech, and talk more sensitively and more reverently than if perforce it confined itself to prose. And conversely, if we ask how poets and their verse won honour and renown,[1] we shall need to give first place to Religion. Religion is like a magic wand; once that wand touches a part of Nature, a new and heavenly light is cast upon it. Thereby we perceive that the analogies and pleasant images are not the meaningless sport or fancy of a clever mind, but are true evidences of Nature's voice—in truth, of Him who created Nature. For this reason great poets have been regarded almost as the high priests of the secular world. In short, Poetry affords to Religion its store of symbols and its metaphors; Religion gives them back to Poetry, but sparkling in their new light, (so to say) more sacraments than symbols.

Religion and Poetry are akin because each is marked by a pure

[1] Horace, *Ars Poetica*, 400.

reserve, a kind of modesty or reverence. To follow Nature sensitively, you need to follow her in veiling part of herself. You are led upwards from beauty to beauty, quietly and serenely, step by step, with no sudden leap from depth to height. Beauty is shy, is not like a man rushing out in front of a crowd. Religion too, if it is wise, models itself upon the ways of Scripture, where the treasure of truth is hidden from the idle and unready, to be seen only when the eye of the mind is pure.   KEBLE. *Praelectiones Academicae. pp. 813–6*; transl. by the editor.

FAITH AND REASON

(Newman preached three sermons upon this theme before the University of Oxford, on 6 January, 13 January, and 21 May 1839. The sermons were intended to be a unity. On 29 June 1840 he preached a further sermon on Implicit and Explicit Reason; and on White Tuesday 1841 a sermon on Wisdom as contrasted with Faith and with Bigotry. These five sermons were printed with others in the volume of 1843 entitled Sermons chiefly on the Theory of Religious Belief. *Despite the* Grammar of Assent, *and his introduction to the later republication of* The Via Media, *these sermons represent his most delicate thought upon the relation between faith and reason and were among the most influential of all the theological expositions of the Oxford Movement. The substance of the first three is here printed—the many omissions being mainly overlapping sections, or sections less relevant to the main thought—together with some explanatory passages added from the fourth, and one passage from his* Arians of the Fourth Century *on the relation of faith to theology.)*

THE PRINCIPLE OF FAITH

Whatever be the particular faculty or frame of mind denoted by the word, certainly Faith is regarded in Scripture as the chosen instrument connecting heaven and earth, as a novel principle of action, most powerful in the influence which it exerts both on the heart and on the Divine view of us, and yet in itself of a nature to excite the contempt or ridicule of the world. These characteristics, its apparent weakness, its novelty, its special adoption, and its efficacy, are noted in such passages as the following: "Have faith in God; for verily I say unto you, that whosoever shall say unto this mountain, Be thou removed and be thou cast into the sea, and shall not doubt in his heart, but shall believe that those things which he saith shall come to pass, he shall have whatsoever he saith. Therefore I say unto you, what things soever ye desire, when ye pray, believe that ye receive them, and ye shall have them." And again: "If thou canst believe, all things are possible to him that believeth." Again: "The preaching of the Cross is to them that perish foolishness, but unto us which are saved it is the power of God. Where is the wise? where is the scribe? where is the disputer of this world? For after that in the wisdom of God the world by wisdom knew not God, it pleased God by the foolishness of preaching to save them that believe." Again: "The word is nigh thee, even in thy mouth and in thy heart, that is, the word of faith which we preach. . . . Faith cometh by hearing, and hearing by the word of God." And again: "Yet a little while, and He that shall come will come, and will not tarry; now the just shall live by faith." . . . And then, soon after, the words of the text: "Now faith is the substance of things hoped for, the evidence of things not seen."[1]

Such is the great weapon which Christianity employs, whether viewed as a religious scheme, as a social system, or as a moral rule; and what it is described in the foregoing texts, it is also said to be expressly or by implication in other passages too numerous to cite. And I suppose that it will not be denied, that the first impression made upon the reader from all these is, that Faith is an instrument of knowledge and action, unknown to the world before, a principle *sui generis*, distinct from those which nature supplies, and in particular (which is the point into which I mean to inquire) independent of what is commonly understood by Reason. Certainly, if after all that is said about Faith in the New Testament, as if it were what may be called a discovery of the Gospel, and a special divine method of salvation; if, after all, it turns out merely to be a believing upon evidence, or a sort of conclusion upon a process of reasoning, a resolve formed upon a calculation, the inspired text is not level to the understanding, or adapted to the instruction, of the unlearned reader. If Faith be such a principle, how is it novel and strange?

U.S. pp. *169–71*

On the other hand, however, it may be urged, that it is plainly impossible that Faith should be independent of Reason, and a new mode

[1] Mark xi. *22–24*; ix. *23*. 1 Cor. i. *18–21*. Rom. x. *8–17*. Heb. x. *37, 38*.

of arriving at truth; that the Gospel does not alter the constitution of our nature, and does but elevate it and add to it; that Sight is our initial, and Reason is our ultimate informant concerning all knowledge. We are conscious that we see; we have an instinctive reliance on our Reason: how can claims of a professed Revelation be brought home to us as Divine, except through these? Faith, then, must necessarily be resolvable at last into Sight and Reason,; unless, indeed, we agree with enthusiasts in thinking that faculties altogether new are implanted in our minds, and that perceptibly, by the grace of the Gospel; faculties which, of course, are known to those who have them without proof; and, to those who have them not, cannot be made known by any. Scripture confirms this representation, as often as the Apostles appeal to their miracles, or to the Old Testament. This is an appeal to Reason; and what is recorded, in some instances, was, probably or certainly (as it is presumed from the necessity of the case) made in the rest, even where not recorded.

Such is the question which presents itself to readers of Scripture, as to the relation of Faith to Reason: and it is usual at this day to settle it in disparagement of Faith—to say that Faith is but a moral quality, dependent upon Reason—that Reason judges both of the evidence on which Scripture is to be received, and of the meaning of Scripture; and then that Faith follows or not, according to the state of the heart; that we make up our minds by Reason without Faith, and then we proceed to adore and to obey by Faith apart from Reason; that, though Faith rests on testimony, not on reasonings, yet that testimony, in its turn, depends on Reason for the proof of its pretensions, so that Reason is an indispensable preliminary.   U.S. pp. 172-3

FAITH NOT GROUNDED ON REASON, THOUGH APPROVED BY REASON

Now, in attempting to investigate what are the distinct offices of Faith and Reason in religious matters, and the relation of the one to the other, I observe, first, that undeniable though it be, that Reason has a power of analysis and criticism in all opinion and conduct, and that nothing is true or right but what may be justified, and, in a certain sense, proved by it, and undeniable, in consequence, that, unless the doctrines received by Faith are approvable by Reason, they have no claim to be regarded as true, it does not therefore follow that Faith is actually grounded on Reason in the believing mind itself; unless indeed to take a parallel case, a judge can be called the origin, as well as the justifier, of the innocence or truth of those who are brought before him. A judge does not make men honest, but acquits and vindicates them: in like manner Reason need not be the origin of Faith, as Faith exists in the very persons believing, though it does test and verify it. This, then, is one confusion, which must be cleared up in the question—the assumption that Reason must be the inward principle of action in religious inquiries or conduct in the case of this or that individual, because, like a spectator, it acknowledges and concurs in what goes on; the mistake of a critical for a creative power.

This distinction we cannot fail to recognize as true in itself, and applicable to the matter in hand. It is what we all admit at once as regards the principle of Conscience. No one will say that Conscience is against Reason, or that its dictates cannot be thrown into an argumentative form; yet who will, therefore, maintain, that it is not an original principle, but must depend, before it acts, upon some previous processes of Reason? Reason analyses the grounds and motives of action: a reason is an analysis, but is not the motive itself. As, then, Conscience is a simple element in our nature, yet its operations admit of being surveyed and scrutinized by Reason; so may Faith be cognizable, and its acts be justified, by Reason, without therefore being, in matter of fact, dependent upon it; and as we reprobate, under the name of Utilitarianism, the substitution of Reason for Conscience, so perchance it is a parallel error to teach that a process of Reason is the *sine qua non* for true religious Faith. When the Gospel is said to require a rational Faith, this need not mean more than that Faith is accordant to right Reason in the abstract, not that it results from it in the particular case.

A parallel and familiar instance is presented by the generally-acknowledged contrast between poetical or similar powers, and the art of criticism. That art is the sovereign awarder of praise and blame, and constitutes a court of appeal in matters of taste; as then the critic ascertains what he cannot himself create, so Reason may put its sanction upon the acts of Faith, without in consequence being the source from which Faith springs.

On the other hand, Faith certainly does seem, in matter of fact, to exist and operate quite independently of Reason. Will any one say that a child or uneducated person may not savingly act on Faith, without being able to produce reasons why he so acts? What sufficient view has he of the Evidences of Christianity? What logical proof of its divinity? If he has none, Faith, viewed as a habit of the mind, does not depend upon inquiry and examination, but has its own special basis, whatever that is, as truly as Conscience has. We see, then, that Reason may be the judge, without being the origin, of Faith; and that Faith may be justified by Reason, without making use of it.   *U.S.* pp. *173-6*

THE EVIDENCE OF FAITH AND THE EVIDENCE OF REASON

The contrast that would be made between them, on a popular view, is this—that Reason requires strong evidence before it assents, and Faith is content with weaker evidence.

For instance: when a well-known infidel of the last century argues, that the divinity of Christianity is founded on the testimony of the Apostles, in opposition to the experience of nature, and that the laws of nature are uniform, those of testimony variable, and scoffingly adds that Christianity is founded on Faith not on Reason, what is this but saying that Reason is severer in its demands of evidence than Faith?

Again, the founder of the recent Utilitarian School insists that all evidence for miracles, before it can be received, should be brought into a court of law, and subjected to its searching forms: this too is to imply that Reason demands exact proofs, but that Faith accepts inaccurate ones.

The same thing is implied in the notion, which men of the world entertain, that Faith is but credulity, superstition, or fanaticism; these principles being notoriously such as are contented with insufficient evidence concerning their objects. On the other hand, scepticism, which shows itself in a dissatisfaction with evidence of whatever kind, is often called by the name of Reason. What Faith, then, and Reason are, when compared together, may be determined from their counterfeits—from the mutual relation of credulity and scepticism, which no one can doubt about.   *U.S.* pp. *176-7*

If this be so, how is it conformable to Reason to accept evidence less than Reason requires? If Faith be what has been described, it opposes itself to Reason as being satisfied with the less where Reason demands the more. If, then, Reason be the healthy action of the mind, then Faith must be its weakness. The answer to this question will advance us one step further in our investigation into the relation existing between Faith and Reason.

Faith, then, I have said, does not demand evidence so strong as is necessary for what is commonly considered a rational conviction, or belief on the ground of Reason; and why? For this reason, because it is mainly swayed by antecedent considerations. In this way it is, that the two principles are opposed to one another: Faith is influenced by previous notices, prepossessions, and (in a good sense of the word) prejudices; but Reason, by direct and definite proof. The mind that believes is acted upon by its own hopes, fears, and existing opinions; whereas it is supposed to reason severely, when it rejects antecedent proof of a fact—rejects everything but the actual evidence producible in its favour. This will appear from a very few words.

Faith is a principle of action, and action does not allow time for minute and finished investigations. We may (if we will) think that such investigations are of high value; though in truth, they have a tendency to blunt the practical energy of the mind, while they improve its scientific exactness; but, whatever be their character and consequences, they are impracticable in action. Diligent collection of evidence, sifting of arguments, and balancing of rival testimonies, may be suited to persons who have leisure and opportunity to act when and how they will; they are not suited to the multitude.

U.S. pp. 178–80

When the probabilities we assume do not really exist, or our wishes are inordinate, or our opinions are wrong, our Faith degenerates into weakness, extravagance, superstition, enthusiasm, bigotry, prejudice, as the case may be; but when our prepossessions are unexceptionable, then we are right in believing or not believing, not indeed without, but upon slender evidence.

Whereas Reason then (as the word is commonly used) rests on the evidence, Faith is influenced by presumptions; and hence, while Reason requires rigid proofs, Faith is satisfied with vague or defective ones.

U.S. p. 181

ST PAUL'S VIEW OF FAITH AGREES WITH THE ABOVE

I would draw attention to the coincidence, for such it would seem to be, of what has been said, with St Paul's definition of Faith in the text. He might have defined it "reliance on the word of another", or "acceptance of a divine message", or "submission of the intellect to mysteries", or in other ways equally true and more theological; but instead of such accounts of it, he adopts a definition bearing upon its nature, and singularly justifying the view which has been here taken of it. "Faith," he says, "is the substance" or realizing "of things hoped for." It is the reckoning that to be, which it hopes or wishes to be; not "the realizing of things proved by evidence". Its desire is its main evidence; or, as the Apostle expressly goes on to say, it makes its own evidence, "being the *evidence* of things not seen". And this is the cause, as is natural, why Faith seems to the world so irrational, as St Paul says in other Epistles. Not that it has no grounds in Reason, that is, in evidence; but because it is satisfied with so much less than would be necessary, were it not for the bias of the mind, that to the world its evidence seems like nothing.   *U.S. p. 182*

IN WHAT SENSE IS FAITH A MORAL PRINCIPLE?

Faith is created in the mind, not so much by facts, as by probabilities; and since probabilities have no definite ascertained value, and are reducible to no scientific standard, what are such to each individual, depends on his moral temperament. A good and a bad man will think very different things probable. In the judgment of a rightly disposed mind, objects are desirable and attainable, which irreligious men will consider to be fancies. Such a correct moral judgment and view of things, is the very medium in which the argument for Christianity has its constraining influence; a faint proof under circumstances being more availing than a strong one, apart from those circumstances. This holds good as regards the matter as well as the evidence of the Gospel. It is difficult to say where the evidence, whether for Scripture or the Creed, would be found, if it were deprived of those adventitious illustrations which it extracts and absorbs from the mind of the inquirer, and which a merciful Providence places there for that very purpose. Texts have their illuminating power, from the atmosphere of habit, opinion, usage, tradition, through which we see them. On the other hand, irreligious men are adequate judges of the value of mere evidence, when the decision turns upon it; for evidence is addressed to the Reason, compels the Reason to assent so far as it is strong, and allows the Reason to doubt or disbelieve so far as it is weak. The blood on Joseph's coat of many colours was as perceptible to enemy as to friend; miracles appeal to the senses of all men, good and bad; and while their supernatural character is learned from that experience of nature which is common to the just and to the unjust, the fact of their occurrence depends on considerations about testimony, enthusiasm, imposture, and the like, in which there is nothing inward, nothing personal. It is a sort of proof which a man does not make for himself, but which is made for him. It exists independently of him, and is apprehended from its own clear and objective character. It is its very boast that it does but require a candid hearing; nay, it especially addresses itself to the unbeliever, and engages to convert him as if against his will. There is no room for choice; there is no merit, no praise or blame, in believing or disbelieving; no test of character in the one or the other. But a man *is* responsible for his faith, because he is responsible for his likings and dislikings, his hopes and his opinions, on all of which his faith depends. And whereas unbelievers do not see this distinction, they persist in saying that a man is as little responsible for his faith as for his bodily functions; that both are from nature; that the will cannot make a weak proof a strong one; that if a person thinks a certain reason goes only a certain way, he is dishonest in attempting to make it go farther; that if he is after all wrong in his judgment, it is only his misfortune, not his fault; that he is acted on by certain principles from without, and must obey the laws of evidence, which are necessary and constant. But in truth, though a given evidence does not vary in force, the antecedent probability attending it does vary indefinitely, according to the temper of the mind surveying it.

U.S. pp. *182–5*

IN WHAT SENSE IS FAITH A SUPERNATURAL PRINCIPLE?

The laws of evidence are the same in regard to the Gospel as to profane matters. If they were the sole arbiters of Faith, of course Faith

could have nothing supernatural in it. But love of the great Object of
Faith, watchful attention to Him, readiness to believe Him near, easi-
ness to believe Him interposing in human affairs, fear of the risk of
slighting or missing what may really come from Him; these are feelings
not natural to fallen man, and they come only of supernatural grace;
and these are the feelings which make us think evidence sufficient,
which falls short of a proof in itself. The natural man has no heart for
the promises of the Gospel, and dissects its evidence without reverence,
without hope, without suspense, without misgivings; and, while he
analyses it perhaps more philosophically than another, and treats it
more luminously, and sums up its result with the precision and propriety of a legal tribunal, he rests in it as an end, and neither attains
the further truths at which it points, nor inhales the spirit which it
breathes.   *U.S.* pp. *185–6*

THE EVIDENCES OF RELIGION

We here see what divines mean, who have been led to depreciate
what are called the Evidences of Religion. The last century, a time
when love was cold, is noted as being especially the Age of Evidences;
and now, when more devout and zealous feelings have been excited,
there is, I need scarcely say, a disposition manifested in various quarters
to think lightly, as of the eighteenth century, so of its boasted demon-
strations. I have not here to make any formal comparison of the last
century with the present, or to say whether they are nearer the truth,
who in these matters advance with the present age, or who loiter behind
with the preceding. I will only state what seems to me meant when
persons disparage the Evidences—viz. they consider that, as a general
rule, religious minds embrace the Gospel mainly on the great antecedent probability of a revelation, and the suitableness of the Gospel to
their needs; on the other hand, that on men of irreligious minds
Evidences are thrown away. Further, they perhaps would say,
that to insist much on matters which are for the most part so useless for
any practical purpose, draws men away from the true view of Christianity, and leads them to think that Faith is mainly the result of argument, that religious Truth is a legitimate matter of disputation, and
that they who reject it rather err in judgment than commit sin. They
think they see in the study in question a tendency to betray the sacredness

and dignity of Religion, when those who profess themselves its champions allow themselves to stand on the same ground as philosophers of the world, admit the same principles, and only aim at drawing different conclusions. For is not this the error, the common and fatal error, of the world, to think itself a judge of Religious Truth without preparation of heart? "I am the good Shepherd, and know My sheep, and am known of Mine." "He goeth before them, and the sheep follow Him, for they know His voice." "The pure in heart see God": "to the meek mysteries are revealed"; "he that is spiritual judgeth all things". "The darkness comprehendeth it not." Gross eyes see not; heavy ears hear not. But in the schools of the world the ways towards Truth are considered high roads open to all men, however disposed, at all times. Truth is to be approached without homage. Every one is considered on a level with his neighbour; or rather the powers of the intellect, acuteness, sagacity, subtlety, and depth, are thought the guides into Truth. Men consider that they have as full a right to discuss religious subjects, as if they were themselves religious. They will enter upon the most sacred points of Faith at the moment, at their pleasure—if it so happen, in a careless frame of mind, in their hours of recreation, over the wine cup. Is it wonderful that they so frequently end in becoming Indifferentists, and conclude that Religious Truth is but a name, that all men are right and all wrong, from witnessing externally the multitude of sects and parties, and from the clear consciousness they possess within that their own inquiries end in darkness?

U.S. pp. *189–91*

YET THE EVIDENCES ARE OF SERVICE

It does not therefore follow that the Evidences may not be of great service to persons in particular frames of mind. Careless persons may be startled by them as they might be startled by a miracle, which is no necessary condition of believing, notwithstanding. Again, they often serve as a test of honesty of mind; their rejection being the condemnation of unbelievers. Again, religious persons sometimes get perplexed and lose their way; are harassed by objections; see difficulties which they cannot surmount; are a prey to subtlety of mind or over-anxiety. Under these circumstances the varied proofs of Christianity will be a stay, a refuge, an encouragement, a rallying point for Faith, a gracious economy; and even in the case of the most established Christian are they a source of gratitude and reverent admiration, and a means of confirming faith and hope. Nothing need be detracted from the use of the Evidences on this score; much less can any sober mind run into the wild notion that actually no proof at all is implied in the maintenance, or may be exacted for the profession of Christianity. I would only maintain that that proof need not be the subject of analysis, or take a methodical form, or be complete and symmetrical, in the believing mind as such; and that probability is its life. I do but say that it is ante-cedent probability that gives meaning to those arguments from facts which are commonly called the Evidences of Revelation; that, whereas mere probability proves nothing, mere facts persuade no one; that probability is to fact, as the soul to the body; that mere presumptions may have no force, but that mere facts have no warmth. A mutilated and defective evidence suffices for persuasion where the heart is alive; but dead evidences, however perfect, can but create a dead faith.

U.S. pp. *191–2*

NEWMAN. *Sermons chiefly on the Theory of Religious Belief.* (*U.S.* No. IX, "Faith and Reason Contrasted as habits of mind.")

A FACULTY PARALLEL TO FAITH IS USED BY NON-RELIGIOUS JUDGMENTS

Men of exact or acute but shallow minds regard the pursuit of truth only as a syllogistic process, and failure in attaining it as arising merely from a want of mental conformity with the laws on which just reasoning is conducted. But surely there is no greater mistake than this. For the experience of life contains abundant evidence that in practical matters, when their minds are really roused, men commonly are not bad reasoners. Men do not mistake when their interest is concerned. They have an instinctive sense in which direction their path lies towards it, and how they must act consistently with self-preservation or self-aggrandisement. And so in the case of questions in which party spirit or political opinion, or ethical principle, or personal feeling, is concerned, men have a surprising sagacity, often unknown to themselves, in finding their own place. However remote the connexion between the point in question and their own creed, or habits, or feelings, the principles which they profess guide them unerringly to their legitimate issues; and thus it often happens that in apparently indifferent practices or usages or expressions, or in questions of science, or politics, or literature, we can almost prophesy beforehand, from their religious or moral views, where certain persons will stand, and often can defend them far better than they defend themselves. The same thing is proved from the internal consistency of such religious creeds as are allowed time and space to develope freely; such as Primitive Christianity, or the Medieval system, or Calvinism—a consistency which nevertheless is wrought out in and through the rude and inaccurate minds of the multitude. Again, it is proved from the uniformity observable in the course of the same doctrine in different ages and countries, whether it be political, religious, or philosophical; the laws of Reason forcing it on into the same developments, the same successive phases, the same rise, and the same decay, so that its recorded history in one century will almost suit its prospective course in the next.

All this shows, that in spite of the inaccuracy in expression, or (if we will) in thought, which prevails in the world, men on the whole do not reason incorrectly. If their reason itself were in fault, they would reason each in his own way: whereas they form into schools, and that not merely from imitation and sympathy, but certainly from internal compulsion, from the constraining influence of their several principles. They may argue badly, but they reason well; that is, their professed grounds are no sufficient measures of their real ones. And in like manner, though the evidence with which Faith is content is apparently inadequate to its purpose, yet this is no proof of real weakness or imperfection in its reasoning. It seems to be contrary to Reason, yet is not; it is but independent and distinct from what are called philosophical inquiries, intellectual systems, courses of argument, and the like.

U.S. pp. *203-5*

DECISIONS FOR ACTION ARE ALWAYS GROUNDED ON SOME ELEMENT INCAPABLE OF PROOF

However full and however precise our producible grounds may be, however systematic our method, however clear and tangible our evidence, yet when our argument is traced down to its simple elements, there must ever something be assumed ultimately which is incapable of proof, and without which our conclusion will be as illogical as Faith is apt to seem to men of the world.

To take the case of actual evidence, and that of the strongest kind. Now, whatever it be, its cogency must be a thing taken for granted; so far it is its own evidence, and can only be received on instinct or prejudice. For instance, we trust our senses, and that in spite of their often deceiving us. They even contradict each other at times, yet we trust them. But even were they ever consistent, never unfaithful, yet their fidelity would not be thereby proved. We consider that there is so strong an antecedent probability that they are faithful, that we dispense with proof. We take the point for granted; or, if we have grounds for it, these either lie in our secret belief in the stability of nature, or in the preserving presence and uniformity of Divine Providence—which, again, are points assumed. As, then, the senses may and do deceive us, and yet we trust them from a secret instinct, so it need not be weakness or rashness, if upon a certain presentiment of mind we trust to the fidelity of testimony offered for a revelation.

Again: we rely implicitly on our memory, and that, too, in spite of its being obviously unstable and treacherous. And we trust to memory for the truth of most of our opinions; the grounds on which we hold them not being at a given moment all present to our minds. We trust to memory to inform us what we do hold and what we do not. It may be said, that without such assumption the world could not go on: true; and in the same way the Church could not go on without Faith. Acquiescence in testimony, or in evidence not stronger than testimony, is the only method, as far as we see, by which the next world can be revealed to us.

The same remarks apply to our assumption of the fidelity of our reasoning powers; which in certain instances we implicitly believe, though we know they have deceived us in others.

Were it not for these instincts, it cannot be doubted but our experience of the deceivableness of Senses, Memory, and Reason, would perplex us much as to our practical reliance on them in matters of this world. And so, as regards the matters of another, they who have not that instinctive apprehension of the Omnipresence of God and His unwearied and minute Providence which holiness and love create within us, must not be surprised to find that the evidence of

Christianity does not perform an office which was never intended for it—viz. recommend itself as well as the revelation. Nothing, then, which Scripture says about Faith, however startling it may be at first sight, is inconsistent with the state in which we find ourselves by nature with reference to the acquisition of knowledge generally—a state in which we must assume something to prove anything, and can gain nothing without a venture.

U.S. pp. 205-7

We are so constituted, that if we insist upon being as sure as is conceivable, in every step of our course, we must be content to creep along the ground, and can never soar. If we are intended for great ends, we are called to great hazards; and, whereas we are given absolute certainty in nothing, we must in all things choose between doubt and inactivity, and the conviction that we are under the eye of One who, for whatever reason, exercises us with the less evidence when He might give us the greater. He has put it into our hands, who loves us; and He bids us examine it, indeed, with our best judgment, reject this and accept that, but still all the while as loving Him in our turn; not coldly and critically, but with the thought of His presence, and the reflection that perchance by the defects of the evidence He is trying our love of its matter; and that perchance it is a law of His Providence to speak less loudly the more He promises. For instance, the touch is the most certain and cautious, but it is the most circumscribed of our senses, and reaches but an arm's length. The eye, which takes in a far wider range, acts only in the light. Reason, which extends beyond the province of sense or the present time, is circuitous and indirect in its conveyance of knowledge, which, even when distinct, is traced out pale and faint, as distant objects on the horizon. And Faith, again, by which we get to know divine things, rests on the evidence of testimony, weak in proportion to the excellence of the blessing attested. And as Reason, with its great conclusions, is confessedly a higher instrument than Sense with its secure premisses, so Faith rises above Reason in its subject-matter, more than it falls below it in the obscurity of its process. And it is, I say, but agreeable to analogy, that divine Truth should be attained by so subtle and indirect a method, a method less tangible than others, less open to analysis, reducible but partially to the forms of Reason, and the ready sport of objection and cavil.

U.S. pp. 208–9

THE NATURE OF REASONING

Reason, according to the simplest view of it, is the faculty of gaining knowledge without direct perception, or of ascertaining one thing by means of another. In this way it is able, from small beginnings, to create to itself a world of ideas, which do or do not correspond to the things themselves for which they stand, or are true or not, according as it is exercised soundly or otherwise. One fact may suffice for a whole theory; one principle may create and sustain a system; one minute token is a clue to a discovery. The mind ranges to and fro, and spreads out, and advances forward with a quickness which has become a proverb, and a subtlety and versatility which baffle investigation. It passes on from point to point, gaining one by some indication; another on a probability; then availing itself of an association; then falling back on some received law; next seizing on testimony; then committing itself to some popular impression, or some inward instinct, or some obscure memory; and thus it makes progress not unlike a clamberer on a steep cliff, who, by quick eye, prompt hand, and firm foot, ascends how he knows not himself, by personal endowments and by practice, rather than by rule, leaving no track behind him, and unable to teach another. It is not too much to say that the stepping by which great geniuses scale the mountains of truth is as unsafe and precarious to men in general, as the ascent of a skilful mountaineer up a literal crag. It is a way which they alone can take; and its justification lies in their success. And such mainly is the way in which all men, gifted or not gifted, reason—not by rule, but by an inward faculty.

Reasoning, then, or the exercise of Reason is a living spontaneous energy within us, not an art. But when the mind reflects upon itself, it begins to be dissatisfied with the absence of order and method in the exercise, and attempts to analyse the various processes which take place during it, to refer one to another, and to discover the main principles on which they are conducted, as it might contemplate and investigate its faculty of memory or imagination. The boldest, simplest, and most comprehensive theory which has been invented for the analysis of the reasoning process, is the well-known science for which we are indebted to Aristotle, and which is framed upon the principle, that every act of reasoning is exercised upon neither more nor less than three terms. Short of this, we have many general words in familiar use to designate particular methods of thought, according to which the mind reasons (that is, proceeds from truth to truth), or to designate particular states of mind which influence its reasonings. Such methods are antecedent probability, analogy, parallel cases, testimony, and circumstantial evidences; and such states of mind are prejudice, deference to authority, party spirit, attachment to such and such principles, and the like. In like manner we distribute the Evidences of Religion into External and Internal; into *a priori* and *a posteriori;* into Evidences of Natural Religion and of Revealed; and so on. Again, we speak of proving doctrines either from the nature of the case, or from Scripture, or from history; and of teaching them in a dogmatic, or a polemical, or a hortatory way. In these and other ways we instance the reflective power of the human mind, contemplating and scrutinizing its own acts.

Here, then, are two processes, distinct from each other—the original process of reasoning, and next the process of investigating our reasonings. All men reason, for to reason is nothing more than to gain truth from former truth, without the intervention of sense, to which brutes are limited; but all men do not reflect upon their own reasonings, much less reflect truly and accurately, so as to do justice to their own meaning; but only in proportion to their abilities and attainments. In other words, all men have a reason, but not all men can give a reason. We may denote, then, these two exercises of mind as reasoning and arguing, or as conscious and unconscious reasoning, or as Implicit Reason and Explicit Reason. And to the latter belong the words, science, method, development, analysis, criticism, proof, system, principles, rules, laws, and others of a like nature.

That these two faculties are not to be confounded together would seem too plain for remark, except that they have been confounded. Clearness in argument certainly is not indispensable to reasoning well. Accuracy in stating doctrines or principles is not essential to feeling and acting upon them. The exercise of analysis is not necessary to the integrity of the process analysed. The process of reasoning is complete in itself, and independent. The analysis is but an account of it; it does not make the conclusion correct; it does not make the inference rational. It does not cause an individual to reason better. It does not give him a sustained consciousness, for good or for evil, that he is reasoning. How a man reasons is as much a mystery as how he remembers. He remembers better and worse on different subject-matters, and he

reasons better and worse. Some men's reason becomes genius in particular subjects, and is less than ordinary in others. The faculty or talent
of reasoning may be distinct in different subjects, though the process of
reasoning is the same. Now a good arguer or clear speaker is but one
who excels in analysing or expressing a process of reason, taken as his
subject-matter. He traces out the connexion of facts, detects principles,
applies them, supplies deficiencies, till he has reduced the whole into
order. But his talent of reasoning, or the gift of reason as possessed by
him, may be confined to such an exercise, and he may be as little expert
in other exercises, as a mathematician need be an experimentalist; as
little creative of the reasoning itself which he analyses, as a critic need
possess the gift of writing poems.   *U.S.* pp. *252-6*

THE RARITY OF METAPHYSICAL PROOF

Let it be considered how rare and immaterial (if I may use the words)
is metaphysical proof; how difficult to embrace, even when presented
to us by philosophers in whose clearness of mind and good sense we
fully confide; and what a vain system of words without ideas such men
seem to be piling up, while perhaps we are obliged to confess that it
must be we who are dull, not they who are fanciful; and that, whatever
be the character of their investigations, we want the vigour or flexi-
bility of mind to judge of them. Or let us attempt to ascertain the
passage of the mind, when slight indications in things present are made
the informants of what is to be. Consider the preternatural sagacity
with which a great general knows what his friends and enemies are
about, and what will be the final result, and where, of their combined
movements—and then say whether, if he were required to argue
the matter in word or on paper, all his most brilliant conjectures
might not be refuted, and all his producible reasons exposed as
illogical.

And, in an analogous way, Faith is a process of the Reason, in which
so much of the grounds of inference cannot be exhibited, so much lies
in the character of the mind itself, in its general view of things, its
estimate of the probable and the improbable, its impressions concerning
God's will, and its anticipations derived from its own inbred wishes,
that it will ever seem to the world irrational and despicable; till, that is,
the event confirms it. The act of mind, for instance, by which an

unlearned person savingly believes the Gospel, on the word of his teacher, may be analogous to the exercise of sagacity in a great statesman or general, supernatural grace doing for the uncultivated reason what genius does for them.   *U.S.* pp. *210–1*

THE VENTURE OF FAITH

According as objects are great, the mode of attaining them is extraordinary; and again, according as it is extraordinary, so is the merit of the action. Here, instead of going to Scripture, or to a religious standard let me appeal to the world's judgment in the matter. Military fame, for instance, power, character for greatness of mind, distinction in experimental science, are all sought and attained by risks and adventures. Courage does not consist in calculation, but in fighting against chances. The statesman whose name endures, is he who ventures upon measures which seem perilous, and yet succeed, and can be only justified on looking back upon them. Firmness and greatness of soul are shown, when a ruler stands his ground on his instinctive perception of a truth which the many scoff at, and which seems failing. The religious enthusiast bends the hearts of men to a voluntary obedience, who has the keenness to see, and the boldness to appeal to, principles and feelings deep buried within them, which they know not themselves, which he himself but by glimpses and at times realizes, and which he pursues from the intensity, not the steadiness of his view of them. And so in all things, great objects exact a venture, and a sacrifice is the condition of honour. And what is true in the world, why should it not be true also in the kingdom of God? We must "launch out into the deep, and let down our nets for a draught"; we must in the morning sow our seed, and in the evening withhold not our hand, for we know not whether shall prosper, either this or that. "He that observeth the wind shall not sow, and he that regardeth the clouds shall not reap." He that fails nine times and succeeds the tenth, is a more honourable man than he who hides his talent in a napkin; and so, even though the feelings which prompt us to see God in all things, and to recognize supernatural works in matters of the world, mislead us at times, though they make us trust in evidence which we ought not to admit, and partially incur with justice the imputation of credulity, yet a Faith which generously apprehends Eternal Truth, though at times it degenerates into superstition, is far better than that cold sceptical, critical tone of mind, which has no inward sense of an overruling ever-present Providence, no desire to approach its God, but sits at home waiting for the fearful clearness of His visible coming, whom it might seek and find in due measure amid the twilight of the present world. *U.S. pp. 212–13*

IT IS NOT MEANT THAT NO EVIDENCE COULD DISPROVE

I do not mean that there is no extent or deficiency of evidence sufficient to convince a man against his will, or at least to silence him; but that commonly the evidence for and against religion, whether true religion or false religion, in matter of fact, is not of this overpowering nature. Neither do I mean that the evidence does not bear one way more than another, or have a determinate meaning (for Christianity and against Naturalism, for the Church and against every other body), but that, as things are, amid the engagements, the confusion, and the hurry of the world, and considering the private circumstances of most minds, few men are in a condition to weigh things in an accurate balance, and to decide, after calm and complete investigations of the evidence. Most men must and do decide by the principles of thought and conduct which are habitual to them; that is, the antecedent judgment with which a man approaches the subject of religion, not only acts as a bearing this way or that—causing him to go out to meet the evidence in a greater or less degree, and no more—but it practically colours the evidence, even in a case in which he has recourse to evidence, and interprets it for him.

This is the way in which judgments are commonly formed concerning facts alleged or reported in political and social matters, and for the same reason, because it cannot be helped. Act we must, yet seldom indeed is it that we have means of examining into the evidence of the statements on which we are forced to act.

U.S. pp. 220–1

UNBELIEF OPPOSED TO REASON

As Faith may be viewed as opposed to Reason, in the popular sense of the latter word, it must not be overlooked that Unbelief is opposed to Reason also. Unbelief, indeed, considers itself especially rational, or critical of evidence; but it criticizes the evidence of Religion, only because it does not like it, and really goes upon presumptions and prejudices as much as Faith does, only presumptions of an opposite nature. This I have already implied. It considers a religious system so improbable, that it will not listen to the evidence of it; or, if it listens, it employs itself in doing what a believer could do, if he chose, quite as well, what he is quite as well aware can be done; viz. in showing that the evidence might be more complete and unexceptionable than it is. On this account it is that unbelievers call themselves rational; not because they decide by evidence, but because, after they had made their decision, they merely occupy themselves in sifting it. This surely is quite plain, even in the case of Hume, who first asks, "What have we to oppose to such a cloud of witnesses", in favour of certain alleged miracles he mentions, "but the absolute impossibility or miraculous nature of the events which they relate? And this surely," he adds, "in the eyes of all reasonable people will alone be regarded as a sufficient refutation"; that is, the antecedent improbability is a sufficient refutation of the evidence. And next, he scoffingly observes, that "our most holy Religion is founded on Faith, not on Reason"; and that "mere Reason is insufficient to convince us of its veracity". As if his infidelity were "founded on Reason", in any more exact sense; or presumptions on the side of Faith could not have, and presumptions on the side of Unbelief might have, the nature of proof.

U.S. pp. 223–4

DOES THIS VIEW OF FAITH LEAD TO BIGOTRY OR SUPERSTITION?

There is one very serious difficulty in the view which I have taken of Faith, which most persons will have anticipated before I allude to it; that such a view may be made an excuse for all manner of prejudice and bigotry, and leads directly to credulity and superstition; and, on the other hand, in the case of unbelief, that it affords a sort of excuse for impenetrable obduracy. Antecedent probabilities may be equally available for what is true, and what pretends to be true, for a revelation and its counterfeit, for Paganism, or Mahometanism, or Christianity. They seem to supply no intelligible rule what is to be believed, and what not; or how a man is to pass from a false belief to a true. If a claim of miracles is to be acknowledged because it happens to be advanced, why not for the miracles of India, as well as for those of Palestine? If the abstract probability of a Revelation be the measure of genuineness in a given case, why not in the case of Mahomet, as well as of the Apostles? How are we to manage (as I may say) the Argument from Presumption for Christianity, so as not to carry it out into an argument against it?

This is the difficulty. It is plain that some safeguard of Faith is needed, some corrective principle which will secure it from running (as it were) to seed, and becoming superstition or fanaticism. All parties who have considered the subject, seem to agree in thinking some or other corrective necessary. *U.S. pp. 225-6*

REASON NOT THE SAFEGUARD OF FAITH

And here reasoners of a school, which has been in fashion of late years, have their answer ready, and can promptly point out what they consider the desired remedy. What, according to them, forms the foundation of Faith, is also its corrective. Faith is built upon Reason, and Reason is its safeguard. Cultivate the Reason, and in the same degree you lead men both to the acknowledgment, and also to the sober use of the Gospel. Their religion will be rational, inasmuch as they know why they believe, and what. The young, the poor, the ignorant, those whose reason is undeveloped, are the victims of an excessive faith. Give them, then, education; open their minds; enlighten them; enable them to reflect, compare, investigate, and infer; draw their attention to the Evidences of Christianity. While, in this way, you bring them into the right path, you also obviate the chance of their wandering from it; you tend to prevent enthusiasm and superstition, while you are erecting a bulwark against infidelity.
U.S. pp. 226-7

I am not unwilling to make myself responsible for the difficulty in question, by denying that any intellectual act is necessary for right Faith besides itself; that it need be much more than a presumption, or that it need be fortified and regulated by investigation; by denying, that is, that Reason is the safeguard of Faith. What, then, is the safeguard, if Reason is not? I shall give an answer, which may seem at once common-place and paradoxical; yet I believe is the true one. The safe-guard of Faith is a right state of heart. This it is that gives it birth; it also disciplines it. This is what protects it from bigotry, credulity, and fanaticism. It is holiness, or dutifulness, or the new creation, or the spiritual mind, however, we word it, which is the quickening and illuminating principle of true Faith, giving it eyes, hands, and feet. It is Love which forms it out of the rude chaos into an image of Christ; or, in scholastic language, justifying Faith, whether in Pagan, Jew, or Christian, is *fides formata charitate.*   U.S. pp. *227-8*

Does a child trust his parents, because he has proved to himself that they are such, and that they are able and desirous to do him good, or from the instinct of affection? We *believe*, because we *love*. How plain a truth! What gain is it to be wise above that which is written? Why, O men, deface with your minute and arbitrary philosophy the simplicity, the reality, the glorious liberty of the inspired teaching? Is this your godly jealousy for Scripture? this, your abhorrence of human ad-ditions?   U.S. p. *229*

The divinely-enlightened mind sees in Christ the very Object whom it desires to love and worship—the Object correlative of its own affec-tions; and it trusts Him, or believes from loving Him.   U.S. p. *230*

HOW IS LOVE THE SAFEGUARD OF FAITH?

Right Faith is the faith of a right mind. Faith is an intellectual act; right Faith is an intellectual act, done in a certain moral disposition. Faith is an act of Reason, viz. a reasoning upon presumptions; right Faith is a reasoning upon holy, devout, and enlightened presumptions. Faith ventures and hazards; right Faith ventures and hazards deliber-ately, seriously, soberly, piously, and humbly, counting the cost and delighting in the sacrifice. As far as, and wherever Love is wanting, so far, and there, Faith runs into excess or is perverted. The grounds of Faith, when animated by the spirit of love and purity, are such as these: —that a revelation is very needful for man; that it is earnestly to be hoped from a merciful God; that it is to be expected; nay, that of the two it is more probable, that what professes to be a revelation should

be or should contain a revelation, than that there should be no revelation at all; that, if Almighty God interposes in human affairs, His inter-
position will not be in opposition to His known attributes, or to His
dealings in the world, or to certain previous revelations of His will;
that it will be in a way worthy of Him; that it is likely to bear plain
indications of His hand; that it will be for great ends, specified or signi-
fied; and moreover, that such and such ends are in their nature great,
such and such a message important, such and such means worthy, such
and such circumstances congruous. I consider that under the guidance
of such anticipations and calculations as these which Faith—not mere
Faith, but Faith working by Love—suggests, the honest mind may,
under ordinary circumstances, be led, and practically is led, into an
acceptable, enlightened, and saving apprehension of divine Truth,
without that formal intimacy and satisfaction with the special evidence
existing for the facts believed, which is commonly called Reasoning, or
the use of Reason, and which results in knowledge. Some instances
will serve to explain how:—

Superstition, in its grossest form, is the worship of evil spirits. What
the Gentiles sacrifice is done (we are told) "to devils, not to God"; their
table is "the table of devils". "They offered their sons and their daugh-
ters unto devils".[1] It is needless to say, that the view above taken of the
nature of Religious Faith has no tendency towards such impieties.
Faith, indeed, considered as a mere abstract principle, certainly does
tend to humble the mind before any thing which comes with a profession of being supernatural; not so the Faith of a religious mind, a
right religious Faith, which is instinct with love towards God and
towards man. Love towards man will make it shrink from cruelty;
love towards God from false worship. This is idolatry, to account
creatures as the primary and independent sources of providence and the
ultimate objects of our devotion. I say, the principle of Love, acting
not by way of inquiry or argument, but spontaneously and as
an instinct, will cause the mind to recoil from cruelty, impurity,
and the assumption of divinity, though coming with ever so superhuman a claim, real or professed. And though there are cases in
which such a recoil is erroneous, as arising from partial views or
misconceptions, yet on the whole it will be found a correct index
of the state of the case, and a safe direction for our conduct.

[1] 1 Cor. x. 20. Ps. cvi. 37.   *U.S.* pp. 232–4

When the barbarous people of Melita saw the viper fasten upon St. Paul's hand, first they considered him a murderer, then a god. What is to be said of their conduct? Plainly it evinced Faith; but was it healthy Faith or perverted? On the one hand, they had a sense of the probability of supernatural interference, such as to lead them to accept this occurrence as more than ordinary, while they doubted and wavered in their intepretation of it according as circumstances varied. Faith accepted it as supernatural; and in matter of fact they were not wrong in the main point. They judged rightly in thinking that God's presence was in some immediate way with St Paul; Reason, following upon Faith, attempted to deduce from it. Their reasoning was wrong, their faith was right. But did it not involve Superstition? We must distinguish here. It is no refinement, surely, to say that they were not superstitious, though their conduct, viewed in itself, was such. Their reasoning was superstitious in *our* idea of Superstition; I mean, with our superior knowledge of religious truth, *we* are able to say that they were seeing in things visible what was not there, and drawing conclusions which were not valid; but it needs to be proved that they acted preposterously or weakly under their circumstances. I am speaking, be it observed, of their incidental reasoning; and concerning this I say that it does not become us, who are blessed with light, which gives us freedom from the creature by telling us definitely where are the paths and dwelling-places of God in the visible world, to despise those who were "seeking Him, if haply they might feel after Him and find Him". Superstition is a faith which falls below that standard of religion which God has given us, whatever it is. We are accustomed naturally and fairly to define, according to our own standard, what are abstractedly superstitions and what are not; but we have no right to apply this standard, in particular cases, to other men whose circumstances are different.

The woman with the issue of blood, who thought to be healed by secretly touching our Lord's garment, may perhaps be more correctly called superstitious than the barbarians of Melita. Yet it is remarkable that even she was encouraged by our Lord, and that on the very ground of her faith. In His judgment, then, a religious state of mind, which is not free from Superstition, may still be Faith—nay, and high Faith. "Daughter," He said, "be of good comfort; thy faith hath made thee whole; go in peace, and be whole of thy plague." I have said that she

showed a more superstitious temper than the people of Melita, inasmuch as what she did was inconsistent with what she knew. Her faith
did not rise to the standard of her own light. She knew enough of the
Good Shepherd to have directed her faith to Him as the one source of
all good, instead of which she lingered in the circumstances and outskirts of His Divine Perfections. She in effect regarded the hem of His
garment as an original principle of miraculous power, and thereby
placed herself almost in the position of those who idolize the
creature. Yet even this seems to have arisen from great humbleness of
mind: like the servants of the ruler of the synagogue, who were then
standing by, she feared probably to "trouble the Master" with her
direct intercession; or like the Apostles on a subsequent occasion, who
rebuked those who brought children for His touch, she was unwilling
to interrupt Him; or she was full of her own unworthiness, like the
centurion who prayed that Christ would not condescend to enter his
roof, but would speak the word instead, or send a messenger. She
thought that a little one, such as herself, might come in for the crumbs
from His table by chance, and without His distinct bidding, by the
perpetual operation and spontaneous exuberance of those majestic
general laws on which He wrought miracles. In all this—in her faith
and her humility, her faith tinged with superstition, her abject humility
—she would seem to resemble such worshippers in various ages and
countries in the Christian Church, as have impaired their simple
veneration of the Invisible, by an undue lingering of mind upon the
outward emblems which they have considered He had blessed.

U.S. pp. 237–40

ST PAUL'S MODE OF ELICITING FAITH

It was not St Paul's method to represent the faith, to which he
exhorted his hearers, as a state of mind utterly alien from their existing
knowledge, their convictions, and their moral character. He drew
them on, not by unsettling them, but through their own system, as
far as might be—by persuasives of a positive nature, and which, while
fitted to attract by their innate truth and beauty, excluded by their very
presence whatever in Paganism was inconsistent with them. What they
already were, was to lead them on, as by a venture, to what they were
not; what they knew was to lead them on, upon presumptions, to what

they as yet knew not. Neither of Jew nor of Gentile did he demand
Faith in his message, on the bare antecedent ground that God was every
where, and therefore, if so be, might be with himself in particular who
spoke to them; nor, again, did he appeal merely to his miraculous
powers; but he looked at men steadfastly, to see whether they had
"faith to be healed"; he appealed to that whole body of opinion,
affection, and desire, which made up, in each man, his moral self;
which, distinct from all guesses and random efforts, set him forward
steadily in one direction, which, if it was what it should be, would
respond to the Apostle's doctrine, as the strings of one instrument
vibrate with another, which, if it was not, would either not accept it,
or not abide in it. He taught men, not only that Almighty God was,
and was every where, but that He had certain moral attributes; that He
was just, true, holy, and merciful; that His representative was in their
hearts; that He already dwelt in them as a lawgiver and a judge, by a
sense of right and a conscience of sin; and that what he himself was then
bringing fulfilled what was thus begun in them by nature, by tokens so
like the truth, as to constrain all who loved God under the Religion
of Nature to believe in Him as revealed in the Gospel.

U.S. pp. 242–3

FAITH AND THE NEED FOR THEOLOGY

Nothing would be more theoretical and unreal than to suppose that
true Faith cannot exist except when moulded upon a Creed, and based
upon Evidence; yet nothing would indicate a more shallow philosophy
than to say that it ought carefully to be disjoined from dogmatic and
argumentative statements. To assert the latter is to discard the science
of theology from the service of religion; to assert the former, is to
maintain that every child, every peasant, must be a theologian. Faith
cannot exist without grounds or without an object; but it does not
follow that all who have faith should recognize, and be able to state
what they believe, and how. Nor, on the other hand, because it is not
identical with its grounds and its object, does it therefore cease to be
true Faith, on its recognizing them? In proportion as the mind reflects
upon itself, it will be able "to give an account" of what it believes and
hopes; as far as it has not thus reflected, it will not be able. Such knowledge cannot be wrong, yet cannot be necessary, while reflection is at

once a natural faculty of our souls, yet needs cultivation. Scripture gives instances of Faith in each of these states, when attended by a conscious exercise of Reason, and when not. When Nicodemus said "No man can do these miracles that Thou doest, except God be with him", he reasoned or argued. When the Scribe said, "There is One God and there is none other but He; and to love Him with all the heart . . . is more than all whole burnt offerings and sacrifices", his belief was dogmatical. On the other hand, when the cripple at Lystra believed, on St Paul's preaching, or the man at the Beautiful gate believed in the Name of Christ, their faith was independent, not of objects or grounds, (for that is impossible), but of perceptible, recognized, producible objects and grounds: they believed, they could not say what or why. True Faith, then, admits but does not require, the exercise of what is commonly understood by Reason.   *U.S.* pp. *249–50*

FAITH AND DOCTRINE

Before the mind has been roused to reflexion and inquisitiveness about its own acts and impressions, it acquiesces, if religiously trained, in that practical devotion to the blessed Trinity, and implicit acknowledgement of the divinity of Son and Spirit, which Holy Scripture at once teaches and exemplifies. This is the faith of uneducated men, which is not the less philosophically correct, nor less acceptable to God, because it does not happen to be conceived in those precise statements, which presuppose the action of the mind on its own sentiments and notions. Moral feelings do not directly contemplate and realize to themselves the objects which excite them. A heathen in obeying his conscience, implicitly worships Him of whom he has never distinctly heard. Again, a child feels not the less affectionate reverence towards his parents because he cannot discriminate in words, nay or idea, between them and others. As, however, his mind opens, he might ask himself concerning the ground of his own emotions and conduct towards them; and might find that these are the correlatives of their peculiar tenderness towards him, long and intimate knowledge of him, and unhesitating assumption of authority over him; all which he continually experiences. And further, he might trace these to the essential relation itself, the gift of life and reason, the inestimable blessing of an indestructible, never-ending existence. And now his reason contemplates the object of those affections, which acted truly from the first, and are not purer or stronger merely for this accession of knowledge. This will tend to illustrate the sacred subject to which we are directing our attention. As the intellect is cultivated and expanded, it cannot refrain from the attempt to analyse the vision which influences the heart, and the object in which it centres; nor does it stop until it has, in some sort, succeeded in expressing in words, what has all along been a principle both of the affections and of practical obedience. But here the parallel ceases; the Object of religious veneration being unseen, and dissimilar from all that is seen, reason can but represent it in the medium of those ideas which the experience of life affords (as we see in the Scripture account, as far as it is addressed to the intellect); and unless these ideas, however inadequate, be correctly applied, they react upon the affections, and deprave the religious principle. This is exemplified in the case of the heathen, who, trying to make their instinctive notion of the Deity an object of reflection, pictured to their minds false images, which eventually gave them a pattern and a sanction for sinning. Thus the systematic doctrine of the Trinity may be considered as the shadow, projected for the contemplation of the intellect, of the object of scripturally-informed piety; a representation, economical; necessarily imperfect, as being exhibited in a foreign medium, and therefore involving apparent inconsistencies or mysteries; given to the Church by tradition contemporaneously with those apostolic writings which are addressed more directly to the heart; kept in the background in the infancy of Christianity, when faith and obedience were vigorous, and brought forward at a time when, reason being disproportionately developed, and aiming at sovereignty in the province of religion, its presence became necessary to expel an usurping idol from the house of God.

If this account of the connexion between the theological system and the Scripture implication of it, be substantially correct, it will be seen how ineffectual all attempts ever will be to obscure the doctrine in mere general language. It is readily granted that the intellectual representation should ever be subordinate to the cultivation of the religious affections. And after all, it must be owned, so reluctant is a well-constituted mind to reflect on its own feelings, that the correct intellectual image, from its hardness of outline, may startle and offend those who have all along acted upon it. Doubtless there are portions of the ecclesiastical doctrine, presently to be exhibited, which may at first sight seem a refinement, merely because the object and bearings of them are not understood without reflexion and experience. But what is left to the Church but to speak out, in order to exclude error? Much as we may wish it, we cannot restrain the rovings of the intellect, or silence its clamorous demand for a formal statement concerning the Object of our worship. If e.g. Scripture bids us adore God, and adore His Son, our reason at once asks, whether it does not follow that there are two Gods; and a system of doctrine becomes unavoidable, being framed, let it be observed, not with a view of explaining, but of arranging the inspired notices concerning the Supreme Being, of providing, not a consistent, but a connected statement. There the inquisitiveness of a pious mind rests, viz. when it has pursued the subject into the mystery which is its limit. But this is not all. The intellectual expression of theological truth not only excludes heresy, it directly assists the acts of religious worship and obedience; fixing and stimulating the Christian spirit in the same way that the knowledge of the one God relieves and illuminates the perplexed conscience of the religious heathen.　　　　　　　NEWMAN. *Arians.* pp. *158–61*

THE PLACE OF ARGUMENT IN RELIGION

Inquiry and argument may be employed, first, in ascertaining the divine origin of Religion, Natural and Revealed; next in interpreting Scripture; and thirdly, in determining points of Faith and Morals; that is, in the Evidences, Biblical Exposition, and Dogmatic Theology. In all three departments there is, first of all, an exercise of implicit reason, which is in its degree common to all men; for all men gain a certain impression, right or wrong, from what comes before them, for or against Christianity, for or against certain interpretations of Scripture, for or against certain doctrines. This impression, made upon their minds, whether by the claim itself of Revealed Religion, or by its documents, or by its teaching, it is the object of science to analyse, verify, methodize, and exhibit. We believe certain things, on certain grounds, through certain informants; and the analysis of these three, the why, the how, and the what, seems pretty nearly to constitute the science of divinity.　　　　　　　　　　　　*U.S.* p. *259*

THE LIMITS OF ARGUMENT IN RELIGION

The great practical evil of method and form in matters of religion—nay, in all moral matters—is obviously this: their promising more than they can effect. At best the science of divinity is very imperfect and inaccurate, yet the very name of science is a profession of accuracy. Other and more familiar objections readily occur; such as its leading to familiarity with sacred things, and consequent irreverence; its fostering formality; its substituting a sort of religious philosophy and literature for worship and practice; its weakening the springs of action by inquiring into them; its stimulating to controversy and strife; its substituting, in matters of duty, positive rules which need explanation for an instinctive feeling which commands the mind; its leading the mind to mistake system for truth, and to suppose that an hypothesis is real because it is consistent: but all such objections, though important, rather lead us to a cautious use of science than to a distrust of it in religious matters. But its insufficiency in so high a province is an evil which attaches to it from first to last, an inherent evil which there are no means of remedying, and which, perhaps, lies at the root of those other evils, which I have just been enumerating. To this evil I shall now direct my attention, having already incidentally referred to it in some of the foregoing remarks.

No analysis is subtle and delicate enough to represent adequately the state of mind under which we believe, or the subjects of belief, as they are presented to our thoughts. The end proposed is that of delineating, or, as it were, painting what the mind sees and feels; now let us consider what it is to portray duly in form and colour things material, and we shall surely understand the difficulty, or rather the impossibility, of representing the outline and character, the hues and shades in which any intellectual view really exists in the mind, or of giving it that substance and that exactness in detail in which consists its likeness to the original, or of sufficiently marking those minute differences which attach to the same general state of mind or tone of thought as found in this or that individual respectively. It is probable that given opinions, as held by individuals, even when of the most congenial views, are as distinct from each other as their faces. Now how minute is the defect in imitation which hinders the likeness of a portrait from being successful! how easy is it to recognize who is intended by it, without allowing that really he is represented! Is it not hopeless, then, to expect that the most diligent and anxious investigation can end in more than in giving some very rude description of the living mind, and its feelings, thoughts, and reasonings? And if it be difficult to analyse fully any state, or frame, or opinion of our own minds, is it a less difficulty to delineate, as Theology professes to do, the works, dealings, providences, attributes, or nature of Almighty God?   *U.S. pp. 262–4*

EVEN THE SCRIPTURE SUBJECT TO SIMILAR LIMITATIONS

In this point of view we may, without irreverence, speak even of the words of inspired Scripture as imperfect and defective; and though they are not subjects for our judgment (God forbid), yet they will for that very reason serve to enforce and explain better what I would say, and how far the objection goes. Inspiration is defective, not in itself, but in consequence of the medium it uses and the beings it addresses. It uses human language, and it addresses man; and neither can man compass, nor can his hundred tongues utter, the mysteries of the spiritual world, and God's dealings in this. This vast and intricate scene of things cannot be generalized or represented through or to the mind of man; and inspiration, in undertaking to do so, necessarily lowers what is divine to raise what is human. What, for instance, is the mention made in Scripture of the laws of God's government, of His providences, counsels, designs, anger, and repentance, but a gracious mode (the more gracious because necessarily imperfect) of making man contemplate what is far beyond him? Who shall give method to what is infinitely complex, and measure to the unfathomable? We are as worms in an abyss of divine works; myriads upon myriads of years would it take, were our hearts ever so religious, and our intellects ever so apprehensive, to receive from without the just impression of those works as they really are, and as experience would convey them to us: sooner, then, than we should know nothing, Almighty God has condescended to speak to us so far as human thought and language will admit, by approximations, in order to give us practical rules for our own conduct amid His infinite and eternal operations.   *U.S. pp. 264–5*

SUMMARY OF THIS VIEW OF FAITH

Such, then, under all circumstances, is real Faith; a presumption, yet not a mere chance conjecture—a reaching forward, yet not of excitement or of passion—a moving forward in the twilight, yet not without clue or direction; a movement from something known to something unknown, kept in the narrow path of truth by the Law of dutifulness which inhabits it, the Light of heaven which animates and guides it—and which, whether feeble and dim as in the Heathen, or bright and vigorous as in the Christian; whether merely the awakening and struggling conscience, or the "minding of the Spirit"; whether as a timid hope, or in the fulness of love; is under every Dispensation, the one acceptable principle commending us to God for the merits of Christ. And it becomes superstition, or credulity, or enthusiasm, or fanaticism, or bigotry, in proportion as it emancipates itself from this spirit of wisdom and understanding, of counsel and ghostly strength, of knowledge and true godliness, and holy fear. And thus I would answer the question how it may be secured from excess, without the necessity of employing what is popularly called Reason for its protection: I mean processes of investigation, discrimination, discussion, argument, and inference. It is itself an intellectual act, and it takes its character from the moral state of the agent. It is perfected, not by mental cultivation, but by obedience. It does not change its nature or its function, when thus perfected. It remains what it is in itself, an initial principle of action; but it becomes changed in its quality, as being made spiritual. It is, as before, a presumption, but the presumption of a serious, sober, thoughtful, pure, affectionate, and devout mind. It acts because it is Faith; but the direction, firmness, consistency, and precision of its acts, it gains from Love.   U.S. pp. 243–4

NEWMAN. *Sermons chiefly on the Theory of Religious Belief.* (*U.S.* Nos. XI and XII.)

GRACE AND KNOWLEDGE

The grace promised us is given, not that we may know more, but that we may do better. It is given to influence, guide, and strengthen us in performing our duty towards God and man; it is given to us as creatures, as sinners, as men, as immortal beings, not as mere reasoners, disputers, or philosophical inquirers. It teaches us what we are, whither we are going, what we must do, how we must do it; it enables us to change our fallen nature from evil to good, "to make ourselves a new heart and a new spirit". But it tells us nothing for the sake of telling it; neither in His Holy Word nor through our consciences has the blessed

Spirit thought fit so to act. Not that the desire of knowing sacred things for the sake of knowing them is wrong. As knowledge about earth, sky, and sea, and the wonders they contain, is in itself valuable, and in its place desirable, so doubtless there is nothing sinful in gazing wistfully at the marvellous providences of God's moral governance, and wishing to understand them. But still God has not given us such knowledge in the Bible; and therefore to look into the Bible for such knowledge, or to expect it in any way from the inward teaching of the Holy Ghost, is a dangerous mistake, and (it may be) a sin. And since men are apt to prize knowledge above holiness, therefore it is most suitably provided, that Trinity Sunday should succeed Whit Sunday; to warn us that the enlightening vouchsafed to us is not an understanding of "all mysteries and all knowledge", but that love or charity which is "the fulfilling of the Law".

NEWMAN. *P.S.* I. p. *234*

APOLOGETICS

Brothers! spare reasoning;—men have settled long
    That ye are out of date, and they are wise;
Use their own weapons; let your words be strong,
    Your cry be loud, till each scared boaster flies;
Thus the Apostles tamed the pagan breast,
They argued not, but preached; and conscience did the rest.

Lyra Apostolica. p. *96*

THE NEED FOR GOD

To understand that we have souls, is to feel our separation from things visible, our independence of them, our distinct existence in ourselves, our individuality, our power of acting for ourselves this way or that way, our accountableness for what we do. These are the great truths which lie wrapped up indeed even in a child's mind, and which God's grace can unfold there in spite of the influence of the external world; but at first this outward world prevails. We look off from self to the things around us, and forget ourselves in them. Such is our state—a depending for support on the reeds which are no stay, and overlooking our real strength—at the time when God begins His process of reclaiming us to a truer view of our place in His great system of providence. And when He visits us, then in a little while there is a stirring within us. The unprofitableness and feebleness of the things of this world are forced upon our minds; they promise but cannot perform, they disappoint us. Or, if they do perform what they promise, still (so it is) they do not satisfy us. We still crave for something, we do not well know what; but we are sure it is something which the world has not given us. And then its changes are so many, so sudden, so silent, so continual. It never leaves changing; it goes on to change, till we are quite sick at heart: then it is that our reliance on it is broken. It is plain we cannot continue to depend upon it, unless we keep pace with it, and go on changing too; but this we cannot do. We feel that, while it changes, we are one and the same; and thus, under God's blessing, we come to have some glimpse of the meaning of our independence of things temporal, and our immortality. And should it so happen that misfortunes come upon us, (as they often do), then still more are we led to understand the nothingness of this world; then still more are we led to distrust it, and are weaned from the love of it, till at length it floats before our eyes merely as some idle veil, which, notwithstanding its many tints, cannot hide the view of what is beyond it; and we begin, by degrees, to perceive that there are but two beings in the whole universe, our own soul, and the God who made it.

Sublime, unlooked-for doctrine, yet most true! To every one of us there are but two beings in the whole world, himself and God; for, as to this outward scene, its pleasures and pursuits, its honours and cares, its contrivances, its personages, its kingdoms, its multitude of busy slaves, what are they to us? nothing—no more than a show: "The world passeth away and the lust thereof." And as to those others nearer to us, who are not to be classed with the vain world, I mean our friends and relations, whom we are right in loving, these, too, after all, are nothing to us here. They cannot really help or profit us; we see them, and they act upon us, only (as it were) at a distance, through the medium of sense; they cannot get at our souls; they cannot enter into our thoughts, or really be companions to us. In the next world it will, through God's mercy, be otherwise; but here we enjoy, not their presence, but the anticipation of what one day shall be; so that, after all, they vanish before the clear vision we have, first, of our own existence, next of the presence of the great God in us, and over us, as our Governor and Judge, who dwells in us by our conscience, which is His representative.   NEWMAN. *P.S.* I. p. *22*

THE STUDY OF THE BIBLE

He who knows beforehand that the Personal Word is everywhere in the written Word, could we but discern Him, will feel it an awful thing to open his Bible; fasting, and prayer, and scrupulous self-denial, and all the ways by which the flesh is tamed to the Spirit, will seem to him no more than natural, when he is to sanctify himself, and draw near with Moses, to the darkness where God is. And this so much the more, the more that darkness is mingled with evangelical light; for so much the more he may hope to see of God; and we know Who it is, that has inseparably connected seeing God with purity of heart. KEBLE. *Tract 89.* p. *138*

Shower on my heart Thy radiance, without which
Thine own sure word were but a barren void.
But ever and anon as Thy calm light
Falls on it, Thy deep fulness comes to view.
Oft clouds and darkness all about thee dwell,
Till thoughts responsive wake with changeful life,
And open all Thy word, as light or shade
Fall on it, and fresh scenes arise to light,
With life and infinite variety,
Ever unfolding, as in scenes of Earth,
Mountains, and plains, and streams, and land, and sea.
As when upon a wild autumnal noon,
Some traveller sits on airy cliffs, and sees
The far-spread range below, where lights and shades
In beauteous interchanges come and go.
One scene comes forth to view, another fades,
Trees on a distant line—then gleaming rocks,
And woods, dwellings of men, and 'tween the hills
O'er-arching, haply glows the opening sea,
And some lone bark in sunshine—then retires
In shade—the nearer object comes to light
Unseen before—and then on either side
The multifarious landscape breaks to sight,
Unseen, till the bright beam expands the view.
Thus the unbounded fulness of Thy Word

Betokens Thy dread Glory veil'd beneath,
Throwing the light and cloud Thy skirts around.

Lend me thy hand, celestial visitant,
Into the inner chambers where thou sittest,
Unfolding lessons of diviner lore!
Touched by the unearthly wand, ethereal doors
Fly open, answering to the wondrous key.
I seem behind this shifting scene of things
Admitted, Heaven's high counsels to behold.
I seem to wander through mysterious ways,
Shadows of other days, and other lights
Around me, such is Thy unfathomed Word;
And oft at every turn myself descry.
Patriarchs, and kings, and prophets, great and good,
Are hurrying all before us to the tomb,
And cry aloud, "we seek another home."
I seem to walk through angel-haunted caves,
Lit by celestial light, not of the sun,
That leadeth to a kingdom far away.
There, as behind this screen and sensual bar
I see a hand that weighs us day by day,
We, wrapt in earthly schemes, are hastening on
And heed not; while Thy judgments walk the earth,
Evils by mortals named, and mercy loves
Beneath a cloud to veil her silver wings,
To me still speaks Thy voice, myself I see,
I see myself in each new scene revealed.

ISAAC WILLIAMS. *The Cathedral.* p. *124*

CONVERSION

In its widest sense "conversion" is a turning towards God: and if, by His mercy, we have been preserved from being turned altogether away from Him, yet none of us can say, that we have been, or are turned to Him, as fully as we might be. It is well if the full purpose of our heart be to Him, if we knowingly keep back nothing from Him, if we labour to fix our unsteadfastness on Him, have no bye-ends, are not seeking, half-consciously, our satisfaction or our reward in anything out of Him. Still we are at best but unsteadfast, seeking to be knit into one in Him; detained and lingering amid this life's joys, or comforts, or ease, and seeking to be quickened in our path to Him; with manifold ends which it is our duty to accomplish, and seeking that all our ends shall have no end but Him. "Who can say I have kept my heart clean, I am pure from sin?" Conversion, then, in its widest sense, is a course of being conformed to God, a learning to have Him more simply in our minds, to be turned wholly to Him, solely to Him, never to part from Him, ever to follow Him, our Sun of Righteousness, wherever His pathway is; in the morning, noon, evening of our life; in His bright shining, or when He hideth His face; opening our hearts to Him, to have their warmth, their health, their life, from Him. And since this were heaven itself, and we have not yet, at the best, "attained, nor are yet perfected", we all, in this sense, ever need conversion; we have ever some weaknesses, from which to seek to be freed, infirmities of which to be healed, bands and chains woven round us by past sins, from which to long to be loosed.

But, besides this, conversion may be taken in a narrower sense, for the first turning of the soul to God after it has been estranged from Him. This, had we been faithful, we never should have needed. In Holy Baptism, we were all "made children of God", and we never need have left our Father's house; we were made "members of Christ", and if we would, His life, into Whom we were then engrafted, would have flowed more fully into us, according to our needs, filling us according to our capacities, hallowing our childhood, strengthening our youth, controlling us in the perils of opening manhood, mastering each wayward thought, subduing each rising appetite. It was pledged to us, had we been willing to receive it. Had we admitted it, it would have flowed on equably and gently through us, and we had never needed that sharp, though wholesome remedy, whereby the way must be again reopened to it, when once we have closed it. We were "made inheritors of heaven"; we need never have stood in fear and alarm, lest we had forfeited it, nor had "sought it carefully with tears". We might have ever looked on humbly to it, not as our right, but as His Who purchased it for us and made it ours, and has given us the earnest of it, and gave us, day by day, the forgiveness of the trespasses we prayed for, that we might not forfeit it. This is the happy lot of those, who, though more or less slowly, still steadfastly on the whole, grow on in their Baptismal grace; with their falls, the giddinesses and forgetfulness of childhood, yet never interposing any such grievous sin, as should check the influx of that life in them. Supported by prayer, strengthened by Confirmation, admitted into closer communion in the Holy Eucharist, they are, line by line, and feature by feature, unobserved, insensibly, because unceasingly, "changed", the Apostle says, "into the same image, from glory to glory, as by the Lord, the Spirit". These need no marked change, because the change we all need is ever going on, unmarked, within them. And many more might these blessed cases be, would parents but more bring home to their memory the blessings pledged in Baptism; that their children have been redeemed out of the evil world, and need not be conformed to it; that they have been received under the protection of the saving Name, and may dwell there in safety "under the shadow of the Almighty"; that weak, frail, wayward, selfwilled, as, through the unsubdued remains of their old nature, they appear and are, they have still lodged within them a hidden strength, mightier than the world and Satan and the powers of darkness, even His strength Who "hath overcome the world", and trampled upon Satan; that He can and will triumph in these His young soldiers, if they are taught even now to fight; that He, by His childhood, has sanctified their childish age; that out of the mouths of such as them He hath perfected praise; that of such as these is the kingdom of heaven.

PUSEY. *P.S.* III. pp. *20–2*

THE ORGAN OF FAITH

Faith is instead of eyes. By faith we see Him who to our eyes of sense is unseen. We behold both backwards and forwards, and round about us, and every way we behold the love of God. And beholding and knowing His love, we ourselves, through His gift, love. Backward, we by faith behold God creating us, and we see our own fall; we behold His holiness, and goodness, and love, forming us to love Him everlastingly; and when we had fallen, by faith we behold Him, the Father, willing that God the Son should take our fallen nature, should be born, despised, tortured, crucified, die for us. By faith we see God the Son willing, for our sakes, to become man. We see our dear Lord and Redeemer on the Cross, as though we were, with St Mary Magdalene, at its foot. Faith has no past nor to come. It sees past and to come in the light of God, and is sure of them; yea, surer than of what it sees. More readily could it doubt that itself is, or that the things it sees are real. More readily could it think that all which it sees around is a dream; all things of nature which are seen with the eyes of the body, a vain show; seeming to be, as in a dream, yet not being, than it could doubt that God IS, or IS what HE hath said that HE IS. For what we see around us we know to be, by our mere powers of nature. Faith is a divine power. They are mere bodily powers, these eyes which shall soon decay, which tell us that the things around us are. Faith is the eye of the soul, which God has given us, to behold Himself. PUSEY. *P.S.* II. p. *1-2*

JUSTIFYING FAITH

The question is, What *is* faith and how can a man tell that he has faith? Some persons answer at once and without hesitation, that "to have faith, is to feel oneself to be nothing, and God every thing; it is to be convinced of sin, to be conscious one cannot save oneself, and to wish to be saved by Christ our Lord; and that it is moreover to have the love of Him warm in one's heart, and to rejoice in Him, to desire His glory, and to resolve to live to Him and not to the world". But I will answer, with all due seriousness, as speaking on a serious subject, that this is *not* faith. Not that it is not necessary (it is very necessary) to be convinced, that we are laden with infirmity and sin, and without health in us, and to look for salvation solely to Christ's blessed sacrifice on the cross; and we may well be thankful if we are thus minded; but that a man may feel all this that I have described, vividly, and still not yet possess one particle of true religious faith. Why? Because there is an immeasurable distance between feeling right and doing right. A man may have all these good thoughts and emotions, yet (if he has not yet hazarded them to the experiment of practice), he cannot promise himself that he has any sound and permanent principle at all. If he has not yet acted upon them, we have no voucher, barely on account of them to believe that they are any thing but words. Though a man spoke like an angel, I would not believe him, on the mere ground of his speaking. Nay, till he acts upon them, he has not even evidence to himself, that he has true living faith. Dead faith (as St James says), profits no man. Of course; the devils have it. What, on the other hand, is *living* faith? Do fervent thoughts make faith *living*? St James tells us otherwise. He tells us *works*, deeds of obedience, are the life of faith. "As the body without the spirit is dead, so faith without works is dead also."[1] So that those who think they really believe, because they have in word and thought surrendered themselves to God, are much too hasty in their judgment. They have done something, indeed, but not at all the most difficult part of their duty, which is to surrender themselves to God in deed and act. They have as yet done nothing to show they will not, after saying "I go", the next moment "go not"; nothing to show they will not act the part of the self-deceiving disciple, who said, "Though I die with Thee, I will not deny Thee"; yet straightway went and denied Christ thrice. As far as we know any thing of the matter, justifying faith has no existence independent of its particular definite acts. It may be described to be the temper under which men obey; the humble and earnest desire to please Christ which causes and attends on actual services. He who does one little deed of obedience, whether he denies himself some comfort to relieve the sick and needy, or curbs his temper, or forgives an enemy, or ask forgiveness for an offence committed by him, or resists the clamour or ridicule of the world, such a one (as far as we are given to judge) evinces more true faith than could be shown by the most fluent religious conversation, the most intimate knowledge of Scripture doctrine, or the most remarkable agitation and change of religious sentiments. Yet how many are there who sit still with folded hands, dreaming, doing nothing at all, thinking they have done every thing, or need do nothing, when they merely have had these good *thoughts*, which will save no one!

NEWMAN. *P.S.* I. pp. *197–9*

JUSTIFICATION BY FAITH

Go where you will, and ask what Christian or what body of Christians you will, what is the source of their justification in the sight of God? and they will all answer with one voice, "We are justified for the sake of the merits of Christ Jesus our Lord, alone, not for our own works or deservings." Ask them again, "Can man of his own natural strength and good works, turn and prepare himself to faith and calling upon God?" All would alike answer, "God forbid that we should so disparage the grace of God as to think so!" Ask them again, "Can we do good works pleasing and acceptable to God, without the grace of

[1] James ii. *26*.

God preventing, co-operating, perfecting?" All would answer, "It were heresy to think so." Or, "Although Christ died for all, is any justified who is not born again in Christ?" All would say, "He is not justified." Or again, "Do works done before the grace of Christ and the inspiration of His Spirit, make men meet to receive grace?" All would say, "They do not." Or further, "Can man, without the grace of God, of his own free-will, move himself towards righteousness in His sight?" All will say, "He is not able." "Is man then called without any merits on his own part?" All will say, "Not through works of righteousness which we have done, but according to His mercy He hath saved us." "But has man then the power, through the quickening and assisting grace of God, to obey that will, or by his own perverse will to reject it?" All will say, "He draweth us with the cords of a man, through our wills and our affections, not without or against them." Or further, "Are sins, or have sins ever been remitted, save freely, by the Divine mercy, for Christ's sake?" All will say, "The Blood of Christ alone cleanseth us from all sins." Or again, "Does an historical faith justify, whereby people intellectually or speculatively believe the truths of God, without love for God, or trust in God, or obedience to Him?" All will say, "With the heart man believeth unto salvation." Faith without love is the faith of devils. And yet all will agree that even this historical faith, whereby the mind assents to the word of God, and the doctrines therein taught by God, even while the life is at variance with the belief, is a gift of God, enlightening the mind, and that it is man's own exceeding fault that it avails not to him to salvation.

Further, all will agree, as matter of undoubted faith that justifying faith must include in itself the belief in all the Articles of the Christian Faith, as far as any may attain to know them, and more especially in the merits of Christ, in Whom we are accepted. All will assent that to believe in God is by believing to love Him, by believing to cleave to Him, by believing to go into Him, and to be incorporated in His members.

Again, all will hold that in this living, justifying faith, there is (at least in a healthy state of the soul) combined a trustful hope or confidence in God, whereby we believe that our sins shall be forgiven us for the sake of Christ, that we ourselves are children of God, adopted through His grace, and that He Who hath loved us so as to make us His, will, unless we forsake Him, love us unto the end.

And yet all believe that this justifying faith does not justify us by any quality of its own, but simply brings us to God, Who, of His own free bounty and love, justifies those who believe in Him, and who, being drawn by Him, hold not back from Him, but come unto Him by Whom they have been called and drawn.

And with, or in, this faith, there must be other qualities, besides the one quality of belief; such as those involved in true repentance; some sorrow for the love of God that we ever offended Him; hatred of the sins whereby we offended Him, and steadfast purpose to forsake them; fear of His judgments; hope of His pardoning mercy. Or, if any prefer so to call it, the faith whereby we are justified, must be a penitent, humble, self- or sin-abhorring, trustful, loving, earnest faith, given to us and produced in us by the grace of God.

To those who so come to God, not with *any* faith or belief, but with this penitent, humble, loving faith, it is (all agree) part of the wisdom and good pleasure of God to forgive their sins, to make them members of Christ, and therewith to give them the earnest or first-fruits of the Spirit; which gifts He does not give to those who come not to Him, or who come to Him unsubmissively or feignedly, as Simon Magus, withholding from Him the full submission of the understanding, or the entireness of their obedience, or halving their affections between Him and Mammon.

Further, all agree that God, in justifying us, not only *declares* us, but *makes* us, righteous. He does not declare us to be that which He does not make us. He makes us that which we were not, but which now, if we are in Him (whatever there still remain of inward corruption) we by His gift are, holy. He does not give us an untrue, unreal, nominal, shadowy righteousness; or He does not impute to us *only* a real outward righteousness, "the righteousness of God in Christ"; for which, being unrighteous still, we are to be accounted righteous. But what He imputes, that He also imparts. He creates in us an inchoate and imperfect, yet still a real and true righteousness; inchoate and imperfect, because "we all", while in the flesh, "in many things offend"; yet real and true, because it is the gift of God, and the first-fruits of His Holy Spirit.

This righteousness, being imperfect, even although the fruit in us of God's Holy Spirit, cannot (all agree) stand the strict judgment of God, if God were to judge without mercy. And yet, since it is real and sincere and true in the judgment of God Himself, He, "the righteous Judge", will own it at the Great Day in those who are found sanctified in Him. He Who, not without our will, but through our new-created and invigorated will, "wrought all our works in us", will "crown in us His own gift", which He gave, and which He guarded in us.

This righteousness, again, (all agree) is maintained and enlarged by faithfulness in using the grace of God, and thereby doing good works acceptable to God in Jesus Christ; as, equally, through neglect of that grace, and through deadly sin, faith itself decays, and although it may, by the grace of God, yet be revived, is for the time (as it was in David) dead.

Now since all Christians are thus far agreed, since we all believe that whoever has been, or will be, accepted by God, has been or will be accepted for the sake of Christ alone; that whatever good there is in any one, is through the grace of God in Christ; that man's best works could not stand the severity of God's judgment; that by faith (itself the gift of God) we come to Him, and through faith in Him we abide in Him; yet that good works done by the grace of Christ, are (when they can be performed) essential to a living faith, and necessary to our salvation, how is it that persons, members of the same Church, living by the same faith in the Son of God, having the same hope in Him, can speak, the one of the other, as though they were heathen or apostates "preaching another gospel", teaching another source of righteousness, than "Christ our Righteousness", or substituting this or that for faith in Christ? How is it that, even as to those who are severed in communion from us, men do not try to understand all things in their best sense, and seem more eager to catch at an argument against them, than patiently to understand their meaning?

All believe that Christ is the Way, the Truth, and the Life, Himself the Way, to Himself the Life. All believe that to do, by His grace, the works which He giveth and willeth us to do, is the way by which we hold on in that Way. He Alone is "the cause of our reigning"; "deeds" done by His grace, are the "way to" His eternal "kingdom"; yet we should not have been in the way, had not He freely placed us in it; we should fail by the way, unless He through His grace strengthened us; we should perish from the way, unless He by His grace retained us; we should be let in the race set before us, so as never to attain, unless He freed us from the burden of our sins. "He who willeth and runneth must glory not in himself, but in Him from Whom he had both to will and to run." Let us adore and thank Him Who is the Way; let us hold on in the way; and we shall see that we have the same hope, trust, stay, our one Lord and God, Who is above all to protect, and through all, by His power and working, and in all by His grace and love.

All is of Christ. His is the grace, which brought us out of the mass of our natural corruption in Adam. His was the new principle of life, which in baptism he imparted to us. His the grace which cherished, nurtured, enlarged, that first gift, or if unhappily we wasted it, through repentance, brought us back, converted, renewed, restored us. His, each gift of superadded grace, whereby He rewards the use which, through His grace, we make of each former grace, bestowing grace for grace. And life eternal too, will be from Him, grace for grace. For, as St Augustine says, "If our good life is nothing else than the grace of God, without doubt eternal life, which is given to a good life, is the grace of God; for it too is given gratis, because that to which it is given, is given gratis. But that to which it is given, is merely grace; but this which is given to it, since it is its reward, is grace for grace, as a reward for righteousness, that that may be true, (since it is true) that God shall render to every man according to his works."

But although faith and works are one whole, yea, "the one work in which all works are, is 'faith, which worketh by love', as the Lord Himself says, 'This is the work of God, that ye believe in Him whom He hath sent,' ", God assigns to us works as the test of our faith, not faith as the test of our works. And this, because it is easy to deceive ourselves as to our faith or our feelings; it is not so easy to deceive ourselves as to our deeds, if we will but look into our consciences by the light of the law of God. It is easy to say, "Lord, Lord"; it is *not* easy, but of the power of the grace of God, to "deny ourselves and take up our cross and follow Him". It is a toilless task to "hear His words and do them not, building a house upon the sand". It is *not* easy to be poor in spirit, and meek, and pure in heart, and to pray without ceasing, and in every thing to give thanks; to resist "the lust of the flesh, and the lust of the eye, and the pride of life", and "keep thyself unspotted from the world". It is easy, while going along the broad way, to call up to oneself, out of some forgotten corner of the heart, a vague belief of the mercy of God in Christ Jesus. It is *not* easy, amid the fire of passion

within, the manifold force of temptation without, the delusive pleasures dancing before our eyes, the treachery of our own hearts, to be
"dead to the world, that we may live to God". It is an easy, costless,
confession, to own ourselves what we are, "unprofitable servants"; it
is hard, first to labour with our whole strength, through the grace of
God, to "do all things whatsoever He hath commanded", and then,
and then only, it will be the fruit of God's grace to own it.

But hard though it be, our Lord, if ye indeed seek Him, will, by His
grace, make it easy. For He saith, "My yoke is easy." Meditate but a
little daily, on the truths of faith. Faith will open to your sight heaven
and your eternal home. Faith will shew to you your Lord at the right
hand of God interceding for you, looking down with pity upon you,
for you pleading those five glorious wounds, which, radiant with the
glory of His Godhead, fill heaven with adoring amazement at the
boundlessness of His love for each one of us. Faith will shew you the
vacant throne, amid the choirs of angels, vacant for each of you, if you
pray for the grace of Christ to persevere unto the end. Faith will shew
you the serene peace, the mutual charity, the adoring love, the blissful
contemplation, the transporting gladness, the pure harmony, the
Divine beauty, the thrilling joy of unutterable thankfulness, the un-
sating fulness of bliss, the indissoluble union with thy Redeemer and
thy God, where the pleasures at His right hand are for evermore.

Then embody thy faith in acts. Faith without acts of faith is but a
dream. If you believest that thy Judge in the Great Day, will reward
deeds of mercy, and punish the unmerciful, deny thyself that thou
mayest shew mercy to Him in His poor. If thou believest that "the pure
in heart shall see God", pray Him who searcheth the heart, to cleanse
thine, and admit not into it any thought which leads to sin. If thou
believest that "the world passeth away", set not thy hopes, thy love,
thy ambition, on this passing world, to pass away with the world on
which thou buildest. If thou believest in eternity, live for eternity.
Sow sparingly, if, so sowing, thou hopest to reap bountifully. Sow to
the flesh, if, so sowing, thou hopest to reap incorruption. "Walk in the
ways of thy heart, and in the sight of thine eyes", if "for these things
God will" *not* "bring thee into judgment". But if thou believe that
"God worketh in us to will and to do of His good pleasure", that He
is the Author, He the Finisher, He the exceeding great Reward of thy

faith, then, what thou doest, do, not for the praise of men, not for thine own exaltation, not for any worldly end, but for God. If God is thine end, then see how thou mayest with a strong hand, by the grace of God, cast forth out of thyself what may displease God; how thou mayest perfect in thyself, by His grace, any grace which God hath given thee; how thou mayest by strong importunity, besiege the love of God, and obtain from Him any grace thou lackest.

So shalt thou find, not in words but in life, that faith and deeds of faith are one, given in one by God to thee, and from thee in one to go back to God. As thou by faith beholdest the greatness of God and of His eternal grace, His ineffable holiness, majesty, glory, goodness, love, thou wilt know and feel the nothingness of all in thyself, whether faith or works, save as they are the gift of God. As thou probest thyself, thou wilt see the more thine own evil. But as thou ownest thine own evil and God's good, He will take away from thee thine evil, and crown in thee His own good; as thou ownest thyself in thyself an unprofitable servant, He owning in thee His own work, will say unto thee, "Well done, good and faithful servant, enter thou into the joy of thy Lord."

PUSEY. *Justification* (1853) pp. *3-10, 42-7*

LOVE AND FAITH

Love is in all true faith, as light and warmth are in the rays of the sun. Light and warmth are in the sun's ray, and the sun's ray brings with it light and warmth; not light and warmth, the sun's ray: yet where the sun's ray is, there are light and warmth, nor can that ray be anywhere without giving light and warmth. Even so, faith it is which brings love, not love, faith; yet faith cannot come into the heart without bringing with it the glow of love, yea, and the light wherewith we see things divine. So soon as faith is kindled in the heart, there is the glow of love; and both come from the same Sun of Righteousness, pouring in faith and love together into the heart, and "there is nothing hid from the heat thereof". In winter, fewer rays come upon any spot of this land from the sun; whence there is then less brightness of light and less glow of heat than in summer; and so the surface of the earth is chilled; and though for a time the frost be melted by that fainter sun, this warmth, coming upon it only for a short time, soon passes away. Even so, there are degrees of faith and love. Yet they may be real faith and love, even when the power of both is lessened, in that the soul does not keep itself or live in the full presence of God. Or, as through a closed window, more light comes than heat, so in some hearts, there may be more of knowledge than of love. And again, as on a cold misty day, when the sun is hidden from our eyes, we are so oppressed by the clamminess of the chill damp upon the surface of our bodies, and by the heavy gloom around, that we scarcely feel the presence of light and heat; and yet the light and heat are there, else we should be in utter darkness and our bodies would die; even so, many hearts, at many times, when some mist hides from them the Presence of their Lord, feel nothing but their own coldness and numbness, and all seems dark around them, and yet in their very inmost selves they believe, and love, else their souls would be dead, and they would be "past feeling", and they would not pine for more light and love. A dead body is in darkness, and seeth not the light of this world, and has an aweful coldness to the touch; yet itself feels not its own coldness, nor knows its own darkness. Even so the dead soul, being without the life of God, feels not its own death, craves not to love more. For He who is Love hath left it, and it hath no power wherewith to desire to love, unless or until the voice of Christ raises it from the dead and awakens it, and it hears His voice, and lives.

PUSEY. *P.S.* II. pp. *6–7*

THE MYSTICAL KNOWLEDGE OF GOD IN THE SOUL

'Tis not the speculation of rude thought
That has the key of Heaven, but Prayer alone;
Prayer through the avenues of this dark world
Leads us thus blind with an ethereal thread,
Makes conscious of His guidance, gives to feel
His nearness which alone is life below.
We ask for Him around, and find Him not—
We ask of all His creatures ranging by,
And all His works, if they have seen His face;
They answer, We are formed and live by Him,
But we behold Him not and know Him not.
We ask of nature, if she hath in her
That which can satisfy the craving soul:

But to our search she giveth no reply.
We ask the Sea, with his abyss of waves,
He answers, It is written, that His paths
Are in the mighty waters, but His ways
Are secret, and His footsteps are not known.
We ask the winds and all the inhabitants
That wing the buoyant air: we ask the Skies,
The Sun, the Moon, the Stars, and they respond,
Of his dread going we have heard the sound,
But He is not in us, nor can we speak
His dwelling-place; we range our order'd watch
Without the flaming walls that hide His courts.

It is reveal'd that in the heart of man
Is set the throne of Him that dwells in Heaven;
The Body is His Temple, and the Soul
His inner shrine; then reverend must we think,
And speak of Him in stillness, for where'er
The heart of man may be there is His God,
Conversing with him in his silent thought;
Judging, controlling, guiding, reigning there.
And therefore 'mid the troubles that surround
To know Thee is to know all blessedness,
And is to be at peace! who dwells in love
Doth dwell in Thee, for Thou art Love Divine;
Thou art around us though we see Thee not,
About our path, about our bed, and Thou
Spiest out all our ways; whom then on earth,
And whom have I in Heaven, but Thee alone?
Around us and within us, as the child
Wrapp'd in the mother's womb and there sustain'd;
Or as the gem transfused with radiant light,
Or cavern'd spunge with the surrounding sea;
Or as the air filling the bird's wing'd frame,
Making it buoyant; or as vital heat
Keeping its watch against chill-creeping death,
E'en so around and in us is our God.
And souls made pure and radiant by His grace,

Are spiritual mirrors to reflect Himself,
E'en as the sea reflects the face of heaven.
                    ISAAC WILLIAMS. *The Baptistery.* pp. *272–4*

DOUBT

Let us but obey God's voice in our hearts, and I will venture to say we shall have no doubts practically formidable about the truth of Scripture. Find out the man who strictly obeys the law within him, and yet is an unbeliever as regards the Bible, and then it will be time enough to consider all that variety of proof by which the truth of the Bible is confirmed to us. This is no practical inquiry for us. Our doubts, if we have any, will be found to arise after disobedience; it is bad company or corrupt books which lead to unbelief. It is sin which quenches the Holy Spirit.

Let us get rid of curious and presumptuous thoughts by going about our business, whatever it is; and let us mock and baffle the doubts which Satan whispers to us by *acting* against them. No matter whether we believe doubtingly or not, or know clearly or not, so that *we act* upon our belief. The rest will follow in time; part in this world, part in the next. Doubts may pain, but they cannot harm, unless we give way to them; and that we ought not to give way our conscience tells us, so that our course is plain. And the more we are in earnest to "work out our salvation", the less shall we care to know how those things really are, which perplex us. At length, when our hearts are in our work, we shall be indisposed to take the trouble of listening to curious truths (if they are but curious) though we might have them explained to us. For what says the Holy Scripture? that of speculations "there is no end", and they are "a weariness of the flesh"; but that we must "fear God and keep His commandments; for this is the whole duty of man".[1]

All God's commands, indeed, ought to be received at once upon faith, though we saw no reason for them. It is no excuse for a man's disobeying them, even if he thinks he sees reasons against them; for God knows better than we do. But in great condescension He has allowed us to see here and there His reasons for what He does and

[1] Eccles. xii. *12, 13.*

enjoins; and we should treasure up these occasional notices as memorials against the time of temptation, that when doubt and unbelief assails us, and we are perplexed at His revealed word, we may call to mind those former instances in our own experience, where what at first seemed strange and hard, on closer consideration was found to have a wise end.

NEWMAN. *P.S.* I. pp. *232, 246–7, 291*[1]

RESERVE IN COMMUNICATING RELIGIOUS KNOWLEDGE

Nature withdraws from human sight
   The treasures of her light,
In earth's deep mines, or ocean's cells,
   Her secret glory dwells.
'Tis darkly thro' night's veil on high
   She shews the starry sky;
And where of beauty ought is found,
   She draws a shade around;
Nor fully e'er unveils to sense
   Steps of bright Providence.

When out of Sion God appear'd
   For perfect beauty fear'd,
The darkness was His chariot,
   And clouds were all about.
Hiding His dread sublimity,
   When Jesus walked nigh,
He threw around His works of good
   A holier solitude,
Ris'n from the grave appear'd to view,
   But to a faithful few.

Alone e'en now, as then of old,
   The pure of heart behold
The soul-restoring miracles
   Wherein His mercy dwells;

[1] Cf. the whole of Newman's sermon entitled *Obedience the remedy for religious perplexity*, P.S. I. No. XVIII.

New marvels unto them reveal'd,
  But from the whole conceal'd.
Then pause, and fear—when thus allowed
  We enter the dark cloud,
Lord, keep our hearts, that soul and eye
  Unharm'd may Thee descry.

ISAAC WILLIAMS. *The Cathedral.* pp. *210–1*

RESERVE AND CREEDS

If I allow my belief, that freedom from symbols and articles is abstractedly the highest state of Christian communion, and the peculiar privilege of the primitive Church, it is not from any tenderness towards that proud impatience of control, in which many exult as in a virtue; but first, because technicality and formality are, in their degree, inevitable results of public confessions of faith; and next, because when confessions do not exist, the mysteries of divine truth, instead of being exposed to the gaze of the profane and uninstructed, are kept hidden in the bosom of the Church far more faithfully than is otherwise possible; and reserved by a private teaching, though the channel of her ministers, as rewards in due measure and season, for those who are prepared to profit by them; those, i.e., who are diligently passing through the successive stages of faith and obedience. And thus, while the Church is not committed to declarations which, most true as they are, still are daily wrested by infidels to their ruin; on the other hand, much of that mischievous fanaticism is avoided, which at present abounds from the vanity of men, who think that they can explain the sublime doctrines and exuberant promises of the Gospel, before they have yet learned to know themselves, and to discern the holiness of God, under the preparatory discipline of the Law and of Natural Religion.

NEWMAN. *Arians.* pp. *41–2*

REVELATION AND SYSTEMS OF DOCTRINE

Clearness and symmetry of doctrine are a dear purchase, when Christian truth and duty must be impaired for their sake. After all, a fragment of the true Temple is worth all the palaces of modern philosophical theology.   KEBLE. *U.S.* p. *357*

PART II

THE AUTHORITY OF THE CHURCH

THE APPEAL TO THE ANCIENT AND UNDIVIDED CHURCH

Let us understand what is meant by saying that Antiquity is of authority in religious questions. . . . Whatever doctrine the primitive ages unanimously attest, whether by consent of the Fathers, or by Councils, or by the events of history, or by controversies, or in whatever way, whatever may fairly and reasonably be considered to be the universal belief of those ages, is to be received as coming from the Apostles. . . . Catholicity, Antiquity, and consent of the Fathers, is the proper evidence of the fidelity or apostolicity of a professed Tradition. Infant baptism, for instance, must have been appointed by the Apostles, or we should not find it received so early, so generally, with such a silence concerning its introduction. The Christian faith is dogmatic, because it has been so accounted in every Church up to this day. The washing of the feet, enjoined in the 13th chapter of St John, is not a necessary rite or a Sacrament, because it has never been so observed:— did Christ or His Apostles intend otherwise, it would follow (what is surely impossible), that a new and erroneous view of our Lord's words arose even in the Apostles' lifetime, and was from the first everywhere substituted for the true. Again; fabrics for public worship are allowable and fitting under the Gospel, though our Lord contrasts worshipping at Jerusalem or Gerizim with worshipping in spirit and in truth, because they ever have been so esteemed. The Sabbatical rest is changed from the Sabbath to the Lord's day, because it has never been otherwise since Christianity was a religion.

It follows that Councils or individuals are of authority, when we have reason to suppose that they are trustworthy informants concerning Apostolical Tradition. . . . On the other hand, the most highly gifted and religious persons are liable to error, and are not to be implicitly trusted where they profess to be recording, not a fact, but their own opinion. Christians know no Master on earth; they defer, indeed, to the judgment, obey the advice, and follow the example, of good men in ten thousand ways, but they do not make their opinions part of what is emphatically called the Faith. Christ alone is the Author and Finisher of Faith in all its senses; His servants do but witness it, and their statements are then only valuable when they are testimonies, not deductions or conjectures.

NEWMAN. *Prophetical Office.* pp. 62–5

THE APPEAL TO ANTIQUITY ONLY IN ESSENTIALS

Some persons are apt to think, when Antiquity is talked about, that it implies an actual return to the exact forms of opinion and modes of feeling which are known to have prevailed in those earlier times; and they forthwith begin to talk about the nineteenth century, and the impossibility of our retrograding, and the folly and disadvantage of too narrow a standard, and the fallacy of thinking that whatever is ancient is, as such, an object of imitation. Simeon on his pillar, Antony in the mountain, Councils in full debate, and popular elections, incense and oil, insufflations and stoles with crosses on them, complete their notion of Ancient Religion, when they hear it recommended. Nothing has been said by those whose writings have been so severely animadverted on lately, to show that they are antiquarian fanatics, urging the ancient doctrine and discipline upon the present age in any other except essential points, and not allowing fully that many things are unessential, even if abstractedly desirable. As to these points, let the age acknowledge and submit itself to them in proportion as it can enter into them with heart and reality; in proportion as the reception of them would be, in its case, the natural development of Church principles.

This should be understood; if persons, in this day, do not feel "sufficiently for such things" spontaneously, we are not going to force such things upon them as a piece of imitation. No good could come of merely imitating the Fathers for imitation's sake; rather, such servility is likely to prevent the age from developing Church principles so freely as it might otherwise do.

We cannot, if we would, move ourselves back into the times of the Fathers: we must, in spite of ourselves, be churchmen of our own era, not of any other, were it only for this reason, that we are born in the nineteenth century, not the fourth.

NEWMAN. *Prospects of the Anglican Church*

WHAT ARE THE ESSENTIALS?

Let it be clearly understood what is meant by the word "fundamentals" or "essentials". I do not mean by it what is "necessary to be believed for salvation by *this particular person or that*." No one but God can decide what compass of faith is required of given individuals. The necessary Creed varies, for what we know, with each individual to whom the Gospel is addressed; one is bound to know and believe more, or more accurately, another less. Even the minutest and most precise details of truth may have a claim upon the faith of a theologian; whereas the peasant or artisan may be accepted on a vague and rudimental faith—which is like seeing a prospect at a distance—such as a child has, who accepts the revealed doctrine in the letter, contemplating and embracing its meaning, not in its full force, but as far as his capacity goes.

Our purpose is to determine merely this—what doctrines the Church Catholic will *teach* indefectibly, what doctrines she must *enforce* as a condition of communion, what doctrines she must rescue from the scrutiny of Private Judgment; in a word, what doctrines are the foundation of the Church.

If the Church Catholic is to be indefectible in faith, we have but to enquire what that common faith is which she now holds everywhere as the original deposit, and we shall have ascertained what we seek. If we adopt this course, we shall find what is commonly called the Creed, to be that in which all branches of the Church agree; and therefore that the fundamental or essential doctrines are those which are contained in the Creed. NEWMAN. *Prophetical Office.* pp. *264–7*

NOT ONLY THE CREED AS A FORM OF WORDS, BUT AS THE WAY IN WHICH THE ANCIENT CHURCH RECEIVED SCRIPTURE

We are naturally, if not reasonably, jealous of the word Tradition, associated as it is in our minds with the undue claims and pernicious errors of Rome. Yet must it not be owned, on fair consideration, that Timothy's deposit did comprise matter, independent of, and distinct from, the truths which are directly Scriptural? that it contained, besides the substance of Christian doctrine, a certain form, arrangement, selection, methodizing the whole, and distinguishing fundamentals; and also a certain system of Church practice, both in government, discipline, and worship; of which, whatever portion we can prove to be still remaining, ought to be religiously guarded by us, even for the same reason that we reverence and retain that which is more properly Scriptural, both being portions of the same divine treasure.

To these conclusions we are led by the consideration, first, that the truths and rules committed to Timothy's charge were at the time almost or wholly unwritten. This is clear from the very date of the Epistles which mention that charge: the latest of which must have been composed many years before St John's Gospel, and in the first of them the deposit in question is spoken of, not as an incomplete thing on its progress towards perfection, but as something so wholly sufficient, so unexceptionably accurate, as to require nothing but fidelity in its transmitters. The holy writings themselves intimate, that the persons to whom they were addressed were in possession of a body of truth and duty, totally distinct from themselves, and independent of them. Timothy, for instance, a few verses after the text, is enjoined to take measures for the transmission, not of holy Scripture, but of the things which he had heard of St Paul among many witnesses.

The fact is clearly demonstrable from Scripture, that as long as the canon of the New Testament was incomplete, the unwritten system served as a test even for the Apostles' own writings. Nothing was to be read, as canonical, except it agreed with the faith delivered once for all to the first generation of the saints. The directions of St Paul on this subject are perfectly clear, and without reserve. "Though we or an angel from heaven preach any other Gospel unto you than that which we have preached unto you, let him be anathema."

I do not see how we can be wrong in inferring, from these and similar passages, that the faith once for all delivered to the saints, in other words, Apostolical Tradition, was divinely appointed in the Church as the touchstone of canonical Scripture itself. No writing, however plausible the appearance of its having come from the Apostles, was to be accepted as theirs, if it taught any other doctrine than what they are first delivered: rather both it and its writers were to be anathema.

This use of apostolical tradition may well correct the presumptuous irreverence of disparaging the Fathers under a plea of magnifying Scripture. Here is a tradition so highly honoured by the Almighty Founder and Guide of the Church, as to be made the standard and rule of His own divine Scriptures. The very writings of the Apostles were to be first tried by it, before they could be incorporated into the canon. Thus the Scriptures themselves, as it were, do homage to the tradition of the Apostles; the despisers, therefore, of that tradition take part, inadvertently or profanely, with the despisers of the Scripture itself.

On the other hand, it is no less evident that Scripture, being once ascertained, became in its turn a test for every thing claiming to be of apostolical tradition. But on this part of the subject there is the less occasion to dwell, it being, I suppose, allowed on all hands.

In truth it may be proved to the satisfaction of any reasonable mind, that not a few fragments yet remain, very precious and sacred fragments, of the unwritten teaching of the first age of the Church. The paramount authority, for example of the successors of the Apostles in Church government; the threefold Order established from the beginning; the virtue of the blessed Eucharist as a commemorative sacrifice; infant Baptism; and above all, the Catholic doctrine of the Most Holy Trinity, as contained in the Nicene Creed. All these, however surely confirmed from Scripture, are yet ascertainable parts of the primitive, unwritten system, of which we yet enjoy the benefit. If any one ask, how we ascertain them; we answer, by application of the well-known rule, *Quod semper, quod ubique, quod ab omnibus*: Antiquity, Universality, Catholicity: tests similar to those which jurists are used to apply to the common or unwritten laws of any realm. If a maxim or custom can be traced back to a time whereof the memory of man runneth not to the contrary; if it pervade all the different courts, established in different provinces for the administration of justice; and, thirdly, if it be gener-

ally acknowledged in such sort, that contrary decisions have been dis-
allowed and held invalid: then, whatever the exceptions to it may be,
it is presumed to be part and parcel of our common law. On principles
exactly analogous, the church practice and rules above mentioned, and
several others, ought, we contend, apart from all Scripture evidence,
to be received as traditionary or common laws ecclesiastical.

It is not, therefore, antecedently impossible that a system of tradition, subsidiary to the Scriptures, might yet exist in the commonwealth
or city of God. The rest is matter of investigation in each case, whether
any given rule, interpretation, or custom, be traditionary in the required sense. But it will not be going too far into particulars, and may
help to the understanding and application of the whole argument, if I
point out three distinct fields of Christian knowledge, in neither of
which can we advance satisfactorily or safely without constant appeal
to tradition, such as has been described.

The first is, the *System and Arrangement of fundamental Articles*, so far
as they have come down to us systematic and arranged. We, that is, all
of the Anglican Church who have had any regular training in theology,
are so early taught to trace the Creed in the Scriptures, and to refer at
once certain portions of both Testaments to certain high mysteries of
the Catholic faith, that it commonly appears to ourselves as though we
had learned those mysteries directly from the Scriptures. But there are
few, surely, who on careful recollection would not be compelled to
acknowledge that the Creed, or some corresponding catechetical instruction, had prepossessed them with these truths, before ever they
thought of proving them from Holy Writ. I need hardly remind you
of the unquestioned historical fact, that the very Nicene Creed itself, to
which perhaps of all *formulae* we are most indebted for our sound belief
in the proper divinity of the Son of God—even this Creed had its
origin, not from Scripture, but from tradition. The three hundred
bishops who joined in its promulgation did not profess to have collected it out of the Bible, but simply to express the faith which each of
them had found in the Church which he had represented, received by
tradition from the Apostles. Nor is this any disparagement to Scripture,
nor need it excite any alarm for the great fundamental verity itself,
which the Creed was meant to assert; any more than it would disparage
the works of God, or shake the foundation of our faith in natural

religion, were one to affirm that the power and Godhead of the Creator, although unquestionably proveable from the things which are made, would yet have remained unknown to the mass of mankind, but for primitive tradition, or subsequent revelation of it.

The second great subject, on which most of us are unconsciously indebted to the ancient Catholic tradition, is the *Interpretation of Scripture*, especially those parts which less obviously relate to the mysteries of the Gospel.

The third great field of apostolical tradition lies among *practical* matters, the *Discipline, Formularies,* and *Rites* of the Church of Christ: in regard of which, reason tells us that the Church Apostolical must here have had *some* method and system; yet it is evident to the very eye that the New Testament exhibits no such system in form, but only fragments and other indications of one in full operation at the time, and well known to those for whom the Apostles were writing. These fragments being found to coincide with similar but more copious indications in later Church records; consideration also being had of the religious reverence wherewith in those ages everything primitive was regarded, and of the charitable jealousy of the Churches, watching each other for the purpose of remonstrating against unwarrantable deviations; we need not fear to accept in its fulness, on all such matters, the well-known rule of St Augustine, which I give in the words of Hooker: "Whatsoever positive order the whole Church everywhere doth observe, the same it must needs have received from the very Apostles themselves; unless, perhaps, some general council were the authors of it." In this kind no one at all versed in Church history can be at a loss for examples of the benefit which the present Church derives from the chain of primitive tradition. Without its aid, humanly speaking, I do not see how we could now retain either real inward communion with our Lord through His Apostles, or the very outward face of God's Church and kingdom among us. Not to dwell on disputable cases: how, but by the tradition and practice of the early Church, can we demonstrate the observance of Sunday as the holiest day, or the permanent separation of the clergy from the people as a distinct order? or where, except in the primitive Liturgies, a main branch of that tradition, can we find assurance that in the Holy Eucharist we consecrate as the Apostles did, and, consequently, that the cup of blessing which we bless is the communion of the Blood of Christ, and the bread which we break the communion of the Body of Christ?

Whether, then, we look to Discipline, to Interpretation, or to Doctrine, every way we see reason to be thankful for many fragments of apostolical practice and teaching, most needful to guide us in the right use of Holy Scripture.

Because it is affirmed that the full tradition of Christianity existed before the Christian Scriptures, and so far independent of them, we are charged with alleging two distinct systems or words of God, the one written, the other unwritten, running as it were parallel to each other quite down to our own time. But this, by the terms of the case, is plainly unwarranted. If a man were to say that the Severn and the Wye rise separately in the same mountain, one higher up than the other, must he therefore maintain that they never meet before they reach the sea? Tradition and Scripture were at first two streams flowing down from the mountain of God, but their waters presently became blended, and it were but a vain and unpractical inquiry, to call upon every one who drinks of them to say, how much of the healing draught came from one source, and how much from the other. On account of those who would poison the stream, it is necessary from time to time to analyse it, and show that it contains no ingredients which were not to be found in one or other of the two fountains; and in so doing, it becomes incidentally manifest, at least in some measure, what portion each of the two has contributed to the general mass; it is manifest, for example, that all necessary *credenda*, all truths essential to salvation, are contained in the Scripture itself; and is it not equally manifest, that many helps of greatest consequence, nay I will say generally necessary, to the right development and application of Scripture, are mostly if not entirely derivable from Tradition? And is it not a poor kind of reasoning to say, Tradition would have been worthless had we been left to it alone, therefore it cannot be of any value, now that Scripture has been all along at hand, to check, to sustain, to interpret, to rectify it, as the several occasions might require?   KEBLE. *U.S.* pp. *188ff, 347–8*[1]

Tradition sometimes means the doctrine held by Christians, as distinguished from the same doctrine written in the Bible. It is also

[1] The sermon was preached on *27 September 1836*, in Winchester Cathedral.

used as equivalent to "custom", as in the Thirty-Fourth Article. Traditions in the former sense may be divided into those which have been commonly maintained in some particular age only, or which a portion of the Church has maintained without separating from the rest, and those which the great body of Christians from the beginning have always held to be articles of the faith. The former class of traditions may be certainly true, but the ecclesiastical authority which supports them can only render them probable. The latter sort of traditions afford an irresistible confirmation of the doctrine of scripture, and a certain test of the correctness of scripture interpretation.

It is not here meant that the real sense of scripture is *obscure in any points of faith*, or that it is essential for each individual, in order to understand the scripture aright in such points, to consult previously the traditions and judgments of the universal Church.

Scripture ought to be of itself sufficient for the overthrow of all errors against faith; but since men are liable to be misled, by the evil interpretations of others, to misunderstand the divine meaning of Scripture, the doctrine or tradition of Christians in all ages, i.e. of the catholic Church, is presented to us as a confirmation of the true meaning of Scripture. It is not meant that this tradition conveys to us the exact interpretation of all the particular texts in the Bible. Its utility is of a simpler and more general character; it relates to the interpretation of Scripture as a whole, to the doctrine deduced from it in general. That doctrine which claims to be deduced from Scripture, and which all Christians believed from the beginning, must be truly scriptural. That doctrine which claims to be deduced from Scripture, and which all the Church from the beginning reprobated and abhorred, must be founded on a perversion and misrepresentation of Scripture.

The difference between the Anglo-catholic and the popular Romish doctrine of tradition is this: The former only admits tradition as confirmatory of the true meaning of Scripture, the latter asserts that it is also *supplementary* to Scripture, conveying doctrines which Scripture has omitted.

That such a universal tradition as determining the meaning of Scripture must be true, is evident. I am not here arguing with infidels, and therefore may assume that Christianity was a revelation; that no revelation has superseded it; that it was to be proposed to men in all ages as the means of salvation; in fine, that some truth was actually revealed. If, then, any given doctrine was universally believed by those Christians who had been instructed by the apostles and the disciples of the apostles; if this doctrine was received by all succeeding generations as sacred and divine, and strictly conformable to those scriptures which were read and expounded in every church; this belief, one and uniform, received in all churches, delivered through all ages, triumphing over the novel and contradictory doctrines which attempted to pollute it, guarded with jealous care, even to the sacrifice of life in its defence, and after a lapse of eighteen hundred years believed as firmly by the over-whelming mass of Christians among all nations as when it was first promulgated; such a doctrine must be a truth of revelation. It rests on evidence not inferior to that which attests the truth of Christianity. Is it possible that the infinite majority of Christians in all ages can have mistaken or adulterated their own religion, a religion which they held to be divine, and on which they believed their salvation to depend? And this while the Scriptures were in their hands, and the care of God was (as Christians believe) extended over His Church—the people whom He chose for Himself? If so, then they may have been equally deceived as to the authenticity of Scripture, as to the truth of the mission of our Saviour; and the whole fabric of revelation totters to its base. Hence I maintain that Christians cannot possibly admit that any doctrine established by universal tradition can be otherwise than DIVINELY, INFALLIBLY, TRUE.

The existence of such a tradition from the beginning is *a matter of fact,* which is to be established on the same sort of evidence as proves any other historical fact. The question is, what were the tenets of the religious community called Christian from the beginning. This is evidently to be proved only by authentic documents, monuments, and facts; and we accordingly adduce the *creeds or professions of faith* acknowledged by the universal church, in proof of her faith on certain points up to the period when she made them; the creeds and liturgies of particular churches, as evidence of their belief as far back as those creeds and liturgies can be traced. We produce the *attestations of particular fathers and councils of bishops* to the contemporary and former belief of the Church, either by direct assertions to that effect, or by the silent testimony to the same afforded by the fact of their own express belief, and the approbation of that belief by the Church generally. We adduce *ancient customs and rites* to the same end; and even *the objections of infidels and of sectaries* concur in establishing what was the real faith of the Catholic Church in all ages.

If proofs like these be rejected on the ground of the uncertainty of all *human testimony*, then there can be no certainty of any of the facts of history; and we are reduced to believe only facts which have come under the cognizance of our own senses. If the testimony of the early Christian writers in this question of fact be rejected, the external evidences of Christianity are subverted. The authenticity of primitive tradition and its records, of Scripture and its doctrines, and of Christianity as a revelation, stand or fall together.

W. PALMER. *Treatise on the Church* (3rd ed. *1872*) vol. 2. pp. *33–6*

Every word of revelation has a deep meaning. It is the outward form of a heavenly truth, and in this sense a mystery or Sacrament. We may read it, confess it; but there is something in it which we cannot fathom, which we only, more or less, as the case may be, not perfectly, enter into. Accordingly, when a candidate for Baptism repeats the Articles of the Creed, he is confessing something incomprehensible in its depth, and indefinite in its extent. He cannot know at the time *what* he is binding on himself, whither he is letting himself be carried. It is the temper of reverent faith to feel this; to feel that in coming to the Church, it stands before God's representative, and that, as in her Ordinances, so in her Creed, there is a something supernatural and beyond us. Another property of faith is the wish to conceive rightly of sacred doctrine, as far as it can conceive at all; and, further, to look towards the Church for guidance how to conceive of it. This is faith, viz. submission of the reason and will towards God, wistful and loving meditation upon His message, childlike reliance on the guide which is ordained by Him to be the interpreter of it. The Church Catholic is our mother; if we attend to this figure, we shall have little practical difficulty in the matter before us. A child comes to his mother for instruction; she gives it. She does not assume infallibility, nor is she infallible; yet it would argue a very unpleasant temper in the child to doubt her word, to require proof of it before acting on it, to go needlessly to other sources of information. Sometimes, perhaps, she mistakes in lesser matters, and is set right by her child; yet this neither diminishes her prerogative of teaching, nor his privilege of receiving dutifully. Now this is what the Church does towards her children, according to the primitive design. She puts before them, first of all, as the elements of her teaching, nothing but the original Creed; her teaching will follow in due time, but as a privilege to children necessarily ignorant, as a privilege which will be welcomed by them, and accepted joyfully, or they would be wanting in that temper of faith which the very coming for Baptism presupposes.   NEWMAN. *Prophetical Office.* pp. *314-5*

PRIVATE JUDGMENT

All parties must be agreed, that without private judgment there is no responsibility; and that in matter of fact, a man's own mind, and nothing else, is the cause of his believing or not believing, and of his acting or not acting upon his belief. Even though an infallible guidance be accorded, a man must have a choice of resisting it or not: he may resist it if he pleases, as Judas was traitor to his master. Romanist, I consider, agrees with Protestant so far; the question in dispute being, what are the *means* which are to direct our choice, and what is the due *manner* of using them. This is the point to which I shall direct my attention.

The means which are given us to form our judgment by, exclusively of such as are supernatural, which do not enter into consideration, are various, partly internal, partly external. The internal means of judging are common sense, natural perception of right and wrong, the affections, the imagination, reason, and the like. The external are such as Scripture, the existing Church, Tradition, Catholicity, Learning, Antiquity, and the National Faith. Popular Protestantism would deprive us of all these external means, except the text of Holy Scripture; as if, I suppose, upon the antecedent notion that, when God speaks by inspiration, all other external means are superseded. But this is an arbitrary decision, contrary to facts; for unless inspiration made use of an universal language, learning at least must be necessary to ascertain the meaning of the particular language selected; and if one external aid be adopted, of course all antecedent objection to any other vanishes. This notion, then, though commonly taken for granted, must be pronounced untenable, nay, inconsistent with itself; yet upon it the prevailing neglect of external assistances, and the exaltation of Private

Judgment, mainly rest. Discarding this narrow view of the subject, let us rather accept all the means which are put within our reach, as intended to be used, as talents which must not be neglected; and, as so considering them, let us trace the order in which they address themselves to the minds of individuals.

Our parents and teachers are our first informants concerning the next world; and they elicit and cherish the innate sense of right and wrong which acts as a guide coordinately with them. By degrees they resign their place to the religious communion, or Church, in which we find ourselves, while the inward habits of truth and holiness which the moral sense has begun to form, react upon that inward monitor, enlarge its range, and make its dictates articulate, decisive, and various. Meantime, the Scriptures have been added as fresh informants, bearing witness to the Church and to the moral sense, and interpreted by them both. Last of all, where there is time and opportunity for research into times past and present, Christian Antiquity, and Christendom, as it at present exists, become additional informants, giving substance and shape to much that before existed in our minds but in outline and shadow.

It is popularly conceived that to maintain the right of private judgment, is to hold that no one has an enlightened faith who has not, as a point of duty, discussed the grounds of it and made up his mind for himself. But to put forward such a doctrine as this, rightly pertains to infidels and sceptics only; and if great names may be quoted in its favour, and it is often assumed to be the true Protestant doctrine, this is surely because its advocates do not weigh the force of their own words. Every one must begin religion by faith, not by reasoning; he must take for granted what he is taught and what he cannot prove; and it is better for himself that he should do so, even if the teaching he receives contains a mixture of error. If he would possess a reverent mind, he must begin by obeying; if he would cherish a generous and devoted spirit, he must begin by venturing something on uncertain information; if he would deserve the praise of modesty and humility, he must repress his busy intellect, and forbear to scrutinize. . . . As the mind expands, whether by education or years, a number of additional informants will meet it; and it will naturally, or rather it ought, according to its opportunities, to exercise itself upon all of these, by way of finding out God's perfect truth.

He may go on to examine the basis of the authority of Scripture or of the Church; and if so, he will do it, not, as is sometimes irreverently said, "impartially" and "candidly", which means sceptically and arrogantly, as if he were the centre of the universe, and all things might be summoned before him and put to task at his pleasure, but with a generous confidence in what he has been taught; nay, not recognizing, as will often happen, the process of enquiry which is going on within him. Many a man supposes that his investigation ought to be attended with a consciousness of his making it; as if it were scarcely pleasing to God unless he all along reflects upon it, tells the world of it, boasts of it as a right, and sanctifies it as a principle. He says to himself and others, "I am examining, I am scrutinizing, I am free to choose or reject, I am exercising the right of Private Judgment". What a strange satisfaction! Does it increase the worth of our affections to reflect upon them as we feel them? Would our mourning for a friend become more valuable by our saying "I am weeping; I am overcome and agonized for the second or third time; I am resolved to weep"? What a strange infatuation, to boast of our having to make up our minds! What! is it a great thing to be without an opinion? Is it a satisfaction to have the truth to find? Who would boast that he was without earthly means, and had to get them as he could? Is heavenly treasure less precious than earthly? Is it anything inspiring or consolatory to consider, as such persons do, that Almighty God has left them entirely to their own efforts, has failed to anticipate their wants, has let them lose in ignorance at least a considerable part of their short life and their tenderest and most malleable years? Is it a hardship or a yoke, on the contrary, to be told what is, in the order of Providence, put before them to believe, whether absolutely true or not, is in such sense from Him, that it will improve their hearts to obey it, and convey to them many truths which they otherwise would not know, and prepare them perchance for the communication of higher and clearer views?

(The popular view of Private Judgment is) that every Christian has the right of making up his mind for himself what he is to believe, from personal and private study of the Scriptures. . . . And much is said in praise of independence of mind, free inquiry, the resolution to judge for ourselves, and the enlightened and spiritual temper which these things are supposed to produce. But this notion is so very preposterous, there is something so very strange and wild in maintaining that every individual Christian, rich and poor, learned and unlearned, young and old, in order to have an intelligent faith, must have formally examined, deliberated, and passed sentence upon the meaning of Scripture for himself, and that in the highest and most delicate and mysterious matters of faith, that I am unable either to discuss or to impute such an opinion to another. . . . Rather let us consider what is called the *right* of Private Judgment; by which is meant, not that all *must*, but that all *may* search Scripture, and determine or prove their creed from it—that is, provided they are duly qualified, for I suppose this is always implied, though persons may differ what those qualifications are. And with this limitation I should be as willing as the most zealous Protestant to allow the principle of Private Judgment in the abstract; and it is something to agree with opponents even in an abstract principle.

The task proposed is such as this—to determine first whether Scripture sets forth any dogmatic faith at all; next, if so, what it is; then, if it be necessary for salvation; then, what are its doctrines in particular. . . . I think it will be granted me, by the most zealous opponent, that the mass of Christians are inadequate to such a task; . . . the great proportion even of educated persons have not the accuracy of mind requisite for determining it. The only question is, whether any accurate creed is necessary for the private Christian; which orthodox Protestants have always answered in the affirmative. Consider then, the orthodox Protestant doctrines; those relating to the Divine Nature, and the economy of redemption, or those, again, arising out of the controversy with Rome. . . . Do you really mean to say, that men and women, as we find them in life, are able to deduce these doctrines from Scripture, to determine how far Scripture goes in implying them, to decide upon the exact weight of its terms, and the danger of this or that deviation from them?

Scripture is not so distinct in its announcements, as readers are morally or intellectually slow in receiving them. And if anyone thinks that this avowal is derogatory to Scripture, I answer that Scripture was never intended to teach doctrine to the many; and if it was not given with this object, it argues no imperfection in it that it does not fulfil it.

I repeat it; while Scripture is written by inspired men, with one and one only view of doctrine in their hearts and thoughts, even the Truth which was from the beginning, yet being written not to instruct in doctrine, but for those who were already instructed in it, not with direct announcements but with intimations and implications of the faith, the qualifications for rightly apprehending it are so rare and high, that a prudent man, to say nothing of piety, will not risk his salvation on the chance of his having them; but will read it with the aid of those subsidiary guides which have ever been supplied as if to meet our need. I would not deny as an abstract proposition that a Christian may gain the whole truth from the Scriptures, but would maintain that the chances are very seriously against a given individual. I would not deny but rather maintain, that a religious, wise and intellectually gifted man will succeed: but who answers to this description but the collective Church? There, indeed, such qualifications might be supposed to exist; what is wanting in one member being supplied by another, and the contrary errors of individuals eliminated by their combination. The Church Catholic may truly be said almost infallibly to interpret Scripture, though from the possession of past tradition, and amid the divisions of the time present, perhaps at no period in the course of the dispensation has she had the need and the opportunity of interpreting it for herself. Neither would I deny that individuals, whether from height of holiness, clearness of intellectual vision, or the immediate power of the Holy Ghost, have been and are able to penetrate through the sacred text into some portions of the divine system beyond without external help; though, since that help has ever been given, as to the Church, so to the individual, it is difficult to prove that the individual has performed what the Church has never attempted. None, however, it would seem, but a complete and accurately moulded Christian, such as the world has never or scarcely seen, would be able to bring out harmoniously and perspicuously the divine characters in full which lie hid from mortal eyes within the inspired letter of the revelation. . . . The Church Catholic, the true prophet of God, alone is able to tell the dream and its interpretation.   NEWMAN. *Prophetical Office.* pp. *157–193*

THE MEANING OF CATHOLIC

Now we may form a clearer notion than is commonly taken of the one Church Catholic which is in all lands. Properly it is not on earth, except so far as heaven can be said to be on earth, or as the dead are still with us. It is not on earth, except in such sense as Christ or His Spirit are on the earth. I mean it is not locally or visibly on earth. The Church is not in time or place, but in the region of spirits; it is in the Holy Ghost; and as the soul of man is in every part of his body, yet in no part, not here nor there, yet everywhere; not in any one part, head or heart, hands or feet, so as not to be in every other; so also the heavenly Jerusalem, the mother of our new birth, is in all lands at once, fully and entirely, as a spirit; in the East and in the West, in the North and in the South—that is, wherever her outward instruments are to be found. The Ministry and Sacraments, the bodily presence of Bishop and people, are given us as keys and spells, by which we bring ourselves into the presence of the great company of saints; they are but the outskirts of it; they are but porches to the pool of Bethesda, entrances into that which is indivisible and one. Baptism admits, not into a mere visible society, varying with the country in which it is administered, Roman here, and Greek there, and English there, but through the English or the Greek or the Roman porch into the one invisible company of elect souls, which is independent of time and place, and untinctured with the imperfections or errors of that visible porch by which entrance is made. And its efficacy lies in the flowing upon the soul of the grace of God lodged in that unseen body into which it opens, not, in any respect, in the personal character of those who administer or assist in it. When a child is brought for Baptism, the Church invisible claims it, begs it of God, receives it, and extends to it, as God's instrument, her own sanctity. When we praise God in Holy Communion, we praise Him with the Angels and Archangels, who are the guards, and with the Saints, who are the citizens of the City of God. When we offer our Sacrifice of praise and thanksgiving, or partake in the sacred elements so offered, we solemnly eat and drink of the powers of the world to come. When we read the Psalms, we use before many witnesses the very words on which those witnesses themselves—I mean, all successive generations of that holy company—have sustained themselves in their own day, for thousands of years past, during their pilgrimage heavenward. When we profess the Creed, it is in no self-willed, arbitrary sense, but in the presence of those innumerable Saints who well remember what its words mean, and are witnesses of it before God, in spite of the heresy or indifference of this or that day. When we stand over their graves, we are in the very vestibule of that dwelling which is "all-glorious within", full of light and purity, and of voices crying, "Lord, how long?" When we pray in private, we are not solitary; others "are gathered together" with us "in Christ's Name" though we see them not, with Christ in the midst of them. When we approach the Ministry He has ordained, we approach the steps of His throne. When we approach the bishops, who are the centres of that Ministry, what have we before us but the Twelve Apostles, present but invisible? When we use the sacred Name of Jesus, or the Sign given us in Baptism, what do we but bid defiance to devils and evil men, and gain strength to resist them? When we protest, or confess, or suffer in the Name of Christ, what are we but ourselves types and symbols of the Cross of Christ, and of the strength of Him who died on it? When we are called to battle for the Lord, what are we who are seen, but mere outposts, the advanced guard of a mighty host, ourselves few in number and despicable, but bold beyond our numbers, because supported by chariots of fire and horses of fire round about the Mountain of the Lord of Hosts under which we stand?

Such is the City of God, the Holy Church Catholic throughout the world, manifested in and acting through what is called in each country the Church visible; which visible Church really depends solely on it, on the invisible—not on civil power, not on princes or any child of man, not on endowments, not on its numbers, not on any thing that is seen, unless indeed heaven can depend on earth, eternity on time, angels on men, the dead on the living. The unseen world through God's secret power and mercy encroaches upon this; and the Church that is seen is just that portion of it by which it encroaches; and thus, though the visible Churches of the Saints in this world seem rare, and scattered to and fro, like islands in the sea, they are in truth the tops of the everlasting hills, high and vast and deeply rooted, which a deluge covers.   NEWMAN. *P.S.* IV. pp. *198–201*

THE MEMORY OF THE CHURCH

What happens in the fortunes of individuals, happens also to the Church. Its pleasant times are pleasant in memory. We cannot know who are great and who are little, what times are serious and what are their effects, till afterwards. Then we make much of the abode, and the goings out and the comings in of those who in their day lived familiarly with us, and seemed like other men. Then we gather up the recollection of what they did here, and what they said there. Then their persecutors, however powerful, are not known or spoken of, except by way of setting off *their* achievements and triumph in the Gospel. "Kings of the earth, and the great men, and rich men, and the chief captains and the mighty men", who in their day so magnified themselves, so ravaged and deformed the Church, that it could not be seen except by faith, then are found in nowise to have infringed the continuity of its outlines, which shine out clear and glorious, or more delicate and tender for the very attempt to obliterate them. It needs very little study of history to prove how really this is the case; how little schism and divisions and disorders and troubles and fears and persecutions and scatterings and threatenings interfere with the presence and the glory of Christ Mystical, as looked upon afterwards, though at the time they almost hid it. Great Saints, great events, great privileges, like the everlasting mountains, grow as we recede from them.

NEWMAN. *P.S.* IV. pp. *299-300*

ON OBEYING THE CHURCH

Much might be said on that mode of witnessing Christ which consists in conforming to His Church. He who simply did what the Church bids him do (if he did no more) would witness a good confession to the world, and one which cannot be hid; and at the same time, with very little, if any, personal display. He does only what he is told to do; he takes no responsibility on himself. The Apostles and Martyrs who founded the Church, the saints in all ages who have adorned it, the Heads of it now alive, all these take from him the weight of his profession, and bear the blame (so to call it) of seeming ostentatious. I do not say, that irreligious men will not call such an one boastful, or austere, or a hypocrite; that is not the question. The question is, whether in God's judgment he deserves the censure; whether he is not as Christ would have him, really and truly (whatever the world may say) joining humility to a bold outward profession; whether he is not, in thus acting, preaching Christ without hurting his own pureness, gentleness, and modesty of character. If indeed a man stands forth on his own ground, declaring himself as an individual a witness for Christ, then indeed he is grieving and disturbing the calm spirit given us by God. But God's merciful providence has saved us this temptation, and forbidden us to admit it. He bids us unite together in one, and to shelter our personal profession under the authority of the general body. Thus, while we show ourselves as lights to the world far more effectively than if we glimmered separately in the lone wilderness without communication, at the same time we do so with far greater secrecy and humility. Therefore it is, that the Church does so many things for us, appoints Fasts and Feasts, times of public prayer, the order of the sacraments, the services of devotion at marriages and deaths, and all accompanied by a fixed form of sound words; in order (I say) to remove from us individually the burden of a high profession, of implying great things of ourselves by inventing for ourselves solemn prayers and praises—a task far above the generality of Christians, to say the least, a task which humble men will shrink from, lest they prove hypocrites, and which will hurt those who do undertake it, by making them rude-spirited and profane. I am desirous of speaking on this subject as a matter of practice; for I am sure, that if we wish really and in fact to spread the knowledge of the Truth, we shall do so far more powerfully as well as purely, by keeping together, than by witnessing one by one. Men are to be seen adopting all kinds of strange ways of giving glory (as they think) to God. If they would but follow the Church; come together in prayer on Sundays and saints' days, nay, every day; honour the rubric by keeping to it obediently, and conforming their families to the *spirit* of the Prayer-book, I say, that on the whole they would practically do vastly more good than by trying new religious plans, founding new religious societies, or striking out new religious views.

NEWMAN. *P.S.* I. pp. *177–9*

APOSTOLIC SUCCESSION

What is the Church of Christ but a pledge and proof of God's never-dying love and power from age to age? He set it up in mercy to mankind, and its presence among us is a proof that in spite of our sins He has not yet forsaken us. "Hitherto hath the Lord helped us". He set it on the foundation of His twelve apostles, and promised that the gates of hell should not prevail against it; and its presence among us is a proof of His power. He set it up to succeed to the four monster kingdoms of this world which then were; and it lived to see those kingdoms crumble into dust and come to nought. It lived to see society new formed upon the model of the governments which last to this day. It lives still, and it is older than them all. Much and rightly as we reverence old lineage, noble birth, and illustrious ancestry, yet the royal dynasty of the apostles is far older than all the kingly families which are now on the earth. Every bishop of the Church whom we behold, is a lineal descendant of St Peter and St Paul after the order of a spiritual birth.

The presence of every bishop suggests a long history of conflicts and trials, sufferings and victories, hopes and fears, through many centuries. His presence at this day is the fruit of them all. He is the living monument of those who are dead. He is the promise of a bold fight and a good confession and a cheerful martyrdom now, if needful, as was done by those of old time. We see their figures on our walls, and their tombs are under our feet; and we trust, nay, we are sure, that God will be to us in our day what He was to them.

NEWMAN. *P.S.* III. pp. *268–70*

"He that despiseth you doth me despise".
Lo! at that call Faith her best robe prepares,
And Heav'n to Earth lets down the eternal stairs,
Through a long line of more than good or wise,
The high-born legates of the appeased skies
Come down their avenue of sacred years;
Each in his hand Messiah's olive bears.
Ye priestly brotherhood, with reverend eyes
Receive a guest from Heav'n, your ancient seat
Open ye, and Religion's deep retreat!
The dust of time is on him, and Christ's mark,
Worldly reproach; he bears the unquenched spark
To kindle into life earth's secret womb—
To lighten or destroy, cheer or consume;
Through chains, fire, sword, he bears thy last reprieve,
"He that receiveth you, doth me receive!"

ISAAC WILLIAMS. *The Cathedral.* pp. *48–9*

THE GIFT OF ORDINATION

A mortal youth I saw
Nigh to God's Altar draw
And lowly kneel, while o'er him pastoral hands
Were spread with many a prayer,
And when he rose up there,
He could undo or bind the dread celestial bands.

When bread and wine he takes,
And of Christ's Passion makes
Memorial high before the mercy throne,
Faith speaks, and we are sure
That offering good and pure
Is more than angels' bread to all whom Christ will own.

'Mid mourners I have stood,
And with sad eye pursued
The coffin sinking in the grave's dark shade:
The immortal life, we know,
Dwells there with hidden glow,
Brightly to burn one day when sun and stars shall fade.

What is this silent might,
Making our darkness light,
New wine our waters, heavenly blood our wine?
Christ with His mother dear,
And all His saints, is here,
And where they dwell is heaven, and what they touch, divine.

KEBLE. *Lyra Innocentium. 26* January *1843*

UNITY

How idle is it to suppose, that to demand assent to a form of words which happens to be scriptural, is therefore sufficient to effect an unanimity in faith and action! If the Church would be vigorous and influential, it must be decided and plain-spoken in its doctrine, and must regard its faith rather as a character of mind than as a notion. To attempt comprehensions of opinion, amiable as the motive frequently is, is to mistake arrangements of words, which have no existence except on paper, for habits which are realities; and ingenious generalizations of discordant sentiments for that practical agreement which alone can lead to cooperation. We may indeed artificially classify light and darkness under one term or formula; but nature has her own fixed courses, and unites mankind by the sympathy of moral character, not by those forced resemblances which the imagination singles out at pleasure in the most promiscuous collection of materials. However plausible may be the veil thus thrown over heterogeneous doctrines, the flimsy artifice is discomposed so soon as the principles beneath it are called upon to move and act. Nor are these attempted comprehensions innocent; for, it being the interest of our enemies to weaken the Church, they have always gained a point, when they have put upon us words for things, and persuaded us to fraternize with those who, differing from us in essentials, yet happen in the excursive range of opinion somewhere to intersect that path of faith, which centres in supreme and zealous devotion to the service of God.

NEWMAN. *Arians.* pp. *162–3*

This union in His Church is God's own gift,
Not to be seiz'd by man's rude sinful hands,
But the bright crown of mutual holiness.

ISAAC WILLIAMS. *The Baptistery* (*1842*) p. X

A FATHER OF THE CHURCH AND HIS UNDERSTANDING: ORIGEN

Into God's word as in a palace fair
Thou leadest on and on, while still beyond
Each chamber, touch'd by holy wisdom's wand,
Another opes, more beautiful and rare,
And thou in each art kneeling down in prayer,
From link to link of that mysterious bond
Seeking for Christ; but O, I fear thy fond
And beautiful torch that with so bright a glare
Lighteth up all things, lest thy heaven-lit brand
And thy serene Philosophy divine

Should take the colourings of earthly thought,
And I, by their sweet images o'er-wrought,
Led by weak Fancy, should let go Truth's hand,
And miss the way into the inner shrine.

Lyra Apostolica, p. *111*

THE CHURCH TO TEACH, THE BIBLE TO PROVE

When I was an undergraduate, I heard Dr Hawkins preach in the University pulpit his celebrated sermon on the subject (of Tradition), and recollect how long it appeared to me, though he was at that time a very striking preacher; but when I read it and studied it as his gift, it made a most serious impression upon me. . . . He lays down a proposition, self-evident as soon as stated, to those who have at all examined the structure of Scripture, viz. that the sacred text was never intended to teach doctrine, but only to prove it, and that, if we would learn doctrine, we must have recourse to the formularies of the Church; for instance to the Catechism and to the Creeds. He considers that, after learning from them the doctrines of Christianity, the enquirer must verify them by Scripture.   NEWMAN. *Apologia pro vita sua*

Surely the sacred volume was never intended, and is not adapted to *teach* us our creed; however certain it is that we can prove our creed from it, when it has once been taught us, and in spite of individual produceable exceptions to the general rule. From the very first, that rule has been, as a matter of fact, for the Church to teach the truth, and then appeal to Scripture in vindication of its own teaching. And from the first, it has been the error of heretics to neglect the information provided for them, and to attempt of themselves a work to which they are unable, the eliciting a systematic doctrine from the scattered notices of the truth which Scripture contains. Such men act, in the solemn concerns of religion, the part of the self-sufficient natural philosopher, who should obstinately reject Newton's theory of gravitation, and endeavour, with talents inadequate to the task, to strike out some theory of motion by himself. The insufficiency of the mere private study of Holy Scripture for arriving at the exact and entire truth which it really contains, is shown by the fact, that creeds and teachers have ever been divinely provided, and by the discordance of opinions which exists wherever those aids are thrown aside; as well as by the very structure of the Bible itself. And if this be so, it follows that, while enquirers and neophytes used the inspired writings for the purposes of morals and for instruction in the rudiments of the faith, they still might heed the teaching of the Church as a key to the collection of passages which related to the mysteries of the gospel; passages which are obscure from the necessity of combining and receiving them all.

NEWMAN. *Arians.* pp. *55–6*

EVANGELISM

If people were now asked, what was the most powerful means of advancing the cause of religion in the world, we should be told that it was eloquence of speech or preaching: and the excellency of speech consists in delivery. . . . Whereas, if we were to judge from Holy Scripture, of what were the best means of promoting Christianity in the world, we should say obedience; and if we were to be asked the second, we should say obedience; and if we were to be asked the third, we should say obedience.

ISAAC WILLIAMS. *Tract 87.* p. *82*

UNCOVENANTED MERCIES

It is often said of us by way of reproach, that we leave Dissenters to the "uncovenanted mercies of God"; nay, in a sense, we leave ourselves; there is not one of us but has exceeded by transgressions its revealed provisions, and finds himself in consequence thrown upon those infinite resources of Divine Love which are stored in Christ, but have not been drawn out into form in the appointments of the Gospel.

NEWMAN. *Justification.* p. *364*

PART III

SANCTIFICATION

THE TWO WAYS

Everything may, and does, minister to heaven or hell. Our health may minister to serenity of mind, or, more often, to self-confidence and want of sympathy; our sickness to resignation or fretfulness; the most sacred losses may lead to penitence, or to repining and feverish tossings, and discontent with God, or again, to hard-heartedness; our good actions may serve to self-display, or the love of Him whom in them we serve; our best earthly affections may be a love in and for God, or be idolatry and a subtle selfishness: our study of nature and of the laws imposed upon nature, may make us fall down and worship Him who gave those laws, or our own understanding, which discovered them; it may be holy or godless; the enjoyment of natural beauties may be pure and holy, or may be mere excitement and sensual; the highest things may be made subservient to the meanest, or the poorest infirmities of our weak nature may minister to the highest; music may be the minstrelsy of the heavenly harps, singing the song of the Lamb, or it may be the excitement and voluptuousness of the day; our knowledge may be mere distraction amid the manifold things of sense, wasting our minds with the husks wherewith we feed it, or it may tend to the love of Him who passeth knowledge; our eating and our drinking may be with the beasts which perish, or they may be types of our heavenly food, our feeding on Him who is the bread of life; unhallowed sleep is the image of eternal death; if we lay down to take our rest in Him, it is repose in the everlasting arms, watched by angels, "visited' it may be "with His visitations to His own",[1] the putting off of weakness; and our waking in the morning, may be the type of the resurrection. Nay, even that dryness of soul, under which God sometimes allows His servants to suffer, but quickens that thirst after

[1] From Launcelot Andrewes' Devotions.

righteousness, which He fills; the very loathsomeness of Satan's touch, defiling the imagination with the memory of former sins, but deepens the penitent's remorse, and that abasement which shall be raised up.

In the midst of such things is our life. We are, day by day, and hour by hour, influenced by every thing around us; rising or falling, sinking or recovering, receiving impressions which are to last for ever; taking our colour and mould from everything which passes around us and in us, and not the less because unperceived; each touch slight, as impressed by an invisible spiritual hand, but, in itself, not the less, rather the more lasting, since what we are yielding ourselves to is, in the end, the finger of God or the touch of Satan. In our rising up or our lying down; our labour or our refreshment; our intercourse with others, or our solitary thoughts; our plans for the future or the duties of the day; our purposes and their fulfilments or their failure, our acting or our suffering, we are receiving moment by moment the hallowed impress of the heavenly hand, conforming our lineaments, one by one, each faculty of our spirit, and this poor earthly tenement of our body itself, to the image of God wherein we were re-created, or we are gradually being dried up and withered by the blasting burning touch of the arch-fiend; each touch is of fire, burning out our proud rebellious flesh, or searing our life; some more miserable falls sink us deeper; some more difficult victories, won by God's help over ourselves, the flesh, the world, and Satan, raise us on the heavenward path; but each sense, at every avenue, each thought, each word, each act, is in its degree doing that endless work; every evil thought, every idle word, and still more, each wilful act, is stamping upon men the mark of the beast; each slightest deed of faith is tracing deeper the seal of God upon their foreheads.   PUSEY. *P.S.* III. pp. *430–2*

There are but two resting-places in the whole range of thought about God; the one a loving, implicit, child-like faith, which, although it understands not, believes every Word of God, because it loves Him, and bends not the thoughts of God to be as its thoughts, but yields and casts down its every thought to be obedient to the thoughts of God; the other, entire unbelief, which ends in dethroning God, making God a part of the world, and itself a part of God. All else is only moving in the one way or the other.

He Who holdeth out the prize willeth that we should win it; He doth not look on only, but by His look giveth courage, and strength, and life. The way looks rugged, only until thou enterest it; its ruggedness is not like the ruggednesses of the world, nor its sweetnesses like the world's sweetness. The way is narrow, but only if thou wouldest carry with thee things which Christ forbids; the Forms along it look austere at a distance only; place thyself at their side, and thou wilt see, they will smile upon thee with a heavenly sweetness. The world's broad way narrows in, perplexes, harasses, distresses, slays; Christ's narrow path widens as thou walkest along it; for He hath taught us how to say "Thy commandment is exceeding broad."[1]

PUSEY. *A.W.* pp. *124–5, 136*

The Church and the world cannot meet without either the world rising or the Church falling; and the world forsooth pleads necessity, and says it cannot rise to the Church, and deems the Church unreasonable when she will not descend instead.   NEWMAN. *P.S.* IV. p. *183*

THE SEVERITY OF THE MORAL LIFE

Doubtless many a one there is, who, on hearing doctrines such as I have been insisting on, says in his heart, that religion is thus made gloomy and repulsive; that he would attend to a teacher who spoke in a less severe way; and that in fact Christianity was not intended to be a dark burdensome law, but a religion of cheerfulness and joy. This is what young people think, though they do not express it in this argumentative form. They view a strict life as something offensive and hateful; they turn from the notion of it. And then, as they get older and see more of the world, they learn to defend their opinion, and express it more or less in the way in which I have just put it. They hate and oppose the truth, as it were upon principle; and the more they are told that they have souls, the more resolved they are to live as if they had not souls. But let us take it as a clear point from the first, and not to be disputed, that religion must ever be difficult to those who neglect it. All things that we have to learn are difficult at first, and our duties to God, and to man for His sake, are peculiarly difficult, because they call upon us to take up a new life, and quit the love of this world for the

[1] Ps. cxix. 96

next. It cannot be avoided; we must fear and be in sorrow, before we can rejoice. The Gospel must be a burden before it comforts and brings us peace. No one can have his heart cut away from the natural objects of its love, without pain during the process and throbbings afterwards. This is plain from the nature of the case: and, however true it be, that this or that teacher may be harsh and repulsive, yet he cannot materially alter things. Religion is in itself at first a weariness to the worldly mind, and it requires an effort and a self-denial in everyone who honestly determines to be religious.   NEWMAN. *P.S.* I. p. *26*

THE CHRISTIAN WAY UNPOPULAR

As a general rule, I would say the Church itself is always hated and calumniated by the world, as being in duty bound to make a bold profession. But whether individual members of the Church are so treated, depends on various circumstances in the case of each. There *are* persons, who, though very strict and conscientious Christians, are yet praised by the world. These are such, as having great meekness and humility, are not so prominent in station or so practically connected with the world as to offend it. Men admire religion, while they can gaze on it as a picture. They think it lovely in books; and as long as they can look upon Christians at a distance, they speak well of them. The Jews in Christ's time built the sepulchres of the prophets whom their fathers killed; then they themselves killed the Just One. They "reverenced" the Son of God before He came, but when their passions and interests were stirred by His coming, then they said, "This is the heir; come, let us kill Him, and the inheritance shall be ours."[1] Thus Christians in active life thwarting (as they do) the pride and selfishness of the world, are disliked by the world, and have "all manner of evil said against them falsely for Christ's sake".[2] Still, even under these circumstances, though they must not shrink from the attack on a personal account, it is still their duty to shelter themselves, as far as they can, under the name and authority of the Holy Church; to keep to its ordinances and rules; and, if they are called to suffer for the Church, rather to be drawn forward to the suffering in the common course of duty, than boldly to take upon them the task of defending it. There is no cowardice in this. Some men are placed in posts of danger, and to

[1] Mark xii. 7.   [2] Matt. v. 11.

these danger comes in the way of duty; but others must not intrude into their honourable office. Thus in the first age of the Gospel, our Lord told His followers to fly from city to city, when persecuted; and even the heads of the Church, in the early persecutions, instead of exposing themselves to the fury of the heathen, did their utmost to avoid it. We are a suffering people from the first; but while, on the one hand, we do not defend ourselves illegally, we do not court suffering on the other. We must witness and glorify God, as lights on a hill, through evil report and good report; but the evil and the good report is not so much of our own making as the natural consequence of our Christian profession.   NEWMAN P.S. I. p. *188*

REPENTANCE

The truest penitence no more comes at first, than perfect conformity to any other part of God's law. It is gained by long practice—it will come at length. The dying Christian will fulfil the part of the returning prodigal more exactly than he ever did in his former years. When first we turn to God in the actual history of our lives, our repentance is mixed with all kinds of imperfect views and feelings. Doubtless there is in it something of the true temper of simple submission; but the wish of appeasing God on the one hand, or an hard-hearted insensibility about our sins on the other, mere selfish dread of punishment, or the expectation of a sudden easy pardon—these, and others like them, influence us, whatever we may say or may think we feel. It is indeed easy enough to have good words put into our mouths, and our feelings roused, and to profess the union of utter self-abandonment and enlightened sense of sin, but this is not really to possess these excellent tempers. Really to gain these is a work of time. It is when the Christian has long fought the good fight of faith, and by experience knows how few and how imperfect are his best services; then it is that he is able to acquiesce, and most gladly acquiesces in the statement, that we are accepted by faith only in the merits of our Lord and Saviour.

NEWMAN. *P.S.* III. pp. *104-5*

SELF-EXAMINATION

As our nightly sleep is an image of death, so the nightly self-examination of a thoughtful person is in some sort an image of the last great day.   *Plain Sermons.* II. p. *251*

OBEDIENCE IN LITTLE

Obey the call, whatever it be. Despise it not because it is little; "whoso despiseth little things", it is said, "shall fall by little and little". "Whoso is faithful in little, is faithful also in much", saith our Lord, "and he that is unfaithful in the least, is unfaithful also in much". Obey the call, whatever it be; if it be but a step, it is still a step in following Christ. Were it a great thing, Satan would scare thee by setting before thee its greatness; if a little thing, he would make thee follow thine own way, because it is little. Advise not with him; if it be little, thank God for leading thee thus gently, and go onwards; if great and hard, look to Him for strength, and through Him it will be easy. Some God leads gently onwards, as the shepherd "leads gently the ewes that are with young"; others He brings back at once with a mighty vehemence. Only whatever He saith unto you, do it. Whoso neglects a thing which he suspects he ought to do, because it seems to him too small a thing, is deceiving himself; it is not too little, but too great for him, that he doth it not. "By small grains of sand", saith an ancient bishop, "may mighty ships be sunk. Drops of rain are small, yet they swell rivers", which will overthrow that house which is not "founded upon the rock; and great is the fall thereof". Small steps lead men often best to the tops of high hills.   PUSEY. *P.S.* III. pp. *410–11*

GROWTH THE EVIDENCE OF LIFE

It follows at once, even though Scripture did not plainly tell us so, that no one is able to prepare himself for heaven, that is, make himself holy, in a short time;—at least we do not see how it is possible; and this, viewed merely as a deduction of reason, is a serious thought. Yet, alas! as there are persons who think to be saved by a few scanty performances, so there are others who suppose they may be saved all at once by a sudden and easily-acquired faith. Most men who are living in neglect of God, silence their consciences, when troublesome, with the promise of repenting some future day. How often are they thus led on till death surprises them! But we will suppose they do begin to repent when that future day comes. Nay, we will even suppose that Almighty God were to forgive them, and to admit them in His holy heaven. Well, but is nothing more requisite? are they in a fit state to *do Him service in heaven*? Is not this the very point I have been insisting on, that they are *not* in a fit state? has it not been shown that, even if admitted there without a change of heart, they would find no pleasure in heaven? and is a change of heart wrought in a day? Which of our tastes or likings can we change at our will in a moment? Not the most superficial. Can we then at a word change the whole frame and character of our minds? Is not holiness the result of many patient, repeated efforts after obedience, gradually working on us, and first modifying and then changing our hearts? We dare not, of course, set bounds to God's mercy and power in cases of repentance late in life, even where He has revealed to us the general rule of His moral governance; yet, surely it is our duty ever to keep steadily before us, and act upon, those general truths which His holy Word has declared. His holy Word in various ways warns us, that, as no one will find happiness in heaven, who is not holy, so no one can learn to be so, in a short time, and when he will. NEWMAN. *P.S.* I. p. *12*

PARTICULAR PROVIDENCE

God "beholds" thee individually, whoever thou art. He 'calls thee by thy name. He sees thee, and understands thee, as He made thee. He knows what is in thee, all thy own peculiar feelings and thoughts, thy dispositions and likings, thy strength and thy weakness. He views thee in thy day of rejoicing and thy day of sorrow. He sympathizes in thy hopes and thy temptations. He interests Himself in all thy anxieties and remembrances, all the risings and fallings of thy spirit. He has numbered the very hairs of thy head and the cubits of thy stature. He compasses thee round, and bears thee in His arms; He takes thee up and sets thee down. He notes thy very countenance, whether smiling or in tears, whether healthful or sickly. He looks tenderly upon thy hands and thy feet; He hears thy voice, the beating of thy heart, and thy very breathing. Thou dost not love thyself better than He loves thee. Thou canst not shrink from pain more than He dislikes thy bearing it; and if He puts it on thee, it is as thou wilt put it on thyself, if thou art wise, for a greater good afterwards. Thou art not only His creature (though for the very sparrows He has a care, and pitied the "much cattle" of Nineveh), thou art man redeemed and sanctified, His adopted son, favoured with a portion of that glory and blessedness which flows from Him everlastingly unto the only-begotten. Thou art chosen to be

His, even above thy fellows who dwell in the east and south. Thou wast one of those for whom Christ offered up His last prayer, and sealed it with His precious blood.   NEWMAN. *P.S.* III. *pp.134–5*

THE CALL

We must know full well of ourselves, that we have been oftentimes called, re-called, re-re-called. We were called at our Baptism, by instruction in our childhood, through parents or God's Ministers, by the prayers we were taught, our Confirmation, our first Communion, the early drawings of our inmost souls, terrors, warnings, hopes, deaths of others or of those beloved, our own sickness, God's pleadings in our consciences, the emptiness and weariness of things present, thoughts of Eternity and Judgment to come, the loathsomeness of sin, the beauty of holiness, the bright light in others, the innocence of children, the sweepings by of time, thoughts of the blissful company of heaven, or of the dreadful fellowship of devils.

If we would hear, surely we might rather say, that God calls us, at all times, in all places, by all things, persons, deeds, words, by night and by day, all our lives long, than dare to say for ourselves before God's all-searching eye, "No man hath hired us." For so it is; when persons have heard the first call, every thing calls them. When the heart is awake, every, the lowest, whisper calls it. When it is alive to God, every work of God, every gift of God, every grace of God, in it or in others, every thing done for or against God, every forgetfulness of God, every coarse or idle word it hears, every hard or thoughtless look it sees, calls it anew to God. For when that one thought, "heaven or hell for ever", for ever the blissful Presence, or the loss of the face of God, everlasting love or everlasting hate, is, by God's Holy Spirit, wrought into the soul, everything may bring it back and forth in us; everything of sense or spirit may call us out of and above this world of sense, up to its Maker, the Father of all spirits and all flesh, our God.

The world is one great mirror. As we are who look into it or on it, so is it to us. It gives us back ourselves. It speaks to us the language of our own hearts. Such as we are, so doth it speak to us of pleasure, gain, honour, vanity, worldly happiness, or of everlasting rest and peace, out of itself, in God. Our inmost self is the key to all. Our ruling thought or passion, the thought or love, that is, which has the mastery of us, and governs us, and occupies our soul, is touched by everything around us. In grief, all things alike, the most joyous or the most sorrowful, suggest to the mourner thoughts of grief; yea, joyous sounds and sights speak mostly, most heavily to it of its own heaviness, or of the absence of the lost object of its love. Self-love sees everything as it bears on self; love of pleasure or of gain looks on all, as it may minister to its pleasure or gain, or to envy those which have what it has not. The heart where God dwelleth, is by all things called anew to God; His blessed Presence draws it by its sweetness: or His seeming Absence by the very void, may absorb it yet more, by the very vehemence of longing, into Himself.

It matters not what things are. Things like or things unlike; things divine or things devilish; the obedience, order, growth, harmony, beauty of nature, or the disobedience, disorder, decay, discord of man, and the loathsomeness of sin; sounds of harmony, which echo, as it were, the choirs of heaven, or sounds of discord, hatred, blasphemy, bad words uttered by the tongue, which "is set[1] on fire of hell"; things good, by their loveliness, or things bad, by their dreadfulness, draw the soul upward to God, or drive it onward, lest, like them, it lose Him.

Every thing preaches Eternity to the awakened soul. All love of gain it sees, preaches of Him, the true riches; all disquiet "about many things", of Him, our only rest; all seeking after pleasure, of Him, the ever-flowing torrent of pleasure; all sickness of soul and body, of Him, our soul's only health; all things passing, of Him, Who Alone abideth. Perhaps no place may more preach to the soul the vanity of all things beneath the sun, and the Verity of Him, the Eternal Verity, Whose and of Whom are all things, as the vast solitude of this great, crowded, tumultuous city[2], "full of stirs",[3] where "all things are full of labour; man cannot utter it; the eye is not satisfied with seeing, nor the ear filled with hearing",[4] where well-nigh all countenances or motions are full of eagerness, anxiety; all bent on something, seeking, but finding not, because they are seeking all things out of God, all but Himself, except when, here and there, they at last become very emptiness, because they know no more what to seek or find, but have lost themselves.

But, chiefly, we know, brethren, in our inmost selves, that whether

[1] S. James iii. 6.   [2] London.   [3] Is. xxii. 2.   [4] Eccl. i. 8.

we have obeyed the call, first or last, or, if any are even yet disobeying it or hearing it listlessly, obeying it for awhile in solemn seasons, and then forgetting it, or thinking they obey it when untempted, and then anon, when the temptation comes, ever anew disobeying, we know that we have been called manifoldly, perhaps our whole lives through. All perhaps can recollect when, in their childhood, some sermon or deep Scripture words touched them, or some grave look or word of parents; or they felt ill at ease, or their soul yearned for something better than this world's poor fleeting vanities; or they felt that within them, not made for this world, which could not rest in it, but soared up and up, as though it would find Him from Whom it came, Whose it is; or they were affrighted within themselves, at thoughts of Judgment; or they were inwardly bidden not to put off turning to God with their whole heart. God adapts His calls to each several soul. He calleth gently or in awe; in love or in some form of displeasure; quickening or checking us; within or without, directly or indirectly, in the secret chambers of the heart or "in the chief place of concourse", "in the openings of the gates", "in the city", "Wisdom", that is Himself, "uttereth Her Words", "How long, ye simple ones, will ye love simplicity, and the scorners delight in their scorning, and fools hate knowledge? Turn you at My reproof; behold, I will pour out My Spirit unto you, I will make known My Words unto you."[1] All things stand at His Command; all hearts are in His Hand, Who made them, and for Whom He made them; all things may be the channels of His Holy Inspirations; all times may be seasons of His grace; all words may convey His voice to the soul. As "all things work together for good to them that love Him,[2]" so may and do all things call us to love Him. All things have, in turn, called to our souls; all, nature, the world, grace or sin, shame at our folly and our very misery, have repeated His Words in our ears, "Why stand ye all the day idle?"

No outward gift is it, for which He calleth thee, which He hath promised thee. He calleth thee to Himself, that He may give Himself unto thee. He calleth thee to give up all which is not He, that He may give thee all which HE IS. He calleth thee to give thee His Likeness.

Pusey. *A.W.* pp. *108–12, 118*

[1] Prov. i. *21–23.*   [2] Rom. viii. *28.*

SUFFERING

It behoves us, brethren, to treat suffering, whether in ourselves or others, in a much more solemn way than the generality even of serious Christians are wont to do. In itself, it were a punishment for sin, oppressive, hopeless; through His mercy in Christ, it is His healing medicine, to burn out our wounds and purify us for His Presence. All are tokens of His Presence, the great Physician of our souls, looking graciously upon our spots and sores, checking our diseases ere they take deep root, or cutting deeply and healthfully into our very souls, if He have compassion upon us, when we have deeply offended Him. All, from the most passing pain of the body to the most deep-seated anguish of the soul, are messengers from Him. Some are spread over life to temper our enjoyments, lest we seek our joys here; some follow closely upon what is wrong (as discomfort upon excess); some gradually thicken upon us, if we neglect the first warnings; some come suddenly on an instant, to startle people out of their lethargy and careless ways, and show them that the life which they are wasting is an earnest thing. Some come in the natural order of His Providence, as the loss of parents, some contrary to what seems that order, as that of children; some are a new thing, as when He makes our sun to go down while it is yet day; some, it seems, are the immediate preparation for His holy Presence; whence, perhaps, old age is so generally a period of suffering, and the last illness has mostly so much of heavy suffering. Yet all, if we will regard it, are His fatherly care, tempering our cup with pain and sorrow, as He sees most needful for us: all, in their degree, loosen our hold of this life (as all pain is an earnest and preparation for our final dissolution); all lead up thitherward, where there shall be no pain: all humble us, as being creatures who require it, and deserve far more; all teach us to look into ourselves, to see for what disease in us this medicine has been sent.

All, then, pain, sickness, weariness, distress, languor, agony of mind or body, whether in ourselves or others, is to be treated reverently, since in it our Maker's hand passes over us, fashioning, by suffering, the imperfect or decayed substance of our souls. In itself, it were the earnest of Hell; through His mercy in Christ, it is a purifying for Heaven. Either way, it is a very solemn act. It is the Cross changed from the instrument of shame, the torture of malefactors, into the source of life. It is His Cross, applied to us, not as once in Holy Baptism, a painless remedy, but "washing away our filth by the Spirit of judgment, and the Spirit of burning".[1]

We must treat it reverently, as in His Presence, Who is causing it; not forming any rash judgment as to those who suffer, as though they "were sinners more than others". It may be that they are saints more than others; and therefore God is "purging them that they may bring forth more fruit", and burning away the remains of corruption from them. Anyhow it is a token that God has not forsaken them, but is still striving with them, and slaying them, if so it be, that they may live to Him. We may not then turn away from suffering in others, we may not mitigate it in ourselves, thoughtlessly. It is a form of God's countenance, and so, whatever we do, must be done as a religious act, with religious prudence. Even in those sad cases in the streets, in which it may become our duty to withhold our alms, both because giving would be rather an occasion of sin, and that we may have more for those who really need it, we ought not to "pass by, on the other side", unconcerned or impatient at their importunity. Even when we must say with the Apostle, "Silver and gold have I none", we should with the Apostle bestow what we have, our prayers. Still less may we turn away from what is loathsome, or offensive, or shocking, or disgusting, in human disease and misery, even though produced by previous sin. Lazarus was "full of sores", just ere the Angels carried him into Abraham's bosom. Each sore may be an earnest of his Saviour's mercy, a touch from His healing hand, by which He is saying to him, "I will, be thou clean." If it were possible, it were better not even to relieve suffering, without sharing it.

When heavier sorrows come, as it is often a privilege to feel ourselves allowed not to stifle them, so is it our wisdom and duty not to distract ourselves from them, nor allow ourselves to be distracted by others' well-meaning kindness. Every sorrow which we meet with is a billow on this world's troublesome sea, which we must cross upon the Cross, to bear us nearer to our home. We may not then remain where we were. We may not, when God's "waves and storms have gone over us",[2] be what we were before. We may and must bear our parts in the world's duties, but—in proportion to its heaviness, and the loudness of God's warning voice in it—not, as we did, in its joys. Each

[1] Is. iv. 4.   [2] Ps. xlii. 7.

trouble is meant to relax the world's hold over us, and our hold upon the world; each loss is sent to make us seek our gain in Heaven; the end of each bereavement is to fix our hearts thither, whither we hope the treasures lent us are removed. Each chastisement is to deepen our repentance for those sins for which God has so chastened us. Sadder far than the sight of any sorrow, is it to see persons, after sorrow, become, in all outward show, what they were before, "recovering their spirits" as it is called; even as the impassive waters are troubled for a while by the stone which severs them, and then become calm and cold as heretofore; sadder far, for it seems like a casting aside God's healing hand, and rising up from under it when He is laying low.

Rather it is a Christian's joy, and comfort, and peace, and health, when God has laid him low, there to lie—humble, in proportion as God has humbled him; to lie low at the foot of His Cross, trusting that by the virtue of that Cross He will raise up those who lie willingly where He has placed them. It is well to be there where God wills. And so whatever it be, sorrow bringing sin to remembrance, or agony for past sin, or dread of Judgment, it is our wisdom not to vent it in excitement, much less to seek to distract it or waste it, but to take it calmly home to our bosoms and treasure it there, jealously watching lest we lose one drop of its wholesome bitterness; not anxious to escape sorrow, but anxious only not to lose its fruits, anxious only to escape with our lives in our hands, out of that place which the Lord will burn up, and from which, with the loss, it may be, of all, He is sending His Angel to rescue us.

PUSEY. *P.S.* III. pp. *129-32, 137-8*

Till we attain, by His mercy, to Himself, and death itself is past, there is often need, amid the many, manifold forms of death, wherewith we are encompassed, for that holy steadfastness of the patriarch's trust, "Though He slay me, yet will I trust in Him." The first trials by which God would win us back to Himself, yea, though they seem to part asunder soul and body, are often not the severest. Near as they touch us, they are, most often, without us. They may change the whole life at once; they may seem to reverse the prophet's words, and "behind" it may seem "as the garden of Eden,[1] before, like a desolate wilderness"; the staggered, dizzied, soul may not dare to look backwards or forwards, to ought which belongs to this earth; they may leave the soul bared of all but itself; yea, scarcely leave itself to itself.

[1] Joel ii. 3.

For, mostly, those severe blows whereby God brings the soul to itself, are a rending from it part of itself, since they are a rending from it, what it loved, as, perhaps more than, itself; as even a heathen calls a friend, "the half[1] of his soul". Yet torn, bleeding, scarce alive, except for suffering, as the soul may thus be; bewildered, dead to all interest, or care, or pleasure in things around it; as if it were dead, yet are these the lightest trials of the returning soul. They reach not still its very inmost self. For to feel a nearness of God, even in chastisement, is a deeper, stiller, aweful indeed, yet more thrilling joy, than the intensest, or the most even tide of joy, on which the soul rested, even as the gift of God. Even in the most penetrating of this life's chastisements, God replaces His gifts with the hope of Himself. Chastisement is blessed to the trusting soul, because, though an aweful form of His Presence, it *is* His Presence. "The Lord,"[2] saith the Psalmist, "hath chastened and corrected me: but He hath not given me over unto death." His very chastening is a token to the soul that it is not abandoned. And gladlier often to the bereaved soul is this one token, than all besides is heavy. What is the intensest blackness, if His bow be in it and span it, and enfold and measure its height and breadth of darkness, by the unfoldings of His Light, the radiant, glorious, pledge of His loving-kindness? To feel is to live. To know that one is chastened, is to know that one is not abandoned. Be any what he may, he feels that he is a son yet. The deeper the iron enters, the deeper he knows is the sore which God would lay open and heal; yet the deeper too the mercy of God, Who gives not over what needeth so deep a cure. So true is that which even a heathen[3] saw from nature, "he draweth strength and courage from the very sword" which wounds him. Here too indeed, is there need of faith and hope. For even these very chastisements of God, when they do not soften, harden. They, like every gift of God, yea, the very Gospel of His Son and the tidings of Redemption, are a savour of "life unto life"[4], or "of death unto death". "The sorrow of the world worketh death".[5] Sorrow which cometh from the love of the world only, hath its end in the world; sorrow, which cometh from the Love of God, or turneth unto the Love of God, hath its end in God. Sorrow of the world maketh rebellious against God; sorrow which subdues unto God,

---

[1] Horace. Odes i. *3*. [2] Ps. cxviii. *18*.
[3] Horace. Odes iv. *4*. [4] 2 Cor. ii. *16*.
[5] 2 Cor. vii. *10*.

is from God. Times of God's sorest Judgments have been times of man's deepest rebellions, and have fostered them. The recklessness of the impenitent has grown, with the sternness of God's calls to penitence. How should it not be? Contempt of God's Judgments is almost beyond the very sin of devils, who "believe and tremble", and is a near fore-runner of the unpardonable sin, casting forth with a strong hand, the last remains of grace from the soul. "In that day,"[1] says the Prophet, "did the Lord God of Hosts call to weeping, and to mourning, and to baldness, and to girding with sackcloth; and behold joy and gladness, slaying oxen, and killing sheep, eating flesh, and drinking wine: let us eat and drink; for to-morrow we shall die. And it was revealed in mine ears by the Lord of Hosts, Surely this iniquity shall not be purged from you till ye die, saith the Lord God of Hosts." Yet since this is so, the more must the penitent think it an undeserved mercy of God, that his own sorrows have not hardened him, the more deeply thank his God that, through the prayers of others perhaps, or of the Church, or out of the abyss of God's forecoming mercy, He, with the chastisement, gave the grace to profit by it.

Yet these outward griefs are often but the "beginning of sorrows". Birth-pangs they often are, through which the soul is, by the Grace of God, born again from its state of death to life in God. These are infan-tine trials fitted for the tenderness of new-born souls. Deeper pains are often reserved, until the soul, grown and strengthened through Grace, can endure a more searching, fiery, cleansing. Outward trials bear with them their own witness; conscience owns them; nature itself approves them; our sense of justice takes their side and calls them good; pious examples of Holy Scripture put words in our mouth and teach us how to use them; God pronounces so manifoldly, "Blessed are those whom He chasteneth." In these, too, the soul itself is not disordered in its inner self. Wounded as it may be to the very "dividing asunder of soul and spirit", yet it is whole in that whereby it judges of itself; it can behold its own wounds and the hand of God, wounding to make whole, slaying to give life.

Deeper and more difficult far are those sorrows wherewith God afflicts the very soul herself, and in divers ways, "makes[2] her to possess

---

[1] Is. xxii. *12–14*.

[2] "Prayer for persons troubled in mind or in conscience", in "Visitation for the Sick", from Job xiii. *26*.

her former iniquities." A bitter thing indeed it is, to have to turn to God with a cold, decayed heart; "an evil thing and bitter" to have destroyed ourselves. Yet having so done, gracious and merciful is it, if Almighty God shew us somewhat of the depth of that bitterness, that we may never know its full bitterness in the depths of Hell. Merciful and very good are all the scourges of the All-Good and All-Merciful. The deeper, the more merciful; the more inward, the more cleansing. The more they enter into the very soul, the more they open it for the healing Presence of God. The more they slay its very self, the more do they convey to it the virtue of Christ's Death. The less it lives, the more Christ liveth in it. Hence it has been seen that God mostly doth not send these trials at first upon the soul, but when it is somewhat strengthened by His grace, to endure this healthful probing and opening for greater grace. The beginnings of conversion mostly have sweetness whereby God allures the soul from the deadening sweetness whereby it destroyed itself. "Gracious is God," saith a holy man,[1] "who doth not suffer us to be tempted above that we are able, nor alloweth the worm of conscience to infest us beyond measure. And especially in the beginnings of conversion, He sootheth our ulcers with the oil of mercy; that neither the amount of the disease, nor the difficulty of the cure, should become known to it, more than is beneficial; yea, rather a sort of ease smileth, as it were, upon it, which afterward disappeareth, when it hath its senses exercised, and thereon, perhaps, strife is appointed to it."

Manifold are these clouds whereby God hides, for the time, the brightness of His Presence, and He seemeth, as it were, to threaten again to bring a destroying flood over our earthliness. Yet one character they have in common, that the soul can hardly believe itself in a state of grace. "If it be so," is the common cry of all, "why am I thus?"[2] Can God indeed dwell in a heart thus defiled? are this and this foulness, the tokens of His Presence? Can God and Satan indeed have power over the heart together? I feel too miserably the presence of one; dare I indeed hope the blessed Presence of the other, unseen, unfelt, unknown? Where is faith, when Satan can, at will, pour in his doubts? Or love, when all seems so dry and cold, and hard thoughts come in unbidden, as though lords and owners of the heart in their own domain? Where is life, when devotion seems so lifeless? Or holiness,

[1] St Bernard. [2] Gen. xxv. 22.

when the soul is trampled upon by unholy thoughts, and its broken fences shut them not out? Where is any cleaving to God, when at Holy Communion itself, some chance thought or sight can part the soul with, if not from, its God? How is the heart broken which can thus rebel? how humble, which can thus judge others, see so acutely others' faults, rebel so proudly against any touch of shame, feel so sensitively to the quick any slight? Where, in all this dreary winter and this chill damp mist, are any tokens of the Presence of that Sun of the soul, which, where it is, encircleth and enlighteneth it from end to end, and there is "nothing hid from the heat thereof".

Hard indeed is it for hope to live, when faith thus seems dead and love grown cold. Hard is it to trust in God, when the soul's very self seems slain; and hope seems forbidden by the very senses, and sight, and conscience, and self-knowledge. How can it be beloved by God, when it seems to itself so hateful? how endured by Him, when it cannot bear itself? Yet on that very ground is it beloved by God, because it hates itself. Deep hatred of what the sinful soul has been, empties it of that self-love which estranges it from its God, and He Who "satisfieth the empty soul", in His time shall fill it with His goodness. Self-hating displeasure at its sin, casts out its idols from His temple, that He again may more fully indwell it. It could not feel the full hatefulness of sin which it obeyed, nor the force of the weight which it resisted not, nor see the dreariness of the dungeon, which had no light in it, nor know the poison it breathed, when it knew not the freshness of gales from Heaven. And so, perhaps most frequently, God for a time casts back the converted soul, and plunges it, as it were, amidst the phantoms of its former foulness, and allows it to be assailed and tortured by them, that it may learn the more to hate what He hates, and so, through its very hatred, may gain the love of what He loves.

Faint not then, thou weary soul, but trust! If thou canst not hope, act as thou wouldest, if thou didst hope. If thou canst see nothing but Hell before thee, shut thine eyes and cast thyself blindly into the infinite abyss of God's mercy, and the everlasting arms will, though thou know it not, receive thee and upbear thee. Hide thee in the cleft of the Rock riven for thee, thy Saviour's wounded side, until this tyranny be overpast. If buffeted by the waves, thou wouldest not let go a rope, which held thee to the Rock! So now, though "all His waves and storms seem to pass over thee", hold thee but the faster to Him Who, unseen, holdeth thee. Without Him, thou couldest not even hate thy sin. Hatred, in thyself, of what is contrary to God, is love of God. If thou canst not love with the affections, love with the will, or will to love. If thou canst not love as thou wouldest, do what thou canst. If thy heart seems to have died within thee, cleave to God with the understanding. If God seem to thy mind, as it were, a phantom which to it has no reality, if thy prayers seem to be but words with no substance, sent idly into the air, not ascending unto thy God; if things unseen seem to thee a dream, things seen the only reality; if fervid words move thee not, thoughts of love kindle thee not, the Passion of Christ melt thee not, yet despond not; but "out of the deep cry unto God, and He will hear thy voice".[1] He has recovered out of deeper depths, for whence is the penitent recovered but out of "the depths of Hell?"[2] "Out of the belly of Hell," says the prophet Jonas,[3] "cried I and Thou heardest my voice. I said, I am cast out of the sight of Thine eyes, yet will I look again towards Thy holy temple. The waters compassed me about, even to the soul: the depths closed me round about; the weeds were wrapped about my head. I went down to the bottoms of the mountains: the earth with her bars was about me for ever; yet hast thou brought up my life from corruption, O Lord, my God. When my soul fainted within me, I remembered the Lord, and my prayer came in unto Thee, into Thine holy temple."

"Though He slay me, I will trust in Him." Seemeth this a great thing, brethren? The great holy words will mean yet more, "Lo! if He slay me, I will trust in Him", not "although" only, but "*because*" He slayeth me. It is life to be touched by the hand of God; to be slain is, through the Cross of Christ, the pledge of the Resurrection. Yes; then may our hearts be strung and nerved, when at His pitiful touch, "the sinew shrinks". It is the Redeemer's hand, which upholds while It seems to cripple, strengthens, while He seemeth to put forth His strength, against our weakness; by His strength we have power with God, while we can only weep and make supplication unto Him.[4] Not sensible comforts, nor delight in prayer, nor His very voice to the heart, nor tokens of His Presence, nor the overflowings of His consolations, *may be* such a proof of His Love for the soul, as the unseen, unfelt, strength by which He keeps the fainting soul in life, to trust in Him. consolation is the stay of the weakness of the creature: desolation was,

[1] Ps. cxxx. *1*.   [2] Prov. ix. *18*.   [3] Jonah ii. *2–7*.   [4] Gen. *32*; Hos. xii. *3, 4*.

for our sake, the choice of the Redeemer. When His human nature was all but perfected and consecrated by suffering; when the last act of obedience to the Father's will "even to the Death of the Cross" was all but completed; when His perfect obedience was effacing the sins of a whole world, then withheld He from His Sacred Humanity the consolation of His Divinity, and, forsaken by man, willed He, to seem to be forsaken by God also. In the entrance on His Ministry, that voice was heard, "This is My Beloved Son, in whom I am well pleased": at its close the voice "My God, My God, why hast Thou forsaken Me?" is followed only by That, "Father, into Thy Hands I commend My Spirit", to give us some glimpse into the meaning of that great word, "Though He slay me, yet will I trust in Him".

"Into His Hands", brethren, let us now, for this year, and for all the years of time, and for eternity, "commend our spirits". Whether for the Church or for ourselves, let us not take ourselves into our own hands, or choose our own lot. "My times are in Thy hands.[1]" He loveth the Church, which He died to purchase, His Own Body, and all the members of His own Body, better than we can; He loveth us better and more wisely than we ourselves. He Who made us, loveth us better than we who unmade ourselves; He Who died for us, better than we who destroyed ourselves; He Who would sanctify us for a holy temple unto Himself, better than we who defiled what He hallowed. Fear we not then any thing which threateneth; shrink we not back from any thing which falleth on us. Rather let us, though with trembling, hold up our hearts to Him, to make them His own, in what way He willeth. "If He willeth that we should be comforted, let us too will it; if that we should have desolation, Lord, let us not draw back from it." Pray we Him, by virtue of His holy circumcision, in what way He seeth good, to circumcise our hearts, to cut yea, burn, if He see needful, in this life, and spare for ever. Let us neither outrun Him, nor hold back; neither step on the waters without His bidding, nor fear if we behold them boisterous; neither be troubled, if for the time He withhold affliction, nor if, without or within, He giveth us of His Cup to drink. Give we Him our hearts, to prepare, in whatever way He will, to be made fit vessels for His Love, yea, for Himself. Circumcise, yea, cut them, Lord, round and round, until none of the vanities or love of this world cling unto them; break and bruise them

[1] Ps. xxxi. *15.*

in pieces, that they never come together again, as they once were; melt them, if Thou see good, in the furnace of affliction, or by the Spirit of burning, until Thou purely purge away their dross; press them, and oppress with anguish, if so only they can be emptied of all which is not Thou, or loved for Thee; give them faintness and weariness, if so only they may "faint for Thy" heavenly "courts", and long to rest in Thee Alone.

Only, O Lord, strengthen our hearts with that Bread which came down from Heaven, to give Life unto the world, even Thyself; give us Thy grace, and so deal with us as Thou willest; "give[1] what Thou commandest, and command what Thou willest"; if Thou slay us, give us trust in Thee; "O Lord, in Thee have I trusted, let me never be confounded", let me not be confounded, for ever! PUSEY. *A.W.* pp. *97-105*

RECOLLECTION

Blessed are those holy hours, in which the soul retires from the world, to be alone with God. God's voice, as Himself, is every where. Within and without He speaks to our souls, if we would hear. Only the din[2] of the world or the tumult of our own hearts, deafens our inward ear to it. Stillness is as His very Presence, for, like the prayer for[3] the prophet's servant, it opens our senses to perceive what was there to behold, only our eyes were holden. "There is neither speech nor language; the voice is not heard"; but "day unto day uttereth speech[4]" to hearts that hearken, "and night unto night sheweth knowledge". All

[2] Christian Year:

"Sin is with man at morning break;
    And, through the livelong day,
Deafens the ear, that fain would wake
    To nature's simple lay.

But when eve's silent footfall steals
    Along the eastern sky,
And, one by one, to earth reveals
    Those purer fires on high,

When, one by one, each human sound
    Dies on the aweful ear,
Then nature's voice no more is drown'd,
    She speaks, and we must hear."
        Fourth Sunday after Trinity.

"There are, in this loud stunning tide
    Of human care and crime,
With whom the melodies abide
    Of the everlasting chime;

Who carry music in their heart,
    Through dusky lane and wrangling
    mart;
Plying their daily task with busier feet,
Because their secret souls a holy strain
    repeat."
        S. Matthew's Day.

[1] St Aug. Conf. x. *29.*   [3] *2* Kings vi. *17.*   [4] Ps. xix. *2.*

God's works, because He has made them, bear the traces of His hand, and speak of Him to the soul which is alone with Him.

Until, in silence, ye enter into that sacred loneliness, ye know not whither ye are going. In loneliness a man knows himself and his God. Enter there with Him, and, by His grace, thou wilt not come forth as thou goest in. As thou wouldest not, in a tempest, be tossed about without compass, neither sun nor stars appearing; so trust thyself no longer to the sea of this troublesome world, not knowing whether thou art indeed, year by year, reaching nearer towards the haven where thou wouldest be. As thou wouldest not leave thy worldly affairs unexamined, lest they go to ruin, be as faithful with thy soul. If thou hast not yet, review once, under the eye of God, thy life as a whole, and see whither it has been and is tending. Bear, in the Presence of God, to know thyself. Then seek to know for what God sent thee into the world; how thou hast fulfilled it; art thou yet what God willed thee to be; what yet lacketh unto thee; what is God's will for thee *now;* what chiefly hinders thee from inward peace; what one thing thou mayest *now* do, by His grace, to obtain His favour, and approve thyself unto Him. Say to Him "Teach me to do Thy will, for Thou art my God", and He will say unto thy soul, "Fear not; I am thy Salvation." He will speak peace unto thy soul; He will set thee in the way; He will speak to thy soul "good words and comfortable words"; He will bear thee above things of sense and praise of man, and things which perish in thy grasp, and give thee, if but afar off, some glimpse of His own unfading, unsetting, unperishing, brightness and bliss, and love. Only, by His grace, take with thee one earnest purpose, to desire to know one will of God for thee, and to do it.

If, at all times, God calleth us to be alone with Him in this sacred season, when He, with such unutterable love, suffered for us; if He, Who loved us all one by one, upon the Cross, and thought of us then, our many grievings of Him, and how He would at last melt our hearts and win us to Himself, calleth us ever at this time to sit under His Cross, and there to long to be healed by Him, and to love Him, how much more now! Since stillness is ever fitting at the season of the Passion, how much more when His hand, in some secret purpose of His chastening love, is so heavy upon those whom with us He redeemed![1]

[1] The famine of *1847.*

It is a blessed provision which the chief pastor of the diocese[1] has made, in opening, day by day, these houses of God, for secret prayer to Him. Here, where he has admitted us so often to pour out our sorrows before Him, here, where in our deep penitential litany and confessions, He has heard our cry for mercy and repentance; here, where He has fed us with "the Bread of Life" and made us forget our sorrows in "the pledges of His love", let us, apart from the din of the world and its interruptions, in union with that sacred loneliness of our Redeemer in the garden for us, anew, in penitence, seek Him.

But if this may not be, it needeth not change of place to be alone with God. We departed not from God, if we ever did depart, with our feet, but with our affections.[2] He is ever near us, if we be near Him. If we turn to Him, or pray Him to turn to us, He, Who turneth us, Himself turneth unto us. He is present, if we open our eyes to behold Him. He is more inward to us than our very souls, for He is within the soul; the very Life by which it lives, the Power whereby it thinks of Him, the Love wherewith it loves Him. Withdraw thy thoughts from the world, and He will stand revealed before thee; pluck out the right eye, which would gaze on and love that which offends Him, and He will cleanse thine inward eye, that thou shalt behold Him; pray Him to close thy ears from hearing words of vanity, and He will open the inward ear of the heart, that thou mayest hear His voice, and it is sweet, and know His voice, and follow Him, and "He will give thee eternal life, and none shall pluck thee out of His hand." Whatsoever thou doest, hush thyself to thine own feverish vanities, and busy thoughts, and cares; in silence seek thy Father's face, and the light of His countenance will stream down upon thee. Business, and labour, and toil, these only shut out the voice of God, when they enter into the heart, and take it up and close it. It is the promise of God, in the Gospel, "Thou shalt hear a voice[3] behind thee, saying, This is the way, walk ye in it, when ye turn to the right hand and when ye turn to the left."

More than they of old may we well commune of Him when we "sit in the house, when we walk by the way, when we lie down, and

---

[1] London. The recommendation to the Clergy to open the Churches for an hour before the service, was then (Lent *1847*) recent.

[2] S. Augustine.   [3] Is. xxx. *21*.

when we rise up".[1] Use a sacred diligence to be with God, and He will, in all things, speak to thee. He will make a secret cell in thine heart, and when thou enterest there, there shalt thou find Him. And if thou have found Him there, all around shall reflect Him, all shall speak of Him, and He speak through all. Outwardly thou mayest be doing the work of thy calling; inwardly, if thou commend thy work to God, thou mayest be with Him in the third Heaven. "Say not in thine heart, Who shall ascend into Heaven? (that is, to bring Christ down from above), or who shall descend into the deep? (that is, to bring up Christ again from the dead). But what saith it, The word is nigh thee, even in thy mouth and in thy heart?"[2] Give thyself to Him, and a crowded street may be a solitude, in which thou mayest be alone with Him. As, even in this house of prayer, when the heart is not set on God, it is often away, while the body is here, so may the body be with thy works, and thy soul with God. Was not thy Lord called not a "carpenter's son" only, but "the carpenter"[3] to teach thee how One, in human flesh, and doing common human deeds, might still be in the bosom of His Father? Did not St Paul and the Apostles work with their own hands, while they were preaching the Gospel? Or think you, whatever the beloved Apostle was doing, his soul was ever absent from Him Whom he loved? Whatever ye do, do it to the glory of God, and ye may even be the more with God, because ye are doing it. David "was following the ewes, great with young ones", a shepherd, when God taught him, "the Lord is my Shepherd", and "took him" to be the shepherd of His people. Amos was a herdsman and a gatherer of sycamore fruit, when the Lord took him, as he followed the flock, and the Lord said unto him, "Go, prophesy unto My people Israel." The Apostles were fishermen, when our Lord said unto them, "Follow Me, and I will make you fishers of men." And so even in our own days, there have been those like any of the poorest of you, who while sweeping the streets, were sustained in their daily weariness by thoughts on the golden streets of the heavenly Jerusalem. And for this very cause did our Lord choose for His parables things of every day sight, that all things of sense might speak to us of Himself and the things of the Spirit.

One thing only deafens us to the Voice of God, untunes all, sets us out of harmony with all, that we should not, in all things, feel the thrill

[1] Deut. xi. *19.*   [2] Rom. x. *6–8.*   [3] S. Mark vi. *3.*

of His love, behold the earnest of Heaven, "our hearts burn within us", and He talk unto us by the way, and our eyes be opened, and we behold Him—sin. Labour by His grace to cleanse away this, pray Him to cleanse it with His precious Blood, commend thyself morning by morning to Him, do thy daily work unto Him, and He will be with thee, as with Adam, in the garden, and thy daily labour shall again be a dressing and keeping of the Paradise of God, where He shall walk with thee. Yea, He hath promised "the tabernacle of God shall be with men, and He will dwell with them, and they shall be His people, and God Himself shall be with them, and be their God".

Above all, treasure any season in which God Himself maketh thee lonely. When He brings thee back into thyself, seek not to go forth out of thyself. Whether it be by sickness, or by bereavement, or by any other sorrow, by want of the sympathy of the world, by distresses which make the heart sick and faint, go not forth out of thyself, but with the Prophet, stand in loneliness "upon thy watch, and set thee upon the tower"; dwell in Him, Who "is a most strong Tower to all them that put their trust in Him"; wherein the righteous runneth and is safe; and "watch to see, what He shall say into thee, and what thou shalt speak, when thou art reproved", and He, while He reproves thee of sin, will shew thee His righteousness, and "be gracious unto thee" and say, "deliver him from going down into the pit, I have found a ransom". "He will allure thee and bring thee into the wilderness, and speak unto thy heart." He will fence thee round, that nothing outward break in upon the sacred stillness of thy soul, which seeketh to be hushed in Him. Where He is, is great peace. Learn to commune with Him in stillness, and He Whom thou hast sought in stillness, will be with thee when thou goest abroad. Go not abroad out of thyself, and He will not depart from thee. He cometh not to us, to leave us, if we would detain Him with us. Gather thyself from time to time in thyself; recall to thyself, "Whose am I? for whom am I doing this? how would God have me do it?" Lift up thine eyes to the holy "pattern shewed thee in the mount", even His, "Who came not to do His own will, but the will of Him Who sent Him." Thy Redeemer, Who would work all thy works in thee, will gather thee up wholly into Himself, all thy thoughts, words, and deeds, that they be thought, spoken, done in Him.   Pusey. *A.W.* pp. *193, 196–201*

THE CLOISTER

Surely if scenes on earth be known
　　Which angels love to haunt and prize
As spots that are most like their own,
　　'Tis in those meek societies,
Where cloistral walls the fancy bar,
And shut out busy sounds of earth afar,
Of strife, of tumult and of war;
E'en like a sheltering citadel
Against surrounding arts of hell;
Or like a temple, rampart-crown'd,
Upon whose battlements in heavenly ground
Angels and happy spirits singing go;
While from the courts of prayer below
Blend with their songs the sounds of penitential woe.

I know not if 'tis well to string the heart
　　In solitude to take her part,
Or silence, which is peopled solitude;
　　I know not if 'tis good.
But this I know, to give up all
Which here on earth men treasure call,
With firm resolve to bid depart
Home ties, with earthly promise rife,
And things that lie most near the human heart;—
To spend the days of this short life
In prayers, and alms, and charities;—
This in its fulness daily is to store,
　　For ever more and more,
　　Where nothing dies.

                    ISAAC WILLIAMS. *The Baptistery*. Part II, pp. *57–60*

THE LIVES OF THE SAINTS

(*Newman began editing a series of* Lives of the Saints *in 1842 and the
first volume appeared in 1844. These are not edifying productions by the
standards of modern critical history; and the lives, together with the*

contemporary Essay on Ecclesiastical Miracles, *are the most cogent evidence for the sceptical interpretation of the Tractarian doctrine of faith, illustrated in part i of this anthology. This sceptical interpretation is not, however, typical of the Movement in its further influence; and therefore I select one of the least credulous and most critical statements of the purpose of the saints' lives, drawn from this series—part of the introduction to the Life of St Neot. This life was written by James Anthony Froude, later the eminent historian, at this time under Tractarian influence; the incompatibility between his critical instincts and his effort to write the legends of St Neot is said to have hastened his revolt against Newman. But Newman at least allowed his authors to write how they pleased; if, like Froude, they were critical of the legends, Newman did not edit their criticism out of his series on grounds of piety. There, in the pious series, stands Froude's appreciation of the saints' legends; and as such it may appear here to represent that more sober attitude of the middle group of Tractarians, men like James Mozley and R. W. Church. Perhaps, whatever its possible weakness, it may be thought a less shallow apprehension of medieval hagiography than the mere hostility displayed in* The Oxford Counter Reformation, *written in Froude's old age).*

The Lives of the Saints are not so much strict biographies, as myths, edifying stories compiled from tradition, and designed not so much to relate facts, as to produce a religious impression on the mind of the hearer. Under the most favourable circumstances, it is scarcely conceivable that uninspired men could write a faithful history of a miraculous life. Even ordinary history, except mere annals, is all more or less fictitious; that is, the facts are related, not as they really happened but as they appeared to the writer; as they happen to illustrate his views or support his prejudices. And if this is so of common facts, how much more so must it be when all the power of the marvellous is thrown in to stimulate the imagination. But to see fully the difficulties under which the writers of these Lives must have laboured, let us observe a few of the ways in which we all, and time for us, treat the common history and incidents of life.

First; We all write Legends. Little as we may be conscious of it, we all of us continually act on the very same principle which made the Lives of Saints such as we find them; only perhaps less poetically.

Who has not observed in himself, in his ordinary dealings with the facts of every-day life, with the sayings and doings of his acquaintance, in short, with every thing which comes before him as a *fact*, a disposition to forget the real order in which they appear, and re-arrange them according to his theory of how they ought to be? Do we hear of a generous self-denying action, in a short time the real doer and it are forgotten; it has become the property of the noblest person we know; so a jest we relate of the wittiest person, frivolity of the most frivolous, and so on; each particular act we attribute to the person we conceive most likely to have been the author of it. And this does not arise from any wish to leave a false impression scarcely from carelessness; but only because facts refuse to remain bare and isolated in our memory; they will arrange themselves under some law or other; they must illustrate something to us—some character—some principle—or else we forget them. Facts are thus perpetually, so to say, becoming unfixed and re-arranged in a more conceptional order. In this way, we find fragments of Jewish history in the Legends of Greece, stories from Herodotus become naturalized in the tradition of early Rome; and the mythic exploits of the northern heroes, adopted by the biographers of our Saxon kings. So, uncertain traditions of miracles, with vague descriptions of name and place, are handed down from generation to generation, and each set of people, as they pass into their minds, naturally group them round the great central figure of their admiration or veneration, be he hero or be he saint. And so with the great objects of national interest. Alfred—"England's darling"—the noblest of the Saxon kings, became mythic almost before his death; and forthwith, every institution that Englishmen most value, of law or church, became appropriated to him. He divided England into shires; he established trial by jury; he destroyed wolves, and made the country so secure, that golden bracelets hung untouched in the open road. And when Oxford was founded, a century was added to its age; and it was discovered that Alfred had laid the first stone of the first college, and that St Neot had been the first Professor of Theology.

Again even in these unpoetical times, go where we will among the country villages, and we still find superstition strong as ever, we must still confess that the last victory of civilization is not yet won, and romance is yet lingering in the embrace of nature. The wild moor, the rock, the river, and the wood, have still their legend, and the Fairy and the Saint yet find a home when the earth is wild and beautiful. Of course they will go with light and modern education, and perhaps it

is as well that it should be so. Even Plato finds that Boreas and Orithuia
is an allegory. But it may still be asked whether there are not times
when the most civilized, the most enlightened philosopher, looking at
Nature as he has to do through his knowledge of Law, and Theory, and
Principle, has not experienced very strange sensations in scenes of
striking beauty, in a thunder storm, or at the sight of the most familiar
place in the light of an unusual sky? Who is there that has searched and
explored and dwindled as he searched so low as never with Wordsworth—

> ————to have "felt a sense sublime
> Of something far more deeply interfused,
> Whose dwelling is the light of setting suns,
> And the round ocean, and the living air,
> And the blue sky, and in the mind of man.
> A motion and a spirit that impels
> All thinking things, all objects of all thought
> And rolls through all things——"

If there be any with power of mind so great that they can keep these
deep emotions fresh and pure, and yet leave them purely spiritual, let
them do so. Such is not the lot of ordinary men. For them at least
Plotinus expressed the very condition of their apprehending them at all
when he said, "that those only could be said to have realized the
spiritual, who had clothed it in form of sense". And so ever children,
and childlike ages, who make up for the want of vigour in the understanding by the strength of their faith and the fervour of poetry and
imagination, go out and robe these vanishing feelings in shape and
colour. The old Greeks saw Naïads sporting in every fountain, and
when the breezes played among the branches of the forest, they heard
the Zephyrs whispering to the Dryads; and the Legends of Saints which
still cling to the scenes of their earthly glory, are but Christian expressions of the same human instinct.

> And those illusions, which excite the scorn
> Or move the pity of unthinking minds,
> Are they not mainly outward ministers
> Of Inward Conscience? with whose service charged
> They come and go, appeared and disappear;
> Diverting evil purposes, remorse

Awakening, chastening an intemperate grief
Or pride of heart abating: and whene'er
For less important ends those phantoms move,
Who would forbid them if their presence serve
Among wild mountains and unpeopled heaths,
Filling a space else vacant to exalt
The form of Nature and enlarge her powers.[1]

Time in another way plays strange tricks with facts, and is ever altering, shifting, and even changing their nature in our memory. Every man's past life is becoming mythic to him; we cannot call up again the feelings of our childhood, only we know that what then seemed to us the bitterest misfortunes, we have since learnt by change of character or circumstance, to think very great blessings; and even when there is no change, and were they to recur again, they are such as we should equally repine at, yet by mere lapse of time sorrow is turned to pleasure, and the sharpest pang at present becomes the most alluring object of our retrospect. The sick bed, the school trial, loss of friends, pain and grief of every kind, become rounded off and assume a soft and beautiful grace. "Time dissipates to shining æther the hard angularity of facts"; the harshest of them are smoothed and chastened off in the past like the rough mountains and jagged rocks in the distant horizon. And so it is with every other event of our lives; read a letter we wrote ten years ago, and how impossible we find it to recognize the writer in our altered selves. Incident after incident rises up and bides its day, and then sinks back into the landscape. It changes by distance, and we change by age. While it was present it meant one thing, now it means another, and to-morrow perhaps something else on the point of vision alters. Even old Nature endlessly and patiently reproducing the same forms, the same beauties, cannot reproduce in us the same emotions we remember in our childhood. Then all was Fairy-land; now time and custom have deadened our sense, and

The things which we have seen we now can see no more.

This is the true reason why men people past ages with the superhuman and the marvellous. They feel their own past was indeed something miraculous, and they cannot adequately represent their feelings except by borrowing from another order of beings.

[1] Wordsworth.

Thus age after age springs up, and each succeeds to the inheritance of all that went before it; but each age has its own feelings, its own character, its own necessities; therefore receiving the accumulations of literature and history, it absorbs and fuses and remodels them to meet the altered circumstances. The histories of Greece and Rome are not yet exhausted, every new historian finds something more in them. Alcibiades and Catiline are not to us what they were to Thucydides and Sallust, even though we use their eyes to look at them. So it has been with facts, and so it always shall be. It holds with the lives of individuals; it holds with histories even where there is contemporary writing, and much more than either, when as with many of the Lives of the Saints, we can only see them as they appeared through the haze of several generations with no other light but oral tradition.

Lives of the Saints, Vol. 2, pp. 74–9

PRAY WITHOUT CEASING

Public prayer may be measured; its hours can be counted; *private* prayer is immeasurable, for it may be at all times; when in company, as well as when alone; amid conversation, as when silent; "when thou sittest in the house, and when thou walkest by the way, and when thou liest down, and when thou risest up"; in the midst of business and employment, as when unoccupied; in short intervals, when for the moment thou seemest to have nothing else to do, or when most employed, that thou mayest do what thy hand findeth to do with all thy might, and "as unto the Lord, not unto men". "Most businesses," says a good Doctor of our Church[1] "have wide gaps, all have some chinks, at which, devotion may slip in. Be we never so urgent, or closely intent upon any work (be we feeding, be we travelling, be we trading, be we studying) nothing can forbid but that we may together wedge in a thought concerning God's goodness, and bolt forth a word of praise for it; but that we may reflect on our sins, and spend a penitential sigh on them; but that we may descry our need of God's help, and dispatch a brief petition. A 'God be praised', a 'Lord have mercy', a 'God bless' or 'God help me', will no wise interrupt or disturb our proceedings."

He then cannot be said to have any care about continual prayer, who

[1] Barrow.

passes any day, between morning and evening, without it; who lets his thoughts run on through the day on his daily business, without checking them to offer at least some brief prayer to God; who begins a work without asking God to bless it; who receives a mercy, or his daily food, without blessing Him; who comes into his daily temptations without asking God to deliver him from them; who is beset by any care, and casts it not on God; who does not labour to fix his heart, like David, upon God, that he may praise Him; who does not consider prayer (whatever he may yet have come up to) as the main business of life, as it will be of life eternal, and so does not wish and strive at least to interpose it at all intervals he may have; who does not, at least, divide each day into portions, and begin, at least, each such portion with some prayer.

Pray morning by morning to be enabled to pray; strive against covetousness, or sensuality, or the cares of this life, which prevent thy thinking upon God; make efforts to win thy soul from the business of this life, if but now and then, for a thought on God; use all the stated means in thy power, and make what thou canst. If thou wakest in the night, pray; when thou wakest in the morning, be thy first thought prayer; bethink thee that the journey is hard for thee, the way slippery, thy feet easily wearied, thy strength small, and haste thee "to the mountain", the Rock of ages, "lest thou be consumed".

And above all, neglect not any thought which God puts into thy heart (as He does oftentimes) to pray. The thought to pray must come from Him; it cannot come from thyself or from the evil one. Pray, wherever thou art, whatever thou art doing; man will not see it, but God will; and thy Father Who seeth in secret Himself shall reward thee openly. The first step on this way of frequent prayer, is the first step on Jacob's ladder, its foot on earth, its top in heaven; look not above, lest thou faint and sink back; nor downwards lest thou turn dizzy; but go on, step by step labouring to make thy prayers more and more continual and fervent, and God shall send His angels to conduct thee, and thy Saviour shall intercede for thee, and the Holy Ghost shall strengthen thee, and thou shalt win thy way step by step, until the cloud of death close round thee, and then thou shalt find that the first step to continual earnest prayer was "the gate of heaven".

PUSEY. *P.S.* III. pp. *229–30, 238*

Meditate daily on the things of Eternity; and by the grace of God, do something daily, which thou wouldest wish to have done, when that day cometh. PUSEY. *P.S.* II. p. *18*

A HABIT OF PRAYER

It is plain to common sense, that the man who has not accustomed himself to the language of heaven will be no fit inhabitant of it when, in the Last Day, it is perceptibly revealed. The case is like that of a language or style of speaking of this world; we know well a foreigner from a native. Again, we know those who have been used to king's courts or educated society, from others. By their voice, accent, and language, and not only so, by their gestures and gait, by their usages, by their mode of conducting themselves and their principles of conduct, we know well what a vast difference there is between those who have lived in good society and those who have not. What indeed is called "*good* society" is often very worthless society. I am not speaking of it to praise it; I only mean, that as what men call refined or courtly manners, are gained only by intercourse with courts and polished circles, and as the influence of the words there used (that is, of the ideas which those words, striking again and again on the ear, convey to the mind) extends in a most subtle way over all that men do, over the turn of their sentences, and the tone of their questions and replies, and their general bearing, and the spontaneous flow of their thoughts, and their mode of viewing things, and the general maxims or heads to which they refer them, and the motives which determine them, and their likings and dislikings, hopes and fears, and their relative estimate of persons, and the intensity of their perceptions towards particular objects; so a habit of prayer, the practice of turning to God and the unseen world, in every season, in every place, in every emergency, (let alone its supernatural effect of prevailing with God—prayer, I say, has what may be called a *natural* effect, in spiritualizing and elevating the soul. A man is no longer what he was before; gradually, imperceptibly to himself, he has imbibed a new set of ideas, and become imbued with fresh principles. He is as one coming from kings' courts, with a grace, a delicacy, a dignity, a propriety, a justness of thought and taste, a clearness and firmness of principle, all his own. Such is the power of God's secret grace acting through those ordinances which He has enjoined us;

such the evident fitness of those ordinances to produce the results which they set before us. As speech is the organ of human society, and the means of human civilization, so is prayer the instrument of divine fellowship and divine training.   NEWMAN. *P.S.* IV. pp. *261-2*

THE ESSENCE OF PRAYER

This sense of nothingness there must be in us, if we would be accepted, not working ourselves up to feel it, or deceiving ourselves, but confessing it the more, if we feel it not, since we have not, for our sins or our pride, obtained of God the grace to feel it. We must confess it by an act of faith, as what we know and believe of ourselves though our hearts be too hard and cold and stony to feel it, and must pray Him, Who brought water out of the stony rock, to moisten our stony hearts with the dew of his Life-giving Spirit, that we may feel it. This is the very essence of all prayer; confession of need to Him, Who Alone hath. The parched and gaping earth, the young raven's cry, the lion's roar, are set forth to us as so many images of our prayer; only they, unreasoning as they be, know what they need, and we, duller still, know not what to ask, and so have the more need to pass by ourselves and cast ourselves on Him, and pray in His Name.

Remember that charity and fasting are the wings of prayer; fasting as a token and means of self-abasement, charity to man as a token of our love to God, Whom we see not, and drawing down His ineffable love to us through Whom we love; charity in forgiving wrong; charity in showing mercy in our prayers, as we hope to have others' prayers for us; charity especially in self-denying almsgiving to Christ's poor. So forgiving, may we be at last forgiven; being "merciful", we may at the last "obtain mercy"; giving, it shall be "given to us, good measure, pressed down and shaken together shall they give into our bosom", even the overflowing love of God, which He will pour into the hearts of those who love in Him, opening them by His love to receive His love, even Himself, Who is Love.   PUSEY. *P.S.* III. pp. *246-7, 260*

DISTRACTIONS IN PRAYER

We cannot keep our thoughts disengaged at prayer, if they are through the day engaged; we cannot keep out vain thoughts then, if at other times we yield to them. The thoughts, to which we have been accustomed during the day, rush in upon us before we are aware, and carry us away. They master us then, because we have yielded to them before; they bind us, as lawful captives, because we have before sold ourselves to them, and taken their wages and their yoke, and have delivered ourselves into their hands. We must live more to God, if we would pray more to God; we must be less engrossed with the world, if we would not have the world thrust itself in upon our prayers and stifle them. He who lives to the world, and he who lives to God, must do mostly the same things; but with the one, the things themselves are the end; with the other, to please God in them. If a duty, to be performed well, must for the time needs take up well-nigh all our thoughts, yet is there to the holy, all the while, a consciousness of the Presence of God, as the unseen Light of his life, just as in this bodily world we may have our eyes fixed on some object of sense, yet we are conscious of the presence of the light of the world. We need not fear lest our duties should be done less thoroughly, if done more calmly, and not for their own sakes but for God's. Rather, in that they are done in God, they will be done more as God wills; self and the wrong bias of our minds will be removed; they will be done truly and rightly, since they will be "wrought in God", Who is Truth and Right.

This, then, is the chief, the most comprehensive remedy against distraction in prayer, to see that we be not distracted amid the manifoldness of the things of sense, at other times; that we make not any thing in this world our end, that we seek not our happiness in it, follow it not eagerly, be not passionately fond of any thing; else we make it our god, and what we have allowed ourselves to be captivated with, i.e. held captive by, will hold our thoughts captive in our prayers too, and bind them down to itself, and will not let them soar freely to our God. We must make our choice. If we *will* be anxious about worldly things, we cannot pray as we ought, though we would.

But still further, even when we would serve God, or do our duty in this life, we must see that we do our very duties calmly. There is a religious, as well as a worldly, distraction. We may mix up self in doing duty, as well as when we make self our end. Religious excitement, or excitement about things of religion, may as effectively bar our praying as eagerness about worldly things. We may be engaged about the things of God, yet our mind may all the while centre in these things, not in God. Sad as it is, people may be engaged in the progress of religion or of truth (it is shocking to say it, yet worse that people should fall into it unwarned), much as persons looking on a game or engaged in one; nay, the temptation is the greater, in that the interests are the more absorbing, and persons themselves are more off their guard, because the subject and the cause are in themselves holy, and it is good to be interested in them, only in a right way. We may be diligent about the duties of our calling, and yet find our pleasure and our reward simply in our success or ingenuity in doing them dexterously. Nay, there is no more frequent snare than doing *what* we ought, but not *as* we ought; putting worldly activity in place of religious diligence. Thus people, in providing for their families, which is a duty, become worldly. In serving the State, which may be a duty, they become ambitious; in doing well what they have to do (which they ought) they become vain; in some way putting self in the place of God. Whatever then be our employment, doing the duty of our callings, or seeking to promote God's truth, or doing good to man, or to prepare, if it may be, for the coming of His kingdom, as citizens or as members of the Church, we must see that we do it soberly, labouring to have our minds fixed, not on the things themselves, but on God, that we look through them to Him for Whom we do them. If our mind be in a whirl, hearing, thinking, speaking, about many things, it matters not whether they relate to the world or the Church, it will be dizzy and distracted, i.e. torn asunder among them when we come to our prayer; and we shall not be able to fix it. If we will be busied and careful about many things, we cannot do the one thing needful, sit at Jesus' feet and hear His words. And hence Holy Scripture joins these two together, calmness or sobriety and prayer; "Be ye therefore sober, and watch unto prayer." "Let your *moderation* be known unto all men. Be anxious for nothing; but in every thing by prayer and supplication with thanksgiving let your requests be made known unto God; and the peace of God shall guard your hearts and thoughts in Christ Jesus." Peace is the beginning and end of prayer; its condition and its reward. Resign yourselves, that ye may pray, and God will guard your thoughts, and hold them to Himself.

If, also, you would guard against wandering in prayer, you must practice yourself in keeping a check upon your thoughts at other times. If, as Scripture saith of the fool, our "eyes are in the ends of the earth", if we let our senses wander after everything which presents itself to them, we are forming in ourselves a habit of distraction, which will oppress us in our prayers too. It is not a light matter that we be gazing on everything which we can see, that we listen to all we may hear, that we keep all the avenues of our senses open, and let what will enter in. Rather Holy Scripture so often says, "They lift up their eyes", as if we should not for ever be gazing around us, but keep them rather staid, until we need them. The compass of our minds is narrow at best, and cannot hold many things; one thing thrusts out another; and if we admit these manifold things into our mind, we shall have small room for its true and rightful Owner and Inmate, God. If we let thoughts chase each other through our minds at will, they will find their accustomed entrance there in our prayers too; if we close not the doors of our minds against them at other times, they will stand wide open then. In this busy age, in which everyone would know about everything, and, like the Athenians, our occupation seems to be to know some new thing, and what conveys news is thought the instrument of knowledge, and knowledge of every sort is thought a good, it is not a light matter, but one to which we must take great heed; what we hear, and admit into our minds. Our minds are holy things; they are the temples of God; and so, for His honour's sake Who has so hallowed them, we should be on our guard what we allow to enter there. We are commanded to beware of idle speaking; beware we also of things which foster it, idle hearing and idle seeing, and knowledge of idle things. As life draws towards its close, God dulls our eyes and ears and all our senses, that, being thus shut out from the outer world, our minds may the more retire from the world, withdraw into their own sanctuary, and there be occupied with Him, and prepare to meet Him. Be this method of His Providence a guide to us. Keep the rein over your own minds; control them; master them; check them, for the very sake of keeping them in check; so shall you the better have them in your power in your prayers too. Be not curious about things which concern you not, what happens in the street, or passes by you, or befalls a neighbour, unless charity require it of you. These things waste the mind more than you can well think. Rather recollect that your concern is not with the world; your home, your hopes, your abiding-place, is not here, but in God; your citizenship is not on earth, but in the Heavens; your places here shall shortly know you no more; the earth shall contain no more of you, than the dust of your bodies, in keeping for you against the Resurrection. Why then so curious about what is nothing to you? Why, alas, but because the mind must be filled with something, and unless it be filled with God, it must deaden its cravings with the nothingnesses of this life? But on that very ground, if it be so filled, it empties itself of God, and, being void of God, cannot pray to God, since prayer is the voice of God within us to Himself.

It is the infrequency of prayer which makes prayer so difficult. It is not a great effort now and then, which makes the things even of this life easy to us; it is their being the habit of our bodies or our minds. It was by continued exercise which we were not aware of, that our bodies, as children, were strengthened; it was by continued practice that we learnt anything. By continued gazing at far-off objects, the eye sees further than others; by continued practice, the hand becomes steadied and obeys the motions of our mind. So and much more must the mind, by continual exercise, be steadied, to fix itself on Him Whom it cannot grasp, and look up to Him Whom it cannot see. Yea, so much the more exceedingly must it with strong effort fix itself by His grace on Him, because we cannot see Him or approach to Him, but by His revealing Himself and coming down to us, and giving us eyes to see and hearts to comprehend; and this He will do only to the earnest and persevering, and to us severally, as we are such. They then will pray best, who, praying truly, pray oftenest.

Neglect nothing which can produce reverence. Pass not at once from the things of this world to prayer, but collect thyself. Think what thou art, what God is; thyself a child, and God thy Father; but also thyself dust and ashes, God, a consuming fire, before Whom angels hide their faces: thyself unholy, God holy; thyself a sinner, God thy Judge. And to this it will help, before you first pray, reverently to repeat your Belief, as confessing before God, all He has wrought for you, and His own Majesty; or as they did of old, to think of the last four things, Death, Judgement, Heaven, Hell; what thou hopest, everlasting life; what thou fearest, unceasing misery; what thou needest, God's pardoning, preventing, assisting, perfecting grace, to save thee from the one, and along a strait and narrow path to guide thee to the other; nay further yet, God's help, that thou mayest fear the one and hope for the other; for the very power to dread hell, or to hope for Heaven, is itself a great gift of God. Then forget not, that of thyself thou canst not pray. Without His softening grace Heaven and hell might stand before us, and we could not pray. There have been who have seen hell before them, clear as any object of man's sight, and could not pray. We come before Him, as helpless creatures, who need to be taught what to ask for, and knowing, to be enabled to ask, and asking, to be enabled to persevere to ask. If we think we can pray of ourselves, we cannot pray. Then, as it should be among our last prayers at night, that God should be in our waking thoughts, and that, when we wake up, we should be with God, so we should be very watchful, how we allow the things of the world to enter into our minds, before our first prayers. We wake morning by morning to a new life. The cares and thoughts of yesterday have been buried in our sleep; the world around us is still hushed; the turmoil of life is not yet come back to haunt us. We should deal reverently then with our first thoughts, beware how we awaken in ourselves any of the trains of plans, or business, or occupations, which take up our day. They are yet at a distance from us, and we have more power over them. Stop their first inroad. Turn from them resolutely to God, before one thought have awakened its fellow; that so thou mayest secure undisturbed thy first prayers, wherein thou committest thy whole self, soul, body, spirit, for the day to God. Then watch thyself, what helps or hinders thee to fix thy mind on God. At times, the mind pours itself out to God, when closing the eyes on the outward world, it fixes itself directly upon God. At times, it prays best, by riveting the eyes on the words of its prayer, making the very senses, which would distract us, the means of fixing the yet more wandering mind itself. At times, we pray best silently; at times, the hearing of the sound of our own prayer impresses it on the mind. If we fail in one way, we should betake ourselves to another, and so God, seeing us in earnest, will the rather have mercy upon us. Then as to the words of our own prayer; we should beware how we pass hastily over any of our prayers. It is not how much we say, but what we pray, which is of real moment. If we are not really masters of our own time, it were better to say but a portion of our prayers, resolving to use what after-time we can find for the rest, than to crowd in more than we can pray aright. It is better to delay some, than, by hurrying, to risk the loss of all; but better still, to pray God to waken us at the time of prayer, and ourselves rise that we may have time. Then, the best models of prayer consist of brief petitions, as suited to men in need; for when they really feel their need, they use not many words. "Lord, save us, we perish", is the cry of need.

Yet we are not to think that by these or any other remedies distraction is to be cured at once. We cannot undo at once the habit, it may be, of years. We must be content to drag with us the chain of our former sins; thankful that God in any degree lightens it and enables us to hold on in our course. Distraction has distressed eminent saints; how much more such as we! Only it is likely that they were more shocked by one worldly thought intruding upon the Holy Presence, than we by many. Distraction will come through weakness, ill-health, fatigue: only pray, guard, strive, against it; humble yourselves under it, and for the past negligences, of which it is mostly the sad fruit; rely less upon yourself, cast yourself more upon God, hang more wholly, upon Him, and long the more for that blessed time, when the redeemed of the Lord shall serve Him day and night without distraction.

PUSEY. *P.S.* III. pp. *270–85*

FORMS

We must begin religion with what looks like a form. Our fault will be, not in beginning it as a form, but in continuing it as a form. For it is our duty to be ever striving and praying to enter into the real spirit of our services, and in proportion as we understand them and love them, they will cease to be a form and a task, and will be the real expression of our minds. Thus shall we gradually be changed in heart from servants into sons of Almighty God. NEWMAN. *P.S.* III p. *100*

Love, from whatever earthly cave he springs,
(That spell of something heavenly dwelling round
Home, friend, or grave endear'd) when he hath found
Meet entrance, he will shake his odorous wings,
And throw a charm o'er thousand meaner things,
O'er whatsoe'er at first he entrance found
Into the soul; in ties associate bound
He lives, and o'er them his own radiance flings.
Then why should not a holier Peace and Mirth
Love those mute forms, which cherished first their birth

And braced them for the withering blasts of earth?
The gladsome soul that her devotion plies,
Bound in the wreath of ancient liturgies,
Why should she not her chain beyond all freedom prize?

                          ISAAC WILLIAMS. *The Cathedral.* p. *12*

FORMS NOT TO BE UNUSED FROM FEAR OF IDOLATRY.
(*A dialogue*)

A   What forbids
But e'en from shades where baneful weeds lie hid,
I still may gather flowers, and bid them grow
In the home vineyard of our mother Church?
These symbols have I gazed on long and oft,
Threading their morals and their mysteries,
And thence beguiled to deeper, holier, thoughts.
And surely heart-expanding Charity,
If aught she finds that ministers to good,
To others would like instruments supply.
For objects pleading through the visual sense
Are stronger than discourses to the ear,
More powerfully they reach and move the soul.

B Yet these appeals to the more sensual eye
Do savour of her[1] worship, in her courts
Imagination holds too high a place,
Leagu'd with material things, and charms the heart
Prone to idolatry, unconscious glides
To sense from spirit: upward to ascend
Is hard; it is on earth to live in Heaven.

A Yes, dangers on each side beset our way;
When zeal, imbued with puritanic leaven,
Clogs up heart-easing Heaven-born poesy,
The soul thus stifled breeds dark mutinies,
Irreverence, irreligion, hollow words,
Hypocrisies; yet on the other side
Let loose it runs on to material things,
And blends with sensuous idolatry.
The Church, 'tis thought, is wakening through the land,

                    [1] The Church of Rome.

And seeking vent for the o'erloaded hearts
Which she has kindled—pours her forth anew—
Breathes life in ancient worship—from their graves
Summons the slumbering Arts to wait on her,
Music and Architecture, varied forms
Of Painting, Sculpture, and of Poetry;
These are allied to sense, but soul and sense
Must both alike find wing and rise to Heaven;
Both soul and body took the Son of man,
Both soul and body must in Him serve God.

ISAAC WILLIAMS. The Baptistery. pp. ix–x

THE WORSHIP OF THE CHURCH

There can be no harm in professing much directly to God, because, while we speak, we know He sees through our professions, and takes them for what they really are, *prayers.* How much, for instance, do we profess when we say the Creed! and in the Collects we put on the full character of a Christian. We desire and seek the best gifts, and declare our strong purpose to serve God with our whole hearts. By doing this, we remind ourselves of our duty; and withal, we humble ourselves by the taunt (so to call it) of putting upon our dwindled and unhealthy forms those ample and glorious garments which befit the upright and full-grown believer.   NEWMAN. *P.S.* I. p. *202*

THE DAILY OFFICE

If a Christian Minister might suitably offer up common prayer by himself three centuries ago, surely he may do so now. If he then was the spokesman of the saints far and near, gathering together their holy and concordant suffrages, and presenting them by virtue of his priesthood, he is so now. The revival of this usage is merely a matter of place and time; and though neither our Lord nor His Church would have us make sudden alterations, even though for the better, yet certainly we ought never to forget what is abstractedly our duty, what is in itself best, what it is we have to aim at and labour towards. If authority were needed, besides our Church's own, for the propriety of Christian Ministers praying even by themselves in places of worship, we have it in the life of our great pattern of Christian faith and wisdom, Hooker. "To what he persuaded others," says his biographer, "he added his own example of fasting and prayer; and did usually every Ember week take from the parish clerk the key of the church-door, into which place he retired every day, and locked himself up for many hours; and did the like most Fridays, and other days of fasting."

That holy man, in this instance, kept his prayers to himself. He was not offering up the Daily Service; but I adduce his instance to show that there is nothing strange or unseemly in a Christian Minister praying in Church by himself; and if so, much less when he gives his people the opportunity of coming if they will. *This*, then, is what I felt and feel:—it is commonly said, when week-day prayers are spoken of, "you will not get a congregation, or you will get but a few"; but they whom Christ has brought near to Himself to be the Stewards of His Mysteries, depend on no man; rather, after His pattern, they are to draw men after them. He prayed alone on the mountain; He prays alone (for who is there to join with Him?), before His Father's throne. He is the one effectual Intercessor for sinners at the right hand of God. And what He is really, such are we in figure; what He is meritoriously, such are we instrumentally. Such are we, by His grace, allowed to occupy His place visibly, however unworthily, in His absence till He come; allowed to depend on Him, and not on our people; allowed to draw our commission from Him, not from them; allowed to be a centre, about which the Church may grow, and about which it really exists, be it great or little.   NEWMAN. *P.S.* III. pp. *341-2*

> And are we then alone on holy ground,
> Most gracious Father? Are we then alone,
> Because the world regards not, and is gone?
> Where are the solemn dead which lie around,
> Are they not with us? Are thy courts not crowned
> With spiritual hosts about? and the sweet tone
> Still lingers round thine altars. Are they flown,
> Bearing no more to see their God disowned?
> Has the great Michael left us, mighty arm,
> Gabriel, our fortitude, and the blest charm
> Of Raphael's healing name? In my heart's fear
> I heard a voice, "Be still, and lowly bend;
> While two or three remain, thy Lord is here,
> And where His presence is, His hosts attend."
>
> ISAAC WILLIAMS. *The Cathedral.* p. *20*

PSALMODY

Come to me Angel guests! whatever springs
In me of passions, or of earthly pride,
Shall flee at sound of your celestial wings;
O gentle Psalmist, other thoughts abide
With thee, how have I scared thee? to my side
Come again, tranquil spirit, oh, unroll
Thy sweet melodious fulness o'er the tide
Of my wild tossing thoughts, touch my sad soul,
And let me own again thy mastering soft control!

                   In that sacred chord
We hear from unseen heights a glorious song,
Of panoplies divine and shield and sword:
Faith in unearthly armour bold and strong,
And strains which to thy ransomed host belong
Then, where from high the showering sunbeams fall
Amid the encircling mists of grief and wrong,
Is seen to use the Eternal City's wall
While earth responds to Heaven and deep to deep doth call.

             ISAAC WILLIAMS. *The Cathedral.* pp. *80, 85*

THE SACRAMENTS

Christ shines through the Sacraments, as through transparent bodies, without impediment. He is the Light and Life of the Church, acting through it, dispensing of His fulness, knitting and compacting together every part of it; and these its Mysteries are not mere outward signs, but (as it were) effluences of grace developing themselves in external forms, as Angels might do when they appeared to men. He has touched them, and breathed upon them, when He ordained them; and thenceforth they have a virtue residing in them, which issues forth and encircles them round, till the eye of faith sees in them no element of matter at all. Once for all He hung upon the cross, and blood and water issued from His pierced side, but by the Spirit's ministration, the blood and water are ever flowing, as though His cross were set up among us, and the baptismal water were but the outward image upon our senses. Thus in a true sense that water is not what it was before, but is gifted with new and spiritual qualities. Not as if its material substance were changed, which our eyes see, or as if any new nature were imparted, but that the lifegiving Spirit, who could make bread of stones, and sustain animal life on them, applies the blood of Christ through it; or according to the doctrine of the text, that He, and not man, is the baptizer.   NEWMAN. *P.S.* III. pp. *302-3*

THE BAPTIZED MAN

Contemplate then thyself, not in thyself, but as thou art in the Eternal God. Fall down in astonishment at the glories which are around thee and in thee, poured to and fro in such a wonderful way that thou art (as it were) dissolved into the kingdom of God, and art as if thou hadst nought to do but to contemplate and feed upon that great vision. This surely is the state of mind the Apostle speaks of in the text, when he reminds us who are justified and at peace with God, that we have access to His royal courts, and stand in His grace, and rejoice in hope of His glory. All the trouble which the world inflicts upon us, and which flesh cannot but feel, sorrow, pain, care, bereavement, these avail not to disturb the tranquillity and the intensity with which faith gazes upon the Divine Majesty. All the necessary exactness of our obedience, the anxiety about failing, the pain of self-denial, the watchfulness, the zeal, the self-chastisements which we practise, no more interfere with this vision of faith, than if they were practised by another, not by ourselves. We are two or three selves at once, in the wonderful structure of our minds, and can weep while we smile, and labour while we meditate.—And if so much is given us by the first Sacrament of the Church, what, think we, is given us in the second?

NEWMAN. *P.S.* IV. pp. *166-7*

PREPARATION FOR HOLY COMMUNION

There is danger in not receiving whenever a person by any means can, because it is despising God's gift, and provoking Him to withdraw it, and give you over to a cold, unloving, careless temper. There is danger in every way of receiving It unduly; and in not receiving It at all, there is starvation and death of the soul. There is danger in every way but *one*; and that is, keeping your hearts diligently; preparing yourselves, when you can, carefully; praying to God fervently, to give you that holy frame of mind, which He will accept; receiving His gifts, whenever they are offered to you, humbly and thankfully; and bringing forth fruit enduringly and increasingly.

God has set dangers on all sides, that we may not shrink back, but may go onward in the one path, which leadeth unto Him. The wilderness shutteth us in; the sea is before, and the enemy behind: but God will place His pillar of fire between the enemy and us, and the sea shall part, and that which was our enemy, shall be our safeguard; a narrow path it is, but the sea which would devour us, should be a wall on the right hand and on the left to fence us in from straying, and protect us against the enemy, so will He conduct us to the promised land. We might have shrunk (who would not have shrunk?) from coming to the all-holy mysteries, but that our Saviour saith, "Except ye eat the Flesh of the Son of Man and drink His Blood, ye have no life in you." Come the, we must; and so, thou with trembling hearts and faint steps, mistrusting ourselves, but trusting in God, we will come. We should mistrust our own weakness, but we should not mistrust God's strength. He invites, who willeth not the sinner's death, who warneth us that He may not strike, who correcteth that He may not destroy. He who hath appointed us this narrow path, will keep therein those who will be kept. He who has made this Heavenly food needful for life, is able to keep us, if we commit ourselves to Him. He who giveth us His Son to dwell in us, how shall He not cleanse us wholly, if we will be cleansed? He who by giving us that Heavenly Body, keepeth us members of that body whereof He is the Head, how shall He not keep those members of Himself? How should Satan have power over the members of Christ? He will make each communion a means to enable you to receive the next more devoutly and profitably. He will increase your longing after that heavenly feast; He will make you more and more members of Him of whom you partake, more fruitful branches of that Vine whose richness He pours into you, richer in faith, stronger amid temptation, more victorious against Satan and yourselves. He will carry you on "from strength to strength, until you appear before" Him, the God of gods, and He remove you from His table here to His glorious presence in Heaven, from faith to sight, from longing to bliss, from spiritual union to see Him eye to eye, from these broken and occasional refreshments to be for ever with Him your Lord. Only come hither with hearty repentance, with lively faith, with real charity, with thankful remembrance of His Death, with steadfast purpose to amend, and as thou drawest near, and art about to partake of the heavenly Food, cast thyself more wholly upon God, pray Him to deepen all that He would have in thee, and to take away all He would not have. Pray Him to increase thy longing, thy sense of need, of thy emptiness and His exceeding fulness, and He will fill thee, He will give thee all thou needest, He will give thee Himself.

If any one feel himself insecure, doubtful about his state, wish himself otherwise, but doubt about his own steadfastness, if he wish to move onwards towards Heaven, but know not how, if he wish to serve God more faithfully, and to have hope in his death, let him come; let him not wait as if he must be fitter to come. "God filleth the hungry, and the rich He sendeth empty away." We come here, not with the riches of our own works, but with our emptiness, and desiring of Him the riches of His grace. He asketh but a penitent earnest heart, conscious of its own weakness and desiring His strength. It is He who calleth thee; bind thyself fast to Him; shrink not; confess to Him thy unworthiness, and desire, if so be, to "touch but the hem of His garment, He will make thee whole". Mistrust thyself, and trust Him. Ask of Him faith, and He will give it thee, and to thy faith He will give thee the pledge of everlasting life, which is in His Son. He will give thee the wedding-garment for His feast. How shouldest thou not be duly prepared, whom He, who inviteth thee, will, if thou ask, prepare? "Whoso cometh unto Me," He says, "I will in no wise cast out."

Let those whose duties are more fixed, at least strive to turn their thoughts to God and into themselves, in the intervals or even in the midst of their worldly callings. Let them do what they can. God is a gracious Master, who accepteth according to what a man hath, not according to what he hath not. Then come in full assurance of faith, with a "fearful", humble "admiration of that heaven" which is opened to you. Come trusting in God, that He who giveth thee His Son will with Him freely give thee all things. Approach as if thou wert coming to the Saviour's side, to drink from it that "Blood which was shed for you and for many for the remission of sins"; and after thou hast received It, beware how thou again profane thyself, whom God has so hallowed. Christ maketh thee, like Saul, a new man, and giveth thee another heart: beware lest, like Saul, thou return to thy former state, lest the Evil Spirit, who has been cast out, "take seven other spirits more wicked than himself, and dwell within thee, and thy last state be worse than the first". "Sin no more, lest a worse thing happen unto thee." Guard diligently that holy thing committed to thee. Return home, like the shepherds who had seen the Saviour, Christ the Lord—glorifying and praising God for all the things which they had seen and heard; be very jealous over thyself, and every inlet and approach of sin, over every thing, which had anything to do with any of thy former sins, over any little acts or thoughts of covetousness or worldliness, or excess, or lightness of mind, or jesting, or thoughtlessness. For it may be that Satan, if he sees thee strengthened thus mightily in the armour of God, will not at once assail thee violently, but will tempt thee to lay aside thine armour piece by piece, until he shall have "made thee naked to thy shame before thine enemies", and slay thee. But as thou art strengthened, walk strongly; "resist the devil, and he will flee from thee"; "draw nigh unto God, and He will draw nigh unto thee". Thou canst not again become what thou wast before; thou must be better or worse. Go on in the strength of that heavenly food unto the Mount of God; so shall our Lord's words be fulfilled in thee, "Whoso eateth My flesh and drinketh My Blood hath eternal life, and I will raise him up at the last day."   Pusey. *P.S.* III. pp. *336-8, 339-40, 342*

HOLY COMMUNION

The Holy Supper is not a gazing up into heaven after Christ. No thoughts of Christ, however holy; no longings after Him, however sanctified; no wish to be with Him, however purified; no thoughts on His Cross and Passion and Precious Death, however devout; no devotion of self to Him; no acknowledgement of Him as our Priest, Prophet, King, and God; no setting Him up in our hearts as (with the Father and the Holy Ghost) the One Object of our love; no reliance upon Him as the only Anchor of our soul, however real, comes up to the truth. We ought to meditate on Him, long for Him, desire to be with Him, rely on Him, devote ourselves to Him, pledge ourselves to obey Him, and do what we have pledged. We should look for His coming, avow Him, be ready in all things, in suffering as in joy, to be partakers with Him, partakers of His Cross, and Death, and Burial. All this we should be at all times, but all this does not make us yet partakers of Him, for man cannot make himself a partaker of Him; He must give Himself. As He gave Himself to the Death upon the Cross for our sins, so in the Holy Eucharist must He, if we are to be partakers of Him, give Himself to us. We have of Him only what He giveth. All Christian graces, although His work, are but messengers to prepare the way before Him. Hope but putteth us in that expectant, longing state which He rewardeth; Faith but openeth the door to receive Him; Love or Charity but cleanseth the chamber of our hearts, which He is to inhabit; Repentance but breaketh the heart, and maketh it that contrite or broken spirit, wherein it pleaseth Him to dwell; but all this is not yet He. He, "the Bread of life, which came down from heaven" must come down also into our hearts, if we are to be partakers of Him. The Communion is not a mere going up of our hearts to Christ, but a coming down of Him to us. Well indeed may the ancient service bid us, "lift up your hearts"; and well may we answer, "we lift them up unto the Lord". Well may we lift them up to meet the Lord, but it is to receive Him that we lift them up, not to embrace Him for ourselves. The outward emblems, bread and wine, which we see, would in themselves not lift us up to Christ, but depress us, except so far as we know them to be emblems and pledges, channels of Him and His Presence to our souls, as they are made to us His Heavenly Body and Blood. Of themselves they are plainly slight and insufficient to convey any spiritual benefit. They are emblems of nothing but His humiliation, forms of earth, such as He took. They tell us that He, Very God, took upon Him a form of earth, and that that form was broken; their very breaking speaks His greater humiliation, and that to receive a humble Saviour, we must also be humbled; that we must not look to gain Him for ourselves, but bow ourselves to the earth, and pray Him to have pity upon and give life to our dust.   PUSEY. *P.S.* III. pp. *351–3*

THE REAL PRESENCE

Although most which is spoken belongs to Christians as belonging already to the household of saints and the family of Heaven and the Communion of Angels and unity with God, still, here as elsewhere in the New Testament, there is a subordinate and subdued notion of sin; and what wraps the Saint already in the third Heaven, may yet uphold us sinners, that the pit shut not her mouth upon us. The same reality of the Divine Gift makes It Angels' food to the Saint, the ransom to the sinner. And both because It is the Body and Blood of Christ. Were it *only* a thankful commemoration of His redeeming love, or *only* a shewing forth of His Death, or a strengthening *only* and refreshing of the soul, it were indeed a reasonable service, but it would have no direct healing for the sinner. To him its special joy is that it is His Redeemer's very broken body, It is His Blood, which was shed for the remission of his sins. In the words of the ancient Church, he "drinks his ransom", he eateth that, "the very Body and Blood of the Lord, the only Sacrifice for sin", God "poureth out" for him yet "the most precious Blood of His Only-Begotten", they "are fed from the Cross of the Lord, because they eat His Body and Blood". PUSEY. *U.S.* pp. *18–9*

What is it that is vouchsafed to us at the Holy Table, when we commemorate the Lord's death? It is "Jesus Christ before our eyes evidently set forth, crucified among us."[1] Not before our bodily eyes; so far, every thing remains at the end of that Heavenly Communion as it did at the beginning. What was bread remains bread, and what was wine remains wine. We need no carnal, earthly, visible miracle to convince us of the Presence of the Lord Incarnate. We have, we trust, more faith than to need to see the heavens open, or the Holy Ghost descend in bodily shape—more faith than to attempt, in default of sight, to indulge our reason, and to confine our notion of the Sacrament to some clear assemblage of words of our own framing. We have faith and love, in St Paul's words, to "*discern* the Lord's Body". He who is at the right hand of God, manifests Himself in that Holy Sacrament as really and fully as if He were visibly there. We are allowed to draw near, to "give, take, and eat" His sacred Body and Blood, as truly as though like Thomas we could touch His hands and thrust our hand into His side. When He ascended into the Mount, "His face did shine as the sun, and His raiment was white as the light."[2] Such is the glorious presence which faith sees in the Holy Communion, though every thing looks as usual to the natural man. Not gold or precious stones, pearls of great price or gold of Ophir, are to the eye of faith so radiant as those lowly elements which He, the Highest, is pleased to make the means of conveying to our hearts and bodies His own gracious self. Not the light of

[1] Gal. iii. *1.*   [2] Matt. xvii. *2.*

the sun sevenfold is so awfully bright and overpowering, if we could see as the Angels do, as that seed of eternal life, which by eating and drinking we lay up in our hearts against the day of His coming. In spite then of all recollections of the past or fear for the future, we have a present source of rejoicing; whatever comes, weal or woe, however stands our account as yet in the books against the Last Day, this we have and this we may glory in, the present power and grace of God in us and over us, and the good hope thence flowing of victory in the end.

NEWMAN. *P.S.* IV. pp. *167-9*

EUCHARISTIC ADORATION

Is it not self-evident that, had there been no abuse, or error, or extravagance connected with the practice, all persons believing and considering the Real Presence of our Lord in Holy Communion, in whatever manner or degree, would in the same manner or degree find it impossible not to use special worship?—the inward worship, I mean, and adoration of the heart: for that, of course, is the main point in question; the posture and mode are secondary and variable, and may and must admit of dispensation.

The simple circumstances of our Lord Christ declaring Himself especially present would, one would think, be enough for this. Why do we bow our knees and pray on first entering the Lord's house? Why do we feel that during all our continuance there we should be, as it were, prostrating our hearts before Him? Why is it well to breathe a short prayer when we begin reading our Bibles, and still as we read to recollect ourselves, and try to go on in the spirit of prayer? And so of other holy exercises: in proportion as they bring with them the sense of His peculiar presence, what can the believer do but adore? I firmly believe that all Christians do so, in the Holy Sacrament most especially, whatever embarrassment many of them may unhappily have been taught to feel touching the precise mode of their adoration.

And this may well be one of the greatest consolations, in the sad controversies and misunderstandings among which our lot is cast. It is as impossible for devout faith, contemplating Christ in this Sacrament, not to adore Him, as it is for a loving mother, looking earnestly at her child, not to love it. The mother's consciousness of her love, and her outward manifestation of it, may vary; scruples, interruptions, bewilderments may occur; but there it is in her heart, you cannot suppress it. So must there be special adoration and worship in the heart of every one seriously believing a special, mysterious presence of Christ, God and man, expressed by the words, *This is My Body*.

I say a *special* adoration and worship, over and above what a religious man feels upon every occasion which helps him to realize, what he always believes, that God is "about his path, and about his bed, and spieth out all his ways"; that in Him he "lives, and moves, and has his being". And this for very many mysterious and overpowering reasons. I will specify three, the most undeniable and irresistible. First the *greatness* of the benefit offered; next, its being offered and brought home to each one *personally* and *individually*; thirdly, the deep *condescension* and *humiliation* on the part of Him who offers the benefit.

KEBLE. *Euch. Ad.* pp. *1–2*

EUCHARISTIC SACRIFICE

The true oblation in the Christian Sacrifice is in no sense earthly or material. It is altogether spiritual: the chief of those spiritual sacrifices in the offering whereof consists the common priesthood of us all. The Eucharist comprehends them all in one, and has besides, peculiar to itself, that which alone causes any of them to be acceptable. For the true oblation in the Eucharist is not the Bread and Wine—that is only as the vessel which contains or the garment which veils it; but that which our Lord by the hands of the priest offers to His Father in the Holy Eucharist, is His own Body and Blood, the very same which He offers and presents to Him—with which, as St Paul says, He appears before Him *now*, night and day continually—in heaven, in commemoration of His having offered it once for all in His Passion and Death on the Cross. It is the one great reality, summing up in itself all the memorial sacrifices of old. In the Christian scheme, it is "proportionable" to them; and of course it stands in the same rank and relation to them, as the other antitypes in the Gospel to their several types and shadows in the law.

The memorial therefore made of Christ before the Father in Holy Communion, is as much more real, more glorious, more blessed, than all the memorial sacrifices of old.

KEBLE. *Euch. Ad.* p. *70*

FREQUENT COMMUNION

Since then, this Divine Sacrament has, as its immediate and proper end, union with Him who hath taken our manhood into God, and the infusion into us of His Spirit and life and immortality, making us one with His glorified Humanity, as He is One in the Godhead with the Father, and, besides this, it is ulteriorly, the cleansing of our sins, the refining our corruptions, the repairing of our decays, what must the loss of the Church of the latter days, in which Communions are so infrequent! How can we wonder that love should have waxed cold, corruptions so abound, grievous falls have been, among our youth, almost the rule, to stand upright the exception, heathen strictness reproach Christian laxity, the Divine life become so rare, all higher instances of it so few and faint, when "the stay and the staff", the strength of that life is willingly forfeited? How should there be the fulness of the Divine life, amid all but a month-long fast from our "daily Bread"? While in the largest portion of the Church, the people mostly gaze at the threshold of the Heaven where they do not enter, what do we? We seem, alas! even to have forgotten, in our very thoughts, that daily Communion, which once was the common privilege of the whole Church, which, when the Eastern Church relaxed in her first love, the Western continued, and which they from whom we have our Communion Service in its present form, at first hoped to restore. It implies a life, so different from this our common-place ordinary tenor, a life so above this world as knit with Him who hath overcome the world; so angelic as living on Him who is Angels' food; a union with God so close; that we cannot mostly, I suppose, imagine to ourselves, how we could daily thus be in Heaven, and in our daily business here below, how sanctify our daily duties, thoughts, refreshment, so that they should be tinged with the hues reflected by our daily Heaven, not that heavenly gift be dimmed with our earthliness; how our souls should through the day shine with the glory of that ineffable Presence to which we had approached, not we approach to it with earth-dimmed souls. It must ever be so; we cannot know the gift of God, if we forget it; we must cease mostly even to long for what we forego. We lose the very sense to understand it.   PUSEY. *U.S.* pp. *27–9*

CONFESSION

Consciences *are* burdened. There is a provision, on the part of God, in His Church, to relieve them. They wish to be, and to know that they are, in a state of grace. God has provided a means, however deeply any have fallen, to replace them in it. They feel that they cannot take off their own burden, loose the chains of their past sins, and set themselves free to serve God. They look for some act out of themselves, if there be one, which shall do this. God has provided it. They want something to sever between past and future, that they may begin anew. By His absolving sentence, God does efface the past. They cannot estimate their own repentance and faith. He has provided physicians of the soul, to relieve and judge for those who "open their griefs" to them. They wish to know how to overcome besetting temptations; God has provided those, experienced in the sad history of man's sins and sorrows, who can tell them how others, through the grace of God, have overcome them.

Such are the cases to which the Church of which we are members, most directly applies the remedy of private Absolution, cases of heavy sin, or of timorous, scrupulous consciences; and this, either previous to the Holy Communion, or at the hour of death. There is a deep instinctive feeling, by which the soul (unless warped by human systems) does long to lay open any oppressive sin, before it comes into the presence of its Judge. Persons, who for a long period of life have carried about them the oppressive consciousness of some past, secret sin, cannot bear it then; those who could not bring themselves to endure the pain and shame of confession in life, still often could not bear the thought of carrying their sin with them, unconfessed, into the very Presence of God.

Our Church explicitly contemplates tender consciences, who need comfort, and peace, and reassurance of the favour of their Heavenly Father. For (blessed be God!) there are those who feel the weight of any slight sin, more than others do "whole cart-loads"; and who do derive comfort and strength from the special application of the power of the keys to their own consciences. The words of our Church are very large; "a full trust in God's mercy and a quiet conscience", "if any by this means cannot quiet his own conscience herein, but requireth further comfort and counsel", "to the avoiding of all scruple and doubtfulness". What Minister of Christ, then, should take upon himself to drive away "His lambs" as if persons were to have less of the Ministry of comfort, the less they had offended God? As if any thing ought, in the estimation of the Christian Minister, to be of slight account, which disturbs the peaceful mirror of the soul, wherein it reflects God! The "benefit of Absolution", then, is intended by our Church, not only for the penitent, who are by it assured of God's acceptance of their repentance, and often by it replaced in a state of grace, but for all who can, through its ministry, approach with lightened, more peaceful hearts to the Holy Communion. Our Church, in leaving her children free, did not mean to stint the use of the gifts entrusted to her, to force all consciences to one level; nor because she does not *require* Confession, therefore, (as some now would seem to interpret her) by an opposite constraint to that which she laid aside, to *hinder* or withhold them from it.

Such a deep need, then, has arisen in the case of our youth. The "world" has ever thought, and will think, that, because children are little, the sins of children are of slight account. Not so conscience and experience, or the Word of God. Every one who has been called upon to minister in this way to human souls, knows too well how years of sin and misery have mostly had their starting-point in some sin of the child. Even amid the deepest wounds of later life, one, perhaps the first grave offence of the child, lives ineffaceably in the memory of the penitent. Years of forgetfulness of self and of God have not been able to blot it out from the memory. As the freshness of early innocence, when the child, yet new from its Maker's Hands, was also newly washed from original guilt, is a bright glad spot, over which the soul ever after yearns with a scared unutterable longing, so that the first breath of graver sin, which tainted that new paradise, leaves a painful memory of its own, single in the soul's history. It may seem strange, that after deep, heathenish sins, that one, in itself so much lighter sin, should stand out so vividly in the memory. But the fact may be of great moral value. It is not an exaggeration, since it recurs again and again, and seems stamped by the Hand of God upon the conscience. It is His witness that childhood is a very sacred age. How should it not be, when He chose it as a type of His disciples, and pronounced such a heavy woe on any one who made "one of these little ones to stumble"? But it is more. It is a witness how fearful, beyond all thought, sin is, when the first grave sin, by which the soul rebelled against God, wounds the soul so deeply; for deep must be the wound which after-years do not efface. Even when the soul has been covered over and over with sores, it has still felt, with a special pain, the wound of the first childish sin.

But more. The young need to be warned, not only against sin, which they know, but against sin which they scarcely suspect to be sin. It will not be thought that such strong language as has been used in this Sermon was used lightly in the House of God, in His immediate Presence, and as by His Minister. It was founded on extensive, painful knowledge. People speak commonly of the evils of Confession, as likely, or in some cases actually having conveyed to the soul, knowledge of evil. And it is painfully true that, in unskilful hands, in other countries, conducted in a dry technical way, it has. But they forget that there are those around youth by whom they are more likely to be taught evil, than by the Priest; there is one nearer still to the soul, whose unceasing object it is, not to guard against it, but to instil and suggest it. Evil is mostly diligent in propagating itself; one evil companion does often a world of evil; the good are tacitly a burthen to the bad, so the bad instinctively seek to make others like themselves. It is a great trial not to be ashamed of ignorance, even of evil. "Amongst my equals," says St Augustine of his heathen youth, "I was ashamed of a less shamelessness." Be the physician removed, lest he inadvertently poison his patients, if there be no risk, that the poison, introduced from other sources shall work more secretly and more fatally! But again this is not the fear to which *our* nation is exposed; it can be avoided by ordinary caution and cleanness of heart. Purity of soul is guarded by Him who gives it; it is not easily injured even by one unskilful; where it exists it carries its own evidence; it is not blighted by all the foulness of the world, much less will it be by the Priests of God.

But be it (as people think) a choice of evils, as there must be evil, wherever there is human infirmity and ignorance, and this there must be in things ministered by man. And yet let people bring before themselves that it is a choice of evil; that all evil and peril does not lie on the side of sacred intercourse with God's Priests; that the world and Satan are busy, and with dreadful success; and then let them weigh which is safest—to leave the soul open to the inroads of the world and Satan, or to guard it, even though "he who is to watch for the soul" be liable to occasional error. The writer is almost ashamed to say so much; but the deep suspicion fostered unhappily in the English mind, by which their holiest earthly affections are enlisted against the very remedy for sore existing evil, made it a duty to speak plainly, and to make one strong protest against it. Let this be said; they who, through ministering to such as after sin have again been brought back to God, have known their whole sorrowful history, have had no doubt that, humanly speaking, in most cases, *early confession would, by the blessing, of Almighty God, have saved them from their sin and misery*; and then let men think whether it be not possible, that this suspicion of confession may be sowed by the father of lies himself, in order to keep his own kingdom undisturbed, and carry on his ravages in the soul unhindered.

We do not disuse medicines for the body because poisons have been administered through carelessness, or disorders wholly mistaken, and so treated as to bring death, not life, or even the infection of mortal diseases been unsuspectingly conveyed; nor do men cease to take advice as to their estates, because ignorant or dishonest lawyers have at times ruined their clients. People are content to run risks in one case, because they value their lives or estates: they magnify the risks in the other, because they either value not their souls, or dislike the cure, or think they cannot be lost. "One we must have," says Bishop Andrewes, "to know thoroughly the state of our lands or goods; one we must have, entirely acquainted with the state of our body: in our souls it holdeth not! I say no more; it were good it did!"

In every thing else, men appeal to experience as the very test of truth; which, then, will they not believe—that men have been wounded? but themselves confess it; or that they are now healed? but of their healing? how, then, is it, that up to this time they were sick, even sinking back into the same sins, and now are whole? This is said, of course, simply as a reason why people should not *a priori* speak against truth which they know not, not as the ground of that truth. Such facts bring the truth home to us individually, as acts of the Providence, or Justice, or Love of Almighty God impress more deeply upon our souls the truths of nature or of grace which we before believed. The ground for belief that "Our Lord Jesus Christ hath left power with His Church to absolve all sinners who truly repent and believe in Him", is His own words, which the Church hath ever understood, as He, in their plain meaning, spake them.

But in all this, nothing has been implied with regard to the *authoritative* restoration of any system of confession. In the abstract, indeed, "with us", as Hooker says, "the Church is not denied to have authority either of abridging or *enlarging* the use and exercise of that power". It is a matter of discipline, open to the Church, to enforce public penance, as in the Ancient Church, or private confession, as now in the Roman Church; or to leave the exercise of it to the consciences of individuals. But no amount of *voluntary* confession involves the restoration of *compulsory*; the one is the prompting of the conscience within, the other the provision of discipline without. And all the indications of God's Providence, for some time past, point to the great restoration of inward life in this portion of His Church, as the inward operation of God the Holy Ghost, not to be promoted by any outward laws or discipline. We need no *organic* change in the Church, no Convocation, no laws, no enforcement of outward directions, no public discipline. It were to begin at the wrong end. What we need is that men's hearts should be restored, the longings after a more inward, or more watchful, more devoted life, fostered, the desire of greater strictness with self, and conformity to the Will of God strengthened, the indistinct feeling after a higher standard of duty confirmed and more defined. The duty of the present day is not to forestall, or calculate, or plan, for the future; but to do that for the present needs, which God gives to be done. Our duties lie severally to individuals, of whom God assigns the charge to any; as a whole we need to follow, not to guide; for That which we should follow is the only sure Guide, the deep Working of the Holy Spirit, which is anew more fully penetrating our whole Church, and lifting it up, as a whole, as the Ark upon the waters.

It cannot surely be meant that if religious parents taught their children to confess their faults to themselves, and then, at a somewhat riper age, transferred them to a minister of God, to open their hearts to him; or if they, who are burthened with the memory of past, heavy sin, and cannot get free from it, long to pour it out before God in the presence of His Priest, and receive through him the sentence of God's forgiveness; or if people find that to take shame is a healthful medicine, or that confession is a quieting of the conscience, a check to the inferior will, that they fall not again and again into the same faults; or that it keeps the heart clean, and that God thereby imparts new energy to serve Him—it cannot be meant that willingness to minister to such cases is an assumption of priestly power, or that to recommend in specific cases a known remedy, is to interfere between the soul and God. Who shall venture to call that "Priestcraft" which is the channel of God's grace to the soul?   PUSEY. *U.S.* No. *2* (Preface)

ABSOLUTION

O Thou the true the good Samaritan,
The Keeper who dost slumber not nor sleep,
I from Thine own the true Jerusalem,
With thy protecting mountains girded round,
Have wander'd down into this lower world,
To Jericho, that city of the moon,
That city of the valleys 'neath the curse—
And wounded by the wayside dying lay.
Thy Priest and Levite give me no relief,
Nor stretch the hand, but pass unheeding by.
Wilt thou not on thy heavenly journey bend,
And come down in thy creature's guise, on us
To look with brotherly and human eyes?
If not unto thy Salem of the hills,
Wherein thy blessed Saints and Angels dwell,
Is there no Inn by the celestial road,
Wherein a wounded man may find repose?
Thou bidd'st the heavy-laden come to thee,
Thou lookest out, and hastenest on the way
To meet the poor returning prodigal.
My sins are more in number than the sands,
More than the sands Thy mercies are to me;
Yea, though my sins are deep as Hell beneath,
Thy pity is more ample than the Heavens.
I count Thy words of promise, Thou hast set
Seventy times seven the measure of our love,
What then shall be the measure of Thine own,
But seven times seventy—Sabbath days of heaven?
Infinite is Thy patience as the Sea,
The Sea of Baptism, sea without a shore,
Thy love is as unbounded as the sky
Reflected in the waves of that calm sea.
    The body of this death doth hem me round,
No part of my whole frame is freed from sin,
No part of Thine is freed from bleeding wounds.
Thy Spirit griev'd to see me leagu'd with death,

Let him not take his everlasting flight:
With fasting and with prayer and painful alms,
Still let me strive to hold and win Thy stay.
Can mothers e'er forget their dear birth-pangs?
I am the child of Thine own bitter pains.
Thou once hast wash'd me with Thine heart's own blood;
Thou since hast often wash'd me with Thy tears;
And drops will wear at length the rocky stone;
Thy promise is to open if I knock,
Yea, Thou Thyself hast knock'd at my dull heart;
By warning—by Thy mercies—by Thy grace—
But I have still refused to let Thee in.
Close not against me the eternal door,
Although my hand is palsied; and in vain
Would I assay to lift it to the door,
But Thou didst heal Thyself the palsied hand.

ISAAC WILLIAMS. *The Baptistery*. pp. *111–3*

ADORNMENT OF CHURCHES

It is maintained that it is not right to expend money in embellishment when the poor are unprovided with room.

This is in some measure true; but then let us be consistent in the application of this rule: let us not apply it merely to the things of God, lest we deprive Him of His due, but to ourselves also.

Enter into our houses; may it not likewise be said, Why is all this cost and unnecessary embellishment, when there are so many of the poor unprovided with necessary food and clothing?

Do we then apply this rule merely to the things of God?

Do we think that nothing is too good for ourselves which we are able to procure; nothing too valuable or handsome which art or skill can supply, and that any thing will do for the service of God, while the poor are unprovided?

Are we to keep the best for ourselves, and to restore to the Giver of all good merely the refuse of His bounty?

The differences of earthly splendour can indeed be nothing to Him whom the heaven of heavens cannot contain; and He is there most graciously present where He is most honoured; but the fact is, that a desire that God should be worshipped in the most worthy manner is the very proof of the right state of the heart. Let me not dwell in cedar while the ark of God dwelleth within curtains, is one of the first expressions of natural piety, and mentioned as highly approved of by God Himself.

It was the good Mary who had chosen the better part, who had saved what she could to embalm our Saviour with very precious ointment.

Plain Sermons. pp. *42-3*

THE SYMBOLIC PATTERN OF A CHURCH

Thou who thy tabernacle mad'st of old
To be a type of things invisible,
And didst within Thy temple come to dwell
Making it holy; I thine altar hold,
And pray Thee, if such prayer be not too bold,
To sanctify each shrine, and mystic cell
Round this thine altar, and baptismal well.
Thou vilest things to thy great ends dost mould—
Accept this offering, and Thy servant spare,
Who this hath built with sin-defiled hands!
And when thine earthly temple, now so fair,
Among the things that have gone by shall be,
And nothing but thy heavenly temple stands,
Pity me in that day, in that day pity me!

Isaac Williams. *The Cathedral,* dedication

FASTING

It must be feared that it is one of the subtlest devices of the Enemy, to persuade us that we may become spiritual, through means merely spiritual; that we can cherish better the things of the Spirit, by neglecting those of the flesh; that we can have the victory over the flesh without fighting against it; that, being in the body, we can transfer the conflict, wholly, to the soul; that we can cultivate spiritual feelings, desires, longings, love, without discipline of the body, which would obstruct them and weigh them down.

It cannot be otherwise. God has wonderfully blended together our souls and bodies, so that they must ever be in harmony with each other, act upon one another; God drawing up the body to the soul, by giving it the mastery, or man drawing down the soul to the body, by making it the slave of the body, whose lord God made it. Nature herself teaches us that we cannot mourn with the soul and be at ease with the body. How does sorrow furrow the cheek, dim the eyes, make the whole frame heavy and languid and weary, dry up and waste the flesh! Feasting and joy, fasting and heaviness, are by nature and our very speech joined together. When we do mourn, dainty meats become loathsome, sweet sounds discordant, fragrant smells oppressive; we refuse our bread, or eat bread of affliction, and drink water of affliction. And shall we then think that we can reverse this law of our nature and pamper our bodies, fare sumptuously every day, and yet be true mourners for our sins, and be in heaviness for them?

If this be any one's first Lent, I would give some simple rules, which might smooth some difficulties. Let it be an act of obedience. A sacred Poet[1] of our own says, "The Scripture bids us fast, the Church says now." Thus shall we do it more simply, not as any great thing; not as of our own will, but as an act of obedience; so will the remarks of others (if such there be) less disturb us, as knowing that we are doing but little, and that not of our own mind. But little in itself, it is connected with high things, with the very height of Heaven and the depths of Hell; our Blessed Saviour and our sins. We fast *with* our Lord, and *for* our sins. The Church brings us nigh to our Lord, Whose Fast and the merits of Whose Fasting and Passion we partake of. We have to "humble our own souls with fasting" for our own sins. Remember we both. Review we our past lives; recall to our remembrance what chief sins we can; confess them habitually and in sorrow, with the use of the Penitential Psalms, and especially that daily medicine of the penitent soul, the fifty-first. Fast we, in token that we are unworthy of God's creatures which we have misused. Take we thankfully weariness or discomfort, as we before sinned through ease and lightness of heart. And thus, owning ourselves unworthy of all, think we on Him, Who, for us, bore all, so shall those precious Sufferings sanctify thy discomfort; the irksomeness shall be gladsome to thee which brings thee nearer to thy Lord.

Then for the mode of fasting, begin gently, it is for the most part the most humble. God leads us in all things step by step. They who begin

[1] G. Herbert.

impetuously, do it mostly over-confidently, and so have often soon grown weary of hardness which they sought to bear in their own strength.   Pusey. *A.W.* pp. *142, 148, 150–1*

HUMILITY

Know thyself. Pray God to show thee thyself. Bear in God's light to see thyself, bared of all outward advantages, what thou thyself hast made thyself, what thou hast been, what thou art. By God's grace, the sight will never again let thee be proud.

Keep ever present with thee the knowledge of thine own infirmity.

Never seek praise, nor speak of any good in thee, except for some good end, nor say, what may draw out praise. Yea, rather if it be useful to speak of thine own experience, it is best mostly to hide, in some true way, that it is thine own.

Do not even blame thyself, if it makes others think thee humble.

Mistrust thyself in everything, and in the very least things, seek, whenever thou canst remember it, the help of God.

Be afraid of the praise of others. If there be good in thee, own it, at least, in thy heart, to be God's, and think of thy evil and thy sins.

Take patiently any humiliation from others. It is a precious gift of God. "Humiliation is the way to humility, as patience to peace, reading to knowledge." If thou endurest not to be humbled, thou canst not be humble.

In all things, humble thyself under the Hand of God. Take all things, through whomsoever they come, from Him.

Do not excuse thyself, if blamed, unless respect or love, or the cause of truth and of God require it. It is more value to thee to detect one grain of fault in thyself, than to show to another that thou deservest not, as it were, a hundredweight of blame.

Be not careful to conceal any ignorance or fault in thee, unless it would hurt another to know that thou hast it.

Do willingly humble offices, humbly.

Give way to all, in all things in which thou mayest.

It is but for a short time, at the longest. Seek here to be humble with the humble JESUS, and He will exalt thee. As thou becomest, by His grace, lowly here, thou shalt be exalted there. *There*, is greatness, which none envies; treasures, of which thou wilt deprive none; joys, in which all will joy with thee. There, not thine own lips or thine own thoughts, but thy Saviour will praise thee. Seek humility, and thou wilt find it; and when thou hast found it, thou wilt love it, and by God's grace, wilt not part with it: with it, thou canst not perish. Yea thou wilt reign for ever with Jesus, Who was humbled for thee, and with the choirs in the heavenly dwellings. For there too, thou wilt be humble, not, as now, in the need of all things, but in the possession of all things, in glory, and honour, and power, and beauty, and know-ledge, and wisdom, of which we have but the faintest shadow here; and all from God and in God. For there, if thou attain, thou shalt cast thy crown before the throne, saying, "Thou art worthy, O Lord, to receive glory, and honour, and power"; and giving back all to God, thou shalt receive all from God, in bliss everlasting, through His Merits, Who humbled Himself to thee, that thou, being humbled with Him there, shouldest enter into His Glory and His Joy.

PUSEY. *P.S.* II. pp. *78-9*

THE HIDDEN LIFE

As this hidden life is obtained by deadness to the world—"ye are dead and your life is hid with Christ in God"—so, by that deadness, is it to be cherished, maintained, perfected. Death to the world is life to God; the life in God deadens to the world. By Baptism we were made partakers of Christ's Death, that we might henceforth share His Life. We were deadened that we might remain dead, and His imparted Life absorb into Itself our whole selves, and quicken us in every part, that we might live to Him, be dead to all out of Him. Since that hour each act of sin (much more if any of us unhappily continued in any course of sin), has been a revival of that which was dead, a minishing of our life. Self-indulgence of every sort, following our own wills, love of pre-eminence, of man's praise, covetousness, self-display, self-applause, deadens our inward life. And so now, each act of obedience, renuncia-tion of ourselves and of self-will, deadness to the world's applause, its idols, its covetousness, to "the lust of the flesh, the lust of the eye, the pride of life", is an increase of our hidden life. The less we live for things outward, the stronger burns our inward life. The more we live amid the distractions of the world, the less vivid is the life of the soul. The more we live to things unseen, the less hold will this world of sense have over us. The more we make anything seen our end, any thing short of approving ourselves to God, the more will our hidden life decay. It matters not wherein we are employed, but how. We may in the most sacred things forget God, or in the most common things serve Him. We may be promoting His Truth, and ourselves be but the unfruitful conduit through which It flows to water the earth; or we may in the meanest things of this earth be living to His Glory and thereby promoting it. Every thing seen, even the outward Coming of God's Kingdom, may make men lose sight of God; in every meanest duty the quickened eye may see Him the Invisible. Self-denying duty, love, and contemplation, together advance this hidden life. Alone, self-denying duty were austere and hard; love were weak and faint; contemplation but imaginative or sensual. Together, self-denial deadens the flesh; deeds of love soften the spirit; contemplation fixes the soul upon God.[1] Without self-denial and love, contemplation could not be; without it, even they would abide on earth. Deeds of self-denying active love may still leave the soul very imperfect in love, unless it habitually and consciously refer them to God as their Beginning and their End; and out of, or amidst, or at intervals from, active service, withdraw from all created things to commune with its God. Even prayer will become lukewarm, unless it be fed by meditation upon God, and the soul be borne, beyond the words of its prayer, to dwell on Him Whom it would love.[2] In

[1] " 'Reading,' i.e. 'the diligent search into the Scriptures with attention of mind', furnishes us the materials and sends us to 'meditation'. 'Meditation' inquires diligently what is to be desired, and digging up, as it were, a hid treasure, finds and points it out; but since of itself it cannot obtain it, sends us to prayer. Prayer with its whole strength lifting itself up to the Lord, obtains that much longed for treasure, the sweetness of contemplation. Contemplation coming rewards the labours of the three preceding, while it satisfieth the thirsty soul with the dew of heavenly sweetness." "Reading without meditation is arid; meditation without reading, erroneous; prayer without meditation is lukewarm; meditation without prayer unfruitful; prayer with devotion obtaineth contemplation; the obtaining of contemplation without prayer is rare or miraculous." Guigo Carthus. Scala Paradisi, c. 1. 10. 11.

[2] "The minds of those who contemplate, although they but slightly see something of the True Light, yet are enlarged in tnemselves by a wonderful expansion. And indeed even of the very things which they see, they can contain but little. For very little is it of Eternity which they contemplating see; but, by that very little, the bosom of their minds is widened to an increase of fervour and of love; and admitting, as it were through a narrow orifice, the Light of Truth, they are thereby in themselves enlarged. Which greatness of contemplation can be given only to those who love." S. Greg. in Ezek., l. ii. hom. 5. § 17.

our very excellencies we need continual checks, lest over-activity make us forget to sit at Jesus' feet, or we think that we are sitting there, while we are seeking only the shade, and shrinking from "the burthen and heat of the day", from thankless toil and drying strife.[1]

This, then, is our office; to see how, day by day, we may be ourselves more hidden from the world, that we may be more with God; how to discharge our duties in it, so as more to forget ourselves and remember God only; to consider this only, how they may be done, so as best to please Him; how self may least mingle in them; to seek no bye-ends of our own, no applause of men, nor our own; rather to seek how we may escape men's praise, that we may win God's; escape men's sight and be seen by our "Father Who seeth in secret" only, and have that in store with Him, which He, "in the last day", "will reward openly"; to be content with the least; desire no more than we have; be thankful to escape the snares of those who have what we have not; be glad, if it may be, to have less, that others may abound; to disburden ourselves of wealth by giving to Christ's poor; forget self in others, love others in God; seek only to be "buried with Christ" from this world and its vanities, hidden in His Tomb, so that all the show and pomps of this world may but flit around us as unreal things, but not catch our gaze, nor draw our hearts, which have been "buried with Him" and are now "risen with Him".

Seek we, then, ever to be hidden more in Him; hidden from the world, and from our own sins, and from the Accuser. Though Satan stand at our right hand, and our own consciences witness against us, and our manifold misdeeds terrify us, yet if we are, at the last, indeed in

---

[1] "The Redeemer of mankind in the day time exhibits His miracles in cities, and spends the night in devotion to prayer upon the mountain, that He may teach all perfect preachers, that they should neither entire leave the active life from love of the speculative, nor wholly slight the joys of contemplation from excess in working; but in quiet imbibe by contemplation, what in employment they may pour back to their neighbours by word of mouth." S. Greg. Mor. vi. § 56. "The right order of living is to stretch forth from the active to the contemplative life. And so again it is mostly of advantage that the mind be turned back from the contemplative to the active; that so the active life may hold the more perfectly what the contemplative has kindled in it. The active life then ought to transmit us to the contemplative, and yet sometimes the contemplative had best recall us to the active out of that which we have beheld in the mind within." Ib., in Ezek., l. 2. hom. 2. § 11.

Him, we are safe. He will say unto us once more, "Behold, I have caused thine iniquity to pass from thee, and I will clothe thee with change of raiment."[1] Seek we, then, day by day, to be more and more hid with Him here, that we may be found hid in Him at the end. Employ we every thing to this end. Year by year, if we look for them, events will come upon us which will sever us from the world, if we grasp it not wilfully. The world goes wrong, and we cannot amend it; it is wilful, and we cannot restrain it; it corrupts itself, and we cannot preserve it; all around is fleeting and shadowy; "nothing continueth in one stay". What we have, we lose; what we seek, disappoints; all "creation is subject to vanity", that we may seek Him Alone, Who Alone is not sought in vain, our Creator and our God. Blessed losses, disappointments, faintings of heart, perishing hopes, if not, like the poor world, we exchange one shadow for another, and forget our sorrow in some fresh source of sorrow.[2] More blessed they who learn betimes that the pure deep yearnings of childhood are not to be satisfied by ought they see, to whom "the depth saith",[3] what ye seek "is not in me; and the sea saith, it is not with me. It cannot be gotten for gold, neither shall silver be weighed for the price thereof"; for nothing earthly can satisfy the soul which is Heavenly; all which passeth away is unreal, and what is unreal cannot satisfy, and all passeth away except the soul and God. Be we not like those who fret and are vexed, or stand amazed at the losses, or sorrows, or pains, which God sends them. But in each seek we for what end He sends it, die more to the world, from which He is detaching us; look we whereunto He is calling us; strive we to forget the world, its pomps, its vanities, its vain desires, its destructive pleasures, its bitter sorrows and more bitter joys, in Him. Contemplating Him and His Cross, each sorrow will but unloose one link of the chain which sin binds round us, and which withholds us from Him; each start or pang of pain will be but His welcome messenger; all shall we gladly share with Him, and in His sufferings forget our own; glad to share here for our own sins' sakes, suffering, sickness, pain, bereavement, sorrow, loss, loneliness, rebuke, contempt—knowing that we are safer thus than in health, reputation, abundance, gladness, enjoyment of all things—glad to share all suffering, which He, for our sakes, suffered, so, for His sufferings' sake, He give "us for a

---

[1] Zech. iii. *4*.   [2] S. Aug. Conf. iv. *8*
[3] Job xxviii. *14, 15*.

prey"[1] our own souls which we had justly forfeited, and the souls which we have loved.

Use we, then, rather the very things of time and sense, whereby others are drawn down to the world, to rise thereby to God. All has been hallowed since they have been used by Him Who, being God, for us became Man. Take we our food as from His Hand, Who is Himself the Food of Angels and our own; lay we down to rest, as longing, although unworthy, to rest in Him; rise we, as from death, to live anew the life in Him; gaze we not on any thing fair, but in it to behold Him; through what is seen, rise we to Him Who is Unseen; in a word, whatever we do, fast we or feast, labour or rest, speak we or be silent, learn or teach, behold what He has spread around us, or close our eyes, seek we, in all, to see Him, to live to Him, and He, Who is our Life, will pour His Hidden Life into our souls, will blind our eyes and stop our ears to this world's tinsel show and false unreal vanities, and open them to hear His own saving cheering voice, and to see the image of His Beauty, and He will pierce us with the sweetness of His love, and lift up our hearts to long for Him, their never-failing, ever-satisfying fulness.

So, while we hide ourselves in Him, shall this bad world lose its hold over us, and appear in our sight more what it is in His. So, while we gaze on His glorious countenance, shall we lose sight of this lower world, and its false glare shall be lost in His brightness. So, shall evil spirits in vain howl around us, evil men in vain seduce us, an evil world in vain allure us, our own evil hearts in vain be ready to betray us; storm, rain, and floods, in vain shall beat upon our house, while we lie safely hid in that Rock Which was pierced for us, to pour forth that Precious Blood Which is our Ransom and our Life, and to be for us "an Hiding-place from the wind, and a Covert from the tempest, the Shadow of a Great Rock in a weary land".[2] PUSEY. *A.W.* pp. *299-305*

LOVE

Faint not, any who would love Jesus, if ye find yourselves yet far short of what He Himself Who is Love saith of the love of Him. Perfect love is Heaven. When ye are perfected in love, your work on earth is done. There is no short road to Heaven or to love. Do what in

---

[1] Jer. xlv. 5.   [2] Is. xxxii. 2.

thee lies by the grace of God, and He will lead thee from strength to strength, and grace to grace, and love to love.

Be diligent by His Grace to do no wilful sin; for sin, wilfully done, kills the soul, and casts out of it the love of God.

Seek to love nothing out of God. God re-makes a broken heart and fills it with love. He cannot fill a divided heart.

Think often, as thou canst, of God. For how canst thou know or love God, if thou fillest thy mind with thoughts of all things under the sun and thy thoughts wander to the ends of the earth, and thou gatherest them not unto God? Nothing (except wilful sin) so keepeth men torpid and lukewarm and holdeth them back from any higher fervour of love, as the being scattered among things of sense, and being taken up with them away from God.

Bring all things, as thou mayest, nigh to God; let not them hurry thee away from Him.

Be not held back by any thought of unworthiness or by failures, from the child-like love of God. When we were dead in trespasses and sins, Christ died for us; when we were afar off, Christ recalled us; when lost, Christ sought us; how much more may we reverently love Him, and hope that we are loved by Him, when He has found us, and we, amid whatever frailties, would love Him by Whom we have been loved!

Be diligent, after thy power, to do deeds of love. Think nothing too little, nothing too low, to do lovingly for the sake of God. Bear with infirmities, ungentle tempers, contradictions; visit, if thou mayest, the sick; relieve the poor; forego thyself and thine own ways for love; and He Whom in them thou lovest, to Whom in them thou ministerest, will own thy love, and will pour His own love into thee. "The love of God," says a holy man,[1] "produceth the love of our neighbour and kindleth it"; the love of our neighbour winneth the love of God.

Where, above all, shouldest thou seek for His love, but in the Feast of His Love? Without It, ye cannot have any true love. In It, Jesus willeth to come to thee, to dwell in thee, to abide in thee. Canst thou be warm, if thou keep away from the sun or the fire? Canst thou have any fire of love, if thou keep away from JESUS? or canst thou think to find Him, if thou seek Him not where He is to be found? He has said:

---

[1] Lorenzo Giustiniani (died 1456).

"Except ye eat the Flesh of the Son of Man and drink His Blood, ye have no life in you." How should ye have life, if ye have not Him Who is Life? How should ye have Him, if ye refuse to come to Him? Come to Him, longing for His Love; come to Him that He may come to you; pray Him to enter into your soul and pour His Love into you, and He will come, and, if you forsake Him not, will dwell in you everlastingly.

"Charity never faileth." How then is all lost, which tendeth not to love! O abyss of love, torrent of pleasure, life of them that believe, paradise of delights, comfort of our pilgrimage, reward of the blessed, root of all good, strength in all strife, rest in all weariness! Why will ye "labour for that which is not bread", and toil for that which satisfieth not; why seek for pleasures which perish in the grasp, and when tasted, become bitterness; why heap up things ye must part with, or why love vanities, when ye have before you love which cannot weary, cannot sate, cannot change, cannot fail; for Love is the Essence, the Bliss, the Being, the Glory of God; and this may be yours for evermore. God in Whom are all things, Who is All-Goodness, willeth that ye love Him eternally, and be eternally filled with His Love, and enter into His Joy, the Joy of the Everlasting Father in His Co-Equal Son through the Spirit, of Both Proceeding, the Bond of Both, and that ye should rest in the Bosom of His Love, and His Love rest upon you and fill you for ever. Will ye not then cast out now, for these few years, what hinders in you the Love of God, that ye may have for ever His Love which passeth all understanding, and be one with God, being filled with the Love of God Who is Love? PUSEY. *P.S.* II. pp. *59–62*

THE PRESENCE OF CHRIST

Oh that there were such an heart in us, to put aside this visible world, to desire to look at it as a mere screen between us and God, and think of Him who has entered in beyond the veil, and who is watching us, trying us, yes, and blessing, and influencing, and encouraging us towards good, day by day! Yet, alas, how do we suffer the mere varying circumstances of every day to sway us! How difficult it is to remain firm and in one mind under the seductions or terrors of the world! We feel variously according to the place, time, and people we are with. We are serious on Sunday, and we sin deliberately on

Monday. We rise in the morning with remorse at our offences and resolutions of amendment, yet before night we have transgressed again. The mere change of society puts us into a new frame of mind; nor do we sufficiently understand this great weakness of ours, or seek for strength where alone it can be found, in the Unchangeable God. What will be our thoughts in that day, when at length this outward world drops away altogether, and we find ourselves where we ever have been, in His presence, with Christ standing at His right hand!

On the contrary, what a blessed discovery is it to those who make it, that this world is but vanity and without substance; and that really they are ever in their Saviour's presence. This is a thought which it is scarcely right to enlarge upon in a mixed congregation, where there may be some who have not given their hearts to God; for why should the privileges of the true Christian be disclosed to mankind at large, and sacred subjects, which are his peculiar treasure, be made common to the careless liver? He knows his blessedness, and needs not another to tell it him. He knows in whom he has believed; and in the hour of danger or trouble he knows what is meant by that peace, which Christ did not explain when He gave it to His Apostles, but merely said it was not as the world could give.   NEWMAN. *P.S.* I. p. *29*

THE BIRTH OF CHRIST IN THE PEACEFUL HEART

Though dark and silent is the room,
The painter and the poet's skill
With other inmates strive to fill,
And all the darkness to illume—
Ashamed of poor humanity
Before the Maker of the sky.
The homely scene they fain would dress
Grieved at the cold and nakedness;
They bring around that wondrous birth
Whate'er of good is found on earth,
And from all hues in fancy's store
Living illumination pour.

Yet rather to the scene be given
The silence of that hour in Heaven.
For what can speak the Infinite?

And what can paint the wondrous light,
Where brighter than ten thousand suns
The stream of burning glory runs
Around His brow, whose viewless glow
To endless worlds doth life bestow?
But if the painter needs must speak,
And poet too would silence break,
We there would paint a heavenly crown,
Opening above, Heaven's Lord to own,
And in dread stillness coming down.

O scene mysterious of all time
What thought can match the dread sublime
Of that the meek reality?
When howling winter hurried by,
And sang Thy birth-night lullaby;
And hungry beasts were prowling round,
In the dead midnight hour profound?

The horned ox is standing by,
And idly feeding without fear,
Looks coldly on, he knows not why,
Nor conscious feels his Maker nigh.
The lamb too lies there bound and dead,
Significance divinely meant,
That life of man must needs be fed,
On death of the meek innocent!
Thus winter's sound and midnight's womb
With sullen cold, and silent gloom,
Welcome Thee to this lowly room.

Little hath Earth to give at best,
But of that little gives the least,
Sullen her mien and cold her cheer,
Her Heavenly Lord to welcome here

★   ★   ★

Alas, and was Thy cradle bare
Of all the welcome earth could spare?

My heart is now a shed more rude
And sterner is the solitude;
Darker my spirit's night, while sound
Remorseful memories, like the wind;
And restless passions, prowling round,
Therein an entrance strive to find.
Wilt Thou within so mean a shed,
So vile a manger lay Thine head?
If so, all things the foulest there
Shall in Thy countenance stand bare,
But should they catch Thy gleam divine
Shall like an eastern palace shine.

ISAAC WILLIAMS. *The Baptistery.* pp. *156–8, 162–4*

JOY

The source of all our joys must not be outward, but from within, from Him: all must come from Him, be enjoyed in Him, in the sense of His Presence, must lead up to Him: (He is our Life, our Lord, the Husband of our spirits). All joy is idolatry which stops short in His creatures; all joy is adulteress joy which joys in aught without Him. The joy, whereof Scripture speaketh, is a deep, tranquil, inward, abiding joy, to which all other joys are to minister, which arises in the Christian from the knowledge that he hath been made a child of God, from the sense of God's continual mercies, from looking to things eternal, from the hope that he is a living member of his redeeming Lord, from looking for his Lord's return; that when this passing scene shall soon be closed, sin and infirmity and negligence will lose their last grasp upon him, the body of this death shall be swallowed up in life, and he shall be translated to the Presence of His Saviour and His God.

This joy, springing, as it does, from the inward fountain placed within the heart, that well of water, which bursteth up into everlasting life, depends not upon anything without. It had its origin in the knowledge of God's mercies in Christ, in having been redeemed out of the evil world, and having been placed by Baptism in Christ's fold; it has been strengthened by every other act of mercy, whether of preserving us in the fold, or recalling us when we had wandered from it; it has increased with every victory which God has enabled the Christian to obtain over the enemies of his salvation, the Devil, the world, and the flesh; it has been strengthened, whenever our Saviour has imparted His precious Body and Blood to us. How then should it depend upon things outward, except as far as they serve to the inward life?

The Christian's joy is in the Creator, the Abiding, Unchangeable, the Living, the True; how should that joy be shaken by His creatures, which, in so far as they are not in Him, are fleeting, changeable, dead, unsubstantial? It is in Him Who is our Abiding place;[1] what can it fear? our Possession;[2] what can it lose? it is our Peace;[3] what can trouble it? it is our Rest; what can disturb it? it is our Life; what can destroy it? How should life, or death, or any other creature be able to separate him from the love of God, which is in Jesus Christ his Lord?

Would that God would open your eyes, yea open more clearly all our half-closed eyes, that we might see things as they are, what we are meant to be, what is in store for us if faithful, what is to each of us the next step to gain it. Not as the world giveth, did our Blessed Saviour give to His disciples (and to us, if we be such) His peace and joy; not as the world giveth, in the things of the world, but in Him; not as the world giveth, sweet to the mouth, but afterwards bitterness, but (more commonly) bitter and painful at first, and then a deep tranquil peace; not as the world giveth, shortly to pass away, but with Himself, in Whom and through Whom we have it, to abide for ever. Oh, seek it not then here. God Himself is the joy of the blessed; God Himself will be thy all, thy food, thy life, the object of thy affections, thy treasure; it will be thy bliss then to have no joy but God's; it is man's real bliss now; why seek it here in any thing but God? It is most like the life to come, to be bared of all bliss but God; that the eye should gaze on, that the ear should hear, the thought dwell on, God alone! Why then heap around us these manifold sources of joy, which distract the mind from God, and not rather in them, if we have them, strive to see, hear, taste, and love only God; if without them, feel that we are, by their very loss, the more severed to God?

Seek not your joy here, and ye shall have it here; seek it not in the world, and though yet in the world, ye shall have it; a foretaste of the

[1] Ps. xc. 4.   [2] Ps. xvi. 5.   [3] Eph. ii. 14.

greater bliss treasured up for those who love Him and keep His commandments. Seek it not in ease, in the lusts of the flesh, the lusts of the eye, and the pride of life, and ye shall have it, whatever outward lot He gives you. Yea He shall teach you, as He has ever taught His children, that it matters not what in this world ye have, enjoy, suffer, win, lose, leave; how the world thinks of us, whether we be looked up to, or looked down on, be thought well or ill of, be praised or dispraised, what our outward station of life is; it matters only what we ourselves *are*, what we believe, think, speak, do; what cometh from within us, not what happeneth to us without us: nay, that true joy is to be found in sorrow rather than in this world's laughter; in poverty rather than in riches; amid losses rather than in gains; amid suffering rather than in ease; under His chastening hand, rather than when left to ourselves; when girt with His Cross, and "led whither we would not", rather than when girding ourselves and, "walking whither we would".

PUSEY. P.S. III. pp. 445–6, 447, 458–60

THE UNION OF THE SOUL WITH GOD

Oh blessedness beyond all thought! Unutterable riches of the mercy of God, to be for ever not our own, but to be His, His by creation, His by redemption, His by re-creation, but His too by His indwelling, His life, His love, His glory, His light, His wisdom, His immortality, within us; yea, all but His infinity, and that the endless object of our enraptured contemplation, never cloying, never exhausted, because He is infinite; to be wholly His, in Him, and yet because we cannot contain Him, to have Him without us, to gaze on with loving adoration and adoring love; by Him and through Him and in Him, to be enabled to see, love, hold, receive Himself; ever receiving, yet never sated; ever contemplating, yet never wearied; ever loving with unchanging, unbroken, undistracted love, because our whole selves shall be in every part, action, affection, indwelt by Him! Oh unutterable blessedness, to be so wholly, inseparably, closely His!

PUSEY. P.S. III. pp. 422–3

INDWELLING

If thou wishest to live more with and to God, and that God should dwell more in thee, and be thy God, these few brief rules may help thee.

Be with God in thy outward works, refer them to Him, offer them to Him, seek to do them in Him and for Him, and He will be with thee in them, and they shall not hinder, but rather invite His Presence into thy soul.

Collect thyself from time to time in God, whatever thou doest, and thou shalt feel Him to be with thee in all.

Seek to see Him in all things, and in all things He will come nigh to thee.

Look to Him and not to man, and thou shalt see His good hand in all evil, His healing hand in all things painful, His Love in all man's unkindness, Himself over-ruling all evil, giving all good.

Then thou must seek His Love for His Love's sake. Not for the praise of man, not for boastfulness, not to be satisfied with ourselves, not to have high places in His Kingdom, not to be above others, or thought well of, not even for inward consolations in themselves, must we desire the secret love of God. Self, not God, is our end, if we seek God for anything except Himself. He loveth not God purely, who loveth God for anything but God. Yet only the humble can so love God. The humble only abase themselves the more, the more good God is to them.

Empty thyself of thyself if thou wouldest that God should fill thee.

PUSEY *P.S.* II. pp. *253-4*

It is the great need of active diligence, not to part with Jesus, when He has once been near us, and visited our souls. On this depends growth in Grace, the Good Pleasure of God, the Love of Christ, Holiness, Everlasting Bliss, Salvation. "Jesus made as though He would have gone further. But they constrained Him, saying, Abide with us, for it is toward evening." So is it with the soul. Jesus visits it many ways. Every visitation of God, in awe and mercy, is a visit of Jesus to the soul. It feels His Presence. It is troubled, and turns to Him; is alarmed at itself, or with fears of Hell, and flees to Him; or He brings before it its own crooked ways and the loathsomeness of its sin, and it would fain escape out of itself to Him; or He gives it thoughts of His Own Everlasting Love, and the bliss of ever loving, ever being beloved; and kindles some longing for Him. Every thing which deadens the soul to the world, or quickens it to heavenly things, is a visit of Jesus. Fast or feast; Lent or Easter; inward joy, or outward sorrow; the hunger of the soul, or His Satisfying it; the restlessness of the soul until it has found God; or the deep, tranquil calm, when His Light dawns on the soul, and it sees and feels that it was made for One Alone, that One Alone can fill it, One Love displaces all besides, One Object of its Faith, Hope, Joy, Praise, its labour or its rest, its speech or its silence, stands, revealed before it; the unformed yearning of the young soul to be wholly God's; or the aching of the heart of elders, that it has ever loved things out of Him; the bright glow of childhood, which says with young Samuel, "Speak, Lord, for Thy servant heareth"; or penitence stricken with Saul to the earth, and crying from the dust, "Lord, what wouldest Thou have me to do?"—every thought of God, every desire to love Him; every hope, fear, misgiving, imagining; every crushing of the heart's bright earthly joys; every gleam of that unsetting Sun which shineth on it from Heaven; the hiding of His face, or the sunshine of His Presence; all are, in different forms, visits of Jesus. Yet in all, we have need to say, "Abide with us, Lord!"

Listen we then to every whisper of our conscience; "do this; do not that; speak not that word of vanity, or unkindness, or untruth, or exaggeration; avoid this or that evil society". It is Jesus Who, within, is speaking to us by His Spirit. Hearken we to every call which rouses us to more diligent, devoted service; to love Him Alone, meditate on His Passion, share His Sufferings, by bearing patiently what He lays upon us, or by denying ourselves for those for whom, with us, He died. It is Jesus saying to us, "O fools and slow of heart to believe all that the Prophets have spoken! Ought not Christ to have suffered these things, and to enter into His Glory?" "And if He entered not into His Own Glory without suffering, think we, without suffering, to enter, not into ours but into His?"[1] He speaketh to us, and cometh to us, and is with us, in every thing by which He would win us back from the world, or draw us to Himself. If a deep Scripture Word pierces our souls as it never did before, He it is Who is speaking to us. He cometh to us in another and another Form, while our eyes are holden; in Sorrow or in Joy; in Fast or Feast; in Humiliation or Forgiveness; in stern words or reproving or gentle tones of love; in awe of His Majesty or the soft whisperings of His Mercy. We may know His Presence by the deep, breathless stirrings of our hearts. He Who made the heart, He it is Who shaketh it. He it is Who bids us "bestir

[1] From St Bernard.

ourselves",[1] "for the Lord goeth out before" us, to subdue our enemies before our face.

Only, in all we say, think, do, fear, hope, enjoy, let us say "Abide with us Lord." We fear our own unsteadfastness; "Lord, abide with us!" The foe is strong, and we, through our sins, weak; "Lord, abide with us", and be our Strength. We are ever subject to change, and ebb, and flow; "Abide with us, Lord", with Whom "is no change".[2] The pleasures of the world would lead us from Thee; "Abide with us, Lord", and be Thou our Joy. The troubles of the world would shake our endurance; "Abide with us, Lord", and bear them in us, as Thou didst bear them for us. Thou art our Refreshment in weariness; Thou our Comfort in trouble; Thou our Refuge in temptation; Thou in death our Life; Thou in Judgment our Redeemer.

If our Lord give thee any fervour in prayer, say to Him "Abide with me, Lord!" Use the fervour He giveth, to stretch on to some higher fervour, to long for some more burning, deeper love; not as though thou couldest gain it for thyself, but, as emboldened by Him Who hath "held[3] out His golden Sceptre" of His Righteousness and Mercy unto thee, that thou mayest "touch it", and ask what thou wilt. For what wouldest thou but what He willeth yet more to give than thou to ask, what, but for His Gift thou couldest not ask, the ineffable Fulness of His Love? "Abide with me, Lord", as Thou hast said, "If[4] ye abide in Me and My Words abide in you, ye shall ask what ye will, and it shall be done unto you." If He permit thee to be tried with dryness of spirit, yet still leaveth in thee a yearning for His Love, and thou seem to have no power to love, (thou couldest not so yearn unless He dwelt in thy heart), say on, "Abide with me, Lord", and He, in His good time, will fill thy hungry, famished, fainting soul, with the abundance of His Goodness. If thou seem to have no token of His Presence, but a hatred of thyself and thy past sin, (thou couldest not have it but for His Presence in thy soul), still say to Him, humbly and lowlily, "Abide with me, Lord", and thy sin shall not again gain the mastery over thee, so long as thou so prayest, and He will turn the intense loathing of thyself and thy past sin into a deep love of Himself, thy Redeemer. If thou art but just and hardly recovered from any ever so deep mire of years of habitual sin, and still tremblest, as though thou wert yet on the brink of the dark lake wherein thou wert plunged and steeped, and as if Satan

[1] 2 Sam. v. 24.   [2] S. James i. 17.   [3] Esther v. 2.   [4] S. John xv. 7.

could put forth his hand to pluck thee back into it, and thy unsteadied step would, through force of passion or a sort of necessity, reel back into it, still say to thy Deliverer, (One only could deliver for a single day from that deep gulf!) "Abide with me, Lord"; and He will keep thee, day by day, as thou prayest, sitting at His Feet and in thy "right mind". Only never lose Him out of thy sight, nor fail to pray "Abide with me", and give me perseverance unto the end and in the end. If the mists of thy besetting master passion seem to drive over thy mind and overcloud it, and thou seem to thyself almost reckless, and as if thou couldest forfeit thy All, but must, in a sort of frenzy, yield to this, pause but a moment, clasp thy hands together and say "Abide with me, Lord!" and a ray of light from Him, the Sun of Righteousness, shall pierce through the darkness which was closing around thee, and thou shalt hate its foulness, and love the pureness of the Light from Above.

And all of us, especially when we pray Him, at Holy Communion, to come under our roof, pray we Him also "Abide with us, Lord", "Why[1] shouldest Thou be as a stranger and as a way-faring man, that turneth aside to tarry for the night?" "Abide with me, Lord", in the Love and Grace I prayed for, "that" I "may bring forth fruit,[2] and my fruit may remain," and the glowing Breath of Thy Spirit "blow[3] upon our garden, that the spices thereof may flow out" in the fragrance of love and deeds of love, to the praise of Him Who gave them. Be very careful that, through forgetfulness or eagerness about common things, or thy bodily food, thou lose not sight of Him; but gather thyself often together into the chamber of thy heart, whither thou hast prayed Him to come; commune with Him there, shew Him thy needs, and pray Him to abide with thee therein, and fill it with His Love. And when thou mayest not receive Him in the Sacrament, pray Him to come and abide with thee by His Spirit.   PUSEY. *A.W.* pp. *274-5, 285-7*

THE VISION OF GOD

If we would truly see Him, we must seek to have the mirror of our hearts cleansed, that it may receive His glorious Image. "The pure in heart," He hath promised, "shall see Him." Of them who love Him and keep His words, He saith, "My Father will love him, and We will come unto him, and make Our abode with him." Love is the eye whereby

[1] Jerem. xiv. *8.*   [2] S. John xv. *16.*   [3] Cant. iv. *16.*

the spirit sees God. Disputing about holy things, (as is now too frequent), but blinds us. If we love and as we love, we shall see and shall receive. While the world jangles, our Lord comes secretly to us, if we, with pure hearts, draw nigh to Him. The Mysteries of Faith must needs be an offence to the wisdom of the world, but we, who truly believe and meditate on the Mystery of the Incarnation, shall not stumble at any other mystery, nor wonder that He chose humble means, the elements of this world, whereby to convey His Presence, when He, the Immortal, Invisible, of the Substance of the Father, took Flesh of our substance, in the Virgin's womb. His Glory is invisible still to the "wise and prudent" of this world, and "revealed unto babes".

But if we would see Him in His Sacraments, we must see Him also, wherever He has declared Himself to be, and especially in His poor. In them also He is "with us" still. And so our Church has united mercy to His poor with the Sacrament of His Body and Blood, and bade us, ere we approach to receive Him, to remember Him in His poor, that so, "loving much", we, who are otherwise unworthy, may be "much forgiven", we, "considering"[1] Him in His "poor and needy", may be permitted to behold Him; and for Him parting with our earthly substance, may be partakers of His Heavenly. Real love to Christ must issue in love to all who are Christ's, and real love to Christ's poor must issue in self-denying acts of love towards them. Casual almsgiving is not Christian charity. Rather, seeing Christ in the poor, the sick, the hungry, the thirsty, the naked, we must, if we can, by ourselves, if not, by others, seek them out, as we would seek Christ, looking for a blessing from it, far greater than any they can gain from our alms. It was promised of old time, as a blessing, "the poor[1] shall never cease out of the land", and now we know the mercy of this mysterious blessing, for they are the Presence of our Lord. "The poor",[2] He saith, "ye have always with you, but Me ye have not always", not in bodily Presence, but in His poor, whom we shall ever have.

The poor of Christ are the Church's special treasure, as the Gospel is their special property, the Church the home of the homeless, the mother of the fatherless. The poor are the wealth, the dowry of the Church; they have a sacred character about them; they bring a blessing with them; for they are what Christ for our sake made Himself. Such

---

[1] Ps. xli. 1. [2] Deut. xv. 11.

as them did He call around Him; such as they, whether by God's outward appointment, or by His Spirit directing men's choice, the "poor,
rich in faith", have been the converters of the world; and we, my
brethren, if we are wise, must seek to be like them, to empty ourselves,
at least, of our abundance; to empty ourselves, rather, of our self-
conceit, our notions of station, our costliness of dress, our jewelry, our
luxuries, our self-love, even as He, on this day, emptied Himself of the
glory which He had with the Father, the Brightness of His Majesty,
the worship of the Hosts of Heaven, and made Himself poor, to make
us rich, and to the truly poor He hath promised the Kingdom of
Heaven; the hungry He will fill, but those in themselves rich, He will
send empty away. Year by year there is more need; the poor are mul-
tiplying upon us, and distress on them; gigantic needs require gigantic
efforts; in these our towns, our Church is losing its best blessing, that
of being the Church of the poor; we know not too often of their
existence; our fair houses are like painted sepulchres, hiding, by a
goodly outside, from our own sight, the misery, and hunger, and cold,
and nakedness, which we love not to look upon, but which will rise in
judgment against our nation, if we heed it not. Realize we that they are
Christ's, yea, that we approach to Christ in them, feed Him, visit Him,
clothe Him, attend on Him, and we shall feel (as Saints, even of the
noble of this world, have felt) that it is a high honour to us to be admitted to them. Such as can, would gladly devote their lives to them.
We all should treat their needs with reverence, not relieving them
coldly, and as a form, but humble ourselves in heart before their
patient suffering; welcome the intercourse with them, as bringing
us nearer unto Christ. In them He comes to us, in them we visit Him;
in them we may find Him; He in them and for them intercedes
for us with the Father; in them He Who gave them to us, the means
and the hearts to relieve them, will receive our gifts; He, before men
and Angels, shall acknowledge as done to Him, what for His sake, we
did to them.

Oh seek we then, at least for ourselves, one by one, while He may
be found, our Lord Who, on this day, sought us in all ways we can.
Seek we Him, in the contemplation of His mysterious mercy; love we
to be alone with Him, to leave the world, at intervals at least, to behold
Him; seek we Him, in His house, whenever two or three may be
gathered there; seek we Him, in the temples of our own hearts, where

He has promised to dwell; seek we Him, with reverence and awe, in His Sacraments, where He has promised to give us His Body and Blood; seek we Him humbly, in His poor, as the source of true riches to us; and on this day let us, who hope to receive Him, return to Him more largely the alms to be offered to Him, for His use in His poor. So may we hope, in all things seeking Him, at length to find Him, yea to be found of Him, and in Him, and being found in Him, to be accepted for His mercy's sake, and He for ever be "God with us", and "we for ever be with the Lord"; loving Him for His mercy, loving Him that He gave us that love, loving Him with everlasting love, and filled and satisfied with His love, Who emptied Himself, that He might give us of His fullness, became the Son of Man, that we might be sons of God.   Pusey. *A.W.* pp. *57–60*

THE SOUL IN HEAVEN

Where is the soul of the devout communicant? in Heaven or on earth? Surely not on earth, which it is taught to forget, through the holy sweetness which streams forth upon it, and the joy which bedews it, that it is washed through its Saviour's Blood. Where is the soul of the penitent, as it poureth forth its sorrows at its Redeemer's feet, mourns, for love of Him, that it ever offended Him, and abashed and affrighted at itself, and knowing not where to hide itself from itself, hides itself under the hem of His garment, yea, would bury itself in His sacred side, Whence issued "the fountain for sin and for uncleanness"?[1] Even a heathen will tell us where. "The soul of one who greatly loveth, is much more in the heart it loveth, than in itself".[2] It is the very character of pure, intense, earthly love, as the image and offspring of Divine, that it is, as it were, out of itself; the heart findeth no rest in itself; it dwelleth not in itself; it is there where it loveth: there it is at ease, there rests, for that careth; it forgetteth itself, seeketh nothing for itself, but only to be there allowed to dwell, where it loveth to be, rather than in itself. And if death, or the Will of God, sever it from that it loves, how does it seem pent within itself, a burthen[3] to itself, unless it can anew go forth out of itself unto Him, the one object of its being, Who made it for Himself. And shall not

[1] Zech. xiii. *1.*   [2] Plato.
[3] See S. Aug. Conf. iv. *6, 7.*

that be much more true of the Love of God, "the soul is much more where it loveth, than where it liveth[1]"? When St Paul was caught up into Paradise, where his body was, he knew not. "Whether in the body, I cannot tell; or whether out of the body, I cannot tell: God knoweth."[2] But where his spirit, where himself was, that he knew. "Such an one was caught up into the third Heaven." And if God have, at any time, vouchsafed unto any of us, any more fervent prayer, any longing for Himself, any desire to escape from the misery which sin brought upon us, any yearning for something which shall satisfy the soul, which things seen cannot satisfy, (because they are of earth, it is of Heaven; they from beneath, it, with its Lord, from above; they of this world, it not of this world); what is all, from the first gushing forth of the tears of penitence, the first restored feeling of child-like love, the first faint trembling hope that it may again call God, Father; even that unspeakable Presence with his Lord, whereby St Paul was caught up into Paradise—what is it all but a going forth out of itself? And to Whom does it, to Whom other can it go? save to Him, Who Himself, by bonds of His Love, draws it; by His Spirit upbears it.

And so when our hearts are most out of ourselves for joy, when we are most longing for that ineffable gift of Himself in His Sacrament, the priest says, "Lift up your hearts", and ye answer, "We lift them up unto the Lord"; "lift up our hearts with our hands unto Him that dwelleth in the Heavens ".[3] Where are they then? with us? Nay, but we have "lifted them up", not in place, but in love; not in space (as if God were in Heaven only, not every where, since in Him "we live and move and have our being"), yet in truth. They are borne out of themselves in thankful love and longing, and are more with Him they would long for, than with our bodies which for the time they inhabit. The spirit, lifted up by the Spirit, is more with the Father of Spirits than with the flesh. The "firstfruits of the Spirit",[4] return unto God Who gave it, the foretaste of the everlasting dwelling with Him, by Whose Love it loves, and is borne to Him.

We cannot of ourselves, go forth of ourselves, any more than we can of ourselves in body leave this earth. But for this cause did our Lord come down to this earth, that He might with us ascend whither He was

---

[1] Anima magis est ubi amat, quam ubi animat. S. Aug.   [2] 2 Cor. xii. 2, 3.
[3] Lam. iii. 41.   [4] Rom. viii. 23.

before, that we might through His Spirit, in spirit thither "ascend" now, "and with Him continually dwell", that hereafter we might in the body also, be "caught up to meet the Lord in the air, and so for ever to be with the Lord".[1] But we can, at least, follow Him Who draweth us. We can, at least, not hold back, when He, as on this day, by the very Mysteries of our Faith, lifts us up above all created things, draws our eyes up and up to follow our ascending Lord out of sight, until we lose ourselves amid the choirs of Angels, as they sing, "Who is the King of Glory? Even the Lord of Hosts, He is the King of Glory".[2]

Oh gaze on for a while there! There behold we the orders of the Angels, the Seraphim with burning love, the Angels round about the throne, and "the seven Spirits of God" before it, and "the ten thousand times ten thousand, and thousands of thousands, who say with a loud voice, Blessing, and honour, and glory, and power, be unto Him that sitteth upon the Throne, and unto the Lamb, for ever and ever", and "the hundred and forty and four thousand, who follow the Lamb whithersoever He goeth", and "the great multitude which no man could number, of all nations, and kindreds, and people, and tongues, who stand before the throne, and before the Lamb, clothed with white robes, and palms in their hands, and crying with a loud voice, "Salvation to our God Which sitteth upon the Throne, and unto the Lamb:"[3] (among them are yourselves, brethren, if ye are, or if with purpose of heart, ye will henceforth be God's), and say ye, "Is it good to be there or here?" not here in this Church of God, which is the Image of Heaven, but here on this earth? Where shall we store our treasures, here or there? Where set our hearts, here or there? In whether of the twain is the full contentment of the heart? Where is the joy that fadeth not, the Sun Who setteth not, the Love Which chilleth not, the Friend Who forsaketh not? Where is thy Redeemer, thy Lord, thy God?

Would we could abide for awhile upon that Holy Mount! Look down from the mountain top upon the sea shore, canst thou see, upon the level beach, which of two sand-grains is higher than the other? When the moon is clad with the full light of the sun, its surface becomes one plane. And shall we, then, on whom the True Sun has not risen only, but hath ascended to the highest Heaven, that all who can love should be drawn unto Him, roll round Him, shall we, in the full glow

[1] I Thess. iv. *17.* [2] Ps. xxiv. *8, 10.* [3] Rev. iv. *5;* v. *6, 11, 13;* xiv. *1;* vii. *9, 10.*

of His light, grope as in darkness? Shall we, whom He has made to "sit with Himself", as on this day, "in Heavenly Places", look up, as if from below, with admiration on any created thing? might not earth itself well disappear from our sight, and our eyes be blinded by that Brightness to all created glory, our ears deafened to all sound except the Harmony of the Love of God? What can be great to him, whose own God is? Surely "all gold is as dust, and the fine gold as the mire of the streets". What were all beside Him, even if it could abide? Surely, as the Heavens are higher than the earth, yea—but what were the height of the Heaven above the earth? The height of the highest created thing were finite; the height of the things of Heaven is infinite: for they are the Love of Christ which passeth knowledge, the depth of the Wisdom of God, which none can reach unto; the Light wherein He dwelleth, which no man can approach unto; the Abyss of that Divinity, which none can search into,[1] save the Co-equal Son and Holy Spirit.

What were all the eminence of the whole world, all the kingdoms of the world and the glory of them, compared with the very lowest place in Heaven? What were all the praises of all mankind, compared with the sweetness of one note of the new song? What all the treasures of riches, compared with the Crown set upon thy head by thy Redeemer's Hand? What all pleasure of sense, by the side of that "pure water of Life?"[2] And yet these sound like created things; the bliss of heaven is no created thing, nor in things created. "The torrent of pleasure" is the Love of God, the Glory of thy Redeemer, the Majesty, Beauty, Holiness, Goodness, All Infinite, because all of the Infinity of God; all, if thou willest with an entire will, are thine; for God shall be "the Strength of thy heart, and thy Portion for ever".

Oh, choose ye then, on this Great Day, if ye have not yet chosen; if ye have, in the light of that Heaven which your Saviour this day opened for you, opens to you, pray ye Him to bind your choice by the bonds of His Everlasting Love. Let not this great sight fade from your eyes. Let not the tinsel of the world dazzle the eyes which were formed to "see the King in His Beauty".[3] Let not the praise of men dull the ears, which were formed to hear the Blissful Words, "Well done, good and faithful servant." Let not cares, riches, pleasures of this world, choke the heart, which was formed to contain the Love of God. Pray, and all is thine. Thine is God Himself, who teacheth thee to pray for

---

[1] I Cor. ii. *10, 11.*   [2] Rev. xxii. *1.*   [3] Is. xxxiii. *17.*

Himself. To pray is to go forth from earth, and to live in Heaven. Learn to commend thy daily acts to God, so shall the dry every-day duties of common life be steps to Heaven, and lift thy heart thither; commend thyself to God in moments of leisure, so shall thy rest be a rest in God, and conduct thee to thine Everlasting Rest. He, thy Head, is Above; shall the heart be any more below?

O! our Saviour, of ourselves we cannot love Thee, cannot follow Thee, cannot cleave unto Thee; but Thou didst come down that we might love Thee, didst ascend that we might follow Thee, didst bind us round Thee as Thy girdle, that we might be held fast unto Thee; Thou Who hast loved us, make us to love Thee; Thou who hast sought us, make us to seek Thee; Thou Who, when lost, didst find us, be Thou Thyself the Way, that we may find Thee, and be found in Thee, our Only Hope, and our Everlasting Joy!   PUSEY. *A.W.* pp. *336–41*

EDITIONS USED

Care in the choice of edition is particularly important with Newman's writings, because he re-edited and sometimes altered them towards the end of his life. I have therefore avoided using the later editions.

FROUDE, J. A.
> A Legend of St. Neot (in Lives of the English Saints, Vol. II, *1844*)

KEBLE, JOHN
> *Praelectiones Academicae.* (*1844*)
> Sermons Academical and Occasional. (*1847*)
> On Eucharistical Adoration. (*1857*)
> *Lyra Innocentium.* (New ed. *1898*)

NEWMAN, J. H.
> Arians of the Fourth Century. (*1833*)
> Lectures on the Prophetical Office of the Church viewed relatively to Romanism and Popular Protestantism. (2nd ed. *1838*)
> Lectures on Justification. (*1838*)
> Prospects of the Anglican Church. (British Critic, April *1839*)
> Parochial Sermons. (*1834–42*)
> Sermons, chiefly on the Theory of Religious Belief, preached before the University of Oxford. (2nd ed. *1844*)
> *Apologia pro vita sua.* (*1864*)
> (ed.) *Lyra Apostolica.* (*1836*)
> (ed.) Tracts for the Times. 5 vols. (*1840*)
> (ed.) Lives of the English Saints. (*1844*)

PALMER, WILLIAM
> A Treatise on the Church of Christ. (3rd ed., revised and enlarged, *1842*)

PUSEY, E. B.
> Sermons during the season from Advent to Whitsuntide. (*1848*)
> Parochial Sermons. (Revised Edition, *1878*)
> Nine Sermons preached before the University of Oxford. (New ed. *1879*)

WILLIAMS, ISAAC
> The Cathedral. (*1838*)
> The Baptistery. (*1842–4*)
> (ed.) Plain Sermons, by contributors to the "Tracts for the Times". (New ed. *1840*)

INDEX OF PERSONS

237

INDEX OF SUBJECTS